Woman Battering: Policy Responses

Edited By Michael Steinman
University of Nebraska - Lincoln

ACJS Series Editor, Anna Kuhl

Academy of Criminal Justice Sciences
Northern Kentucky University
402 Nunn Hall
Highland Heights, KY 41076

Anderson Publishing Co.
Criminal Justice Division
P.O. Box 1576
Cincinnati, OH 45201-1576

Woman Battering: Policy Responses

ISBN 0-87084-807-0

Library of Congress Catalog Number 90-84733

Kelly Humble *Managing Editor* *Project Editor* Gail Eccleston

Cover Design by John H. Walker

Preface

As Series Editor, it is a distinct pleasure to introduce the third volume in the conjoint Monograph Series between the Academy of Criminal Justice Sciences and Anderson Publishing Company: Michael Steinman's *Woman Battering: Policy Responses*. This volume continues the tradition of bringing together findings on the cutting edge of the field set by the first two volumes. This volume presents research which assesses the effectiveness of current intervention techniques in the area of woman battering.

Mike has gathered respected scholars and/or practitioners in the field who are active in the evaluation and/or delivery of interventions by the criminal justice system specific to woman battering. This book is unique in the field of family violence in that it covers the police, prosecutors, the courts, and the use of protection orders, as well as program effectiveness for both battered women and battering men.

The first volume in the series is Ralph Weisheit's *Drugs, Crime and the Criminal Justice System*, and the second is Robert Bohm's *The Death Penalty in America: Current Research*. Future volumes will cover "Police Administration" (by Gary Cordner and Donna Hale) and "Gun Control" (by Gerald Robin). Please keep these volumes in mind either as reference books or as you plan your future classes.

Anna F. Kuhl
Eastern Kentucky University

Acknowledgments

I want to express my gratitude to each of the contributing authors for participating in this project as well as to the series editor, Anna Kuhl, Ed Latessa and Vince Webb of the Academy of Criminal Justice Sciences, and Bill Simon of Anderson Publishing for their help and advice.

In addition, I owe many thanks to a number of people for their support. They are Kit Boesch, the human dynamo who is Lancaster County's director of human services, Lincoln Police Chief Al Curtis, Lancaster County Sheriff Ron Tussing, County Attorney Mike Heavican, and last but certainly not least, my wife Linda, a Lincoln Police Sergeant, and my son Jon.

—Michael Steinman

Contents

1

The Public Policy Process and Woman Battering: Problems and Potentials

Michael Steinman
University of Nebraska—Lincoln

INTRODUCTION

Every year, millions of women, children, and the elderly are criminally assaulted or abused by their closest relations or those with whom they live. Today, an unprecedented number and diversity of interventions are being delivered to protect the victims of this violence and to punish or treat offenders. This book's contributors assess how well most types of interventions are working with respect to one form of family violence, woman battering. Taken together, its twelve original chapters evaluate what responders (public and private, criminal justice and social service) are doing to help battered women and to stop battering. All the authors are respected scholars and/or practitioners in the disciplines that shape the design and delivery of the interventions they examine.

A number of chapters assess criminal justice responses. They cover the police, prosecutors, the courts, and the use of protection orders. Other chapters examine the effectiveness of programs for battered women (shelters, victim advocacy, and counseling) and for batterers (diversion, probation, and therapy). And one chapter analyzes the relationship between child abuse and battering and discusses what can be done to prevent abused children from becoming violent adults.

Public opinion and government traditionally tolerated woman battering. Only relatively recently has pressure been successfully exerted in this country, notably by women's groups, to change public opinion and to persuade government to protect victims and to punish batterers. This success is producing major changes in policies, procedures, and workloads. However, these changes do not ensure that government will be able to stop, let alone lower, the incidence of battering. Our knowledge of the public policy process and of battering suggests that getting results will be at least as difficult, if not more, than getting the public and government to acknowledge battering as a problem. This chapter examines the public policy process and relates it to efforts to stop battering.

THE PUBLIC POLICY PROCESS

The decisions and actions of government constitute public policy. Weber wrote that "government has a monopoly of the legitimate use of physical force" (Gerth & Mills, 1958:78). In other words, public policy is binding. We must obey it or risk being punished. Policy has this authority because it is supposed to represent and promote the public interest. The public policy process includes all the attitudes, expressions of opinion, and behaviors that influence what government does.

Historically, Americans have wanted government to solve problems in a rational way. We have expected public officials to have the time, knowledge, intelligence, and other resources to identify and analyze public problems objectively, to determine the causes of these problems and design remedies for them, and to mobilize public opinion to support their efforts (Lindblom, 1980:Chapter 3). Expectations of a rational policy process are often tied to a belief that government can work nonincrementally, that it can solve problems once and for all.

Rational expectations about government are rooted in our history. The immigrant experience has had a profound impact on our national culture. Immigrants have always been motivated by a powerful drive to create "more perfect" lives for themselves. They have typically sought to do this by trying to understand their problems in order to determine how to resolve them. This practical concern for what works is consistent with a desire to be rational. Most of us are children of the Age of Reason seeking to know the world so we can manipulate it productively. We expect government to do the same. The utopian rhetoric of our leaders who vow to clean the air, balance the budget, and stop crime reinforces this expectation.

Government's use of bureaucracy reinforces public expectations of rationality. Government uses bureaucracies to administer policy, to teach acceptable and unacceptable attitudes and behaviors, and to provide continuity. Bureaucracies also make policy when they decide how and when to apply laws in specific situations. While Americans have a tradition of bashing bureaucracies, we are also attracted to them because many of their features (e.g., meritocratic hiring and standard operating procedures) promise rational action.

Despite the powerful appeal of rational action, we do not have a rational policy process. Disagreements about whether and why specific problems exist and are important and whether they are the government's responsibility block the emergence of consensus about public goals and about how to achieve them.

Agreement is more common about general than specific problems. We agree that "crime" is a problem but disagree about the gravity of specific types of crime. Disagreements occur because specific problems tend to be more or less salient, understandable, and important to different people. Income, education, gender, expertise, age, affiliations, upbringing, and other factors fragment perceptions, information, values, and preferences. These and other factors influence people to define problems differently, to prefer competing resolutions, and to disagree whether problems exist, are public, and are important. Most public problems are "messes" (Dunn, 1981). The more we study them, the more we disagree about them. This affects policy-making and execution. That a policy exists does not mean it will be enforced well, or at all.

Government's structure magnifies the effects of different opinions and priorities. The writers of the Constitution tried to make government accountable by fragmenting it to ensure the representation of diverse views. They created a national government separate from the states with three independent branches and shared powers. These arrangements require officials with different jobs, terms, and constituencies to compromise. Compromise legitimates disagreement, hinders major change, and is the antithesis of applying rational decision rules to solve problems. Shared power systems exist on the state and local levels too with the same divisive effects.

In sum, the policy process is marked by inadequate information, disagreements about specific ends and means, and competition to shape binding determinations of the public interest. To protect themselves, public officials usually avoid adopting and enforcing wholly new policies. The typical "new" policy is a modification of current policy and a product of compromise. This produces an incremental policy process in which successes and failures come in small doses and participants try to "satisfice" (Simon, 1955) by promoting their interests as best they can.

WOMAN BATTERING

This book defines woman battering as violence by men against women "intimates regardless of their marital status or living arrangements" (Lerner, 1986:250). The focus is on male violence because men are the offenders and women are the victims in the overwhelming number of cases treated by public authorities, shelters, and anger control programs. The following paragraphs describe battering briefly.

Battering incidents often have three phases (L. Walker, 1979, 1984). The first contains threats and insults to which victims typically react by trying to please or calm offenders. The failure of such efforts leads to a second phase of uncontrolled verbal and physical violence that shocks and confuses victims. Physical injuries, when they occur, tend to occur at this time. The last phase is one of contrition. Expressing surprise at their behavior, offenders make sincere apologies, are loving, and try to convince victims that they will stop behaving violently. This phase, combined with victims' shock, unwillingness to see that they have misjudged offenders, and a tendency to blame themselves for what happened, keeps many victims from leaving offenders and from seeking outside help.

Over time, women in violent relationships report diminishing success in defusing men's anger and less contrition from them. In addition, motivated by their own insecurities, many offenders try to dominate their victims' lives. This makes many victims feel isolated and leads many to think that they have no one to approach for help (Ball & Wyman, 1977-1978). Isolation is a special problem for women who need offenders for financial support. Walker concludes that isolation and financial dependence lead many victims to feel helpless (1977).

Such circumstances help explain why many victims stay with offenders. Victims often have nowhere to go and little or no money, fear more violence if they try to leave, are afraid of being alone, worry about their children, and fear the stigma of a failed relationship (Roy, 1977). Women who stay with abusers often say they want to help men solve the problems that "make" them abusive (e.g., substance abuse), attribute battering to external causes (e.g., job pressure), define their situations as normal, blame themselves for the violence, or invoke higher loyalties like a commitment to marriage as an institution (Ferraro & Johnson, 1983). These rationalizations, a fear of reprisal, and other factors are examined in Chapter 6 and help explain why reported abuse rates are well under actual rates. The National Crime Survey found that 48 percent of all battering from 1978 to 1982 was not reported (Langan & Innes, 1986).

MAKING BATTERING A PUBLIC PROBLEM

Society and government have only recently begun defining battering as a public problem and a crime. That it is acquiring such status is a result of efforts that have had to overcome a number of major obstacles. One was (is) a myth that abuse is relatively rare and limited to alcoholics and psychopaths, particularly from poor and "disorganized families" (Finkelhor, 1983:22). Victim denials and rationalizations, low rates of reported abuse, and the involvement of low-income people in most reported cases have contributed to this myth. Another obstacle was (is) that justice agencies have categorized battering under other types of crime. Martin notes that this made it difficult to find "convincing statistics to back up [the] contention that [battering] was a national social problem of epidemic proportions" (1985:1).

Victim denials and rationalizations and low-reported rates also fostered a myth that victims are masochists, that they stay with offenders because they like being hurt. This myth remains an obstacle to generating concern for victims. Having little education, few community contacts, and little sense of personal efficacy, many victims cannot help themselves let alone try to make their situations understandable to others.

These hurdles are largely products of historical norms favoring patriarchal power (e.g., Dobash & Dobash, 1979) and limited government (as expressed in Thomas Jefferson's belief that "the least government is the best government"). The former gives men power over women. As a former Detroit police official put it, "The man is the boss, the owner; the female is the subordinate" (Martin, 1976:97). The latter helps protect this relationship by defining government's role narrowly and putting victims beyond government's protective reach. The old maxim that "a man's home is his castle" restates both norms by acknowledging a man's final authority in "his" home and government's obligation not to interfere with it. These norms are so strong that many victims do not seek public help because they think battering is a private matter (Langan & Innes, 1986) and many witnesses do not call police when offenders and victims cohabit (Berk, Berk, Newton & Loseke, 1984). They also help explain why many people have rated battering as less serious than crimes involving strangers (Bureau of Justice Statistics, 1984; Rossi, Waite, Bose & Berk, 1974).

Not surprisingly, given the force of these historical norms, most justice officials have not defined battering as a crime or kept records of its incidence. Indeed, they have opposed treating it as a crime by arguing that doing so causes more violence and wastes time since most victims do not cooperate with them. As a result, inaction has been a characteristic response of the police (Roy, 1977; Sherman, 1980; Vanfossen, 1979) and prosecutors and courts (Field & Field, 1973; Lerman, 1986).

Police reactions to treating battering as a crime are critical because of their gatekeeping role. Many officers have defined battering as a private matter (Berk & Loseke, 1981; Berk, Rauma, Loseke & Berk, 1982), doubted the utility of making arrests (Jaffe, Wolfe, Telford & Austin, 1986), and treated battering less seriously than they could have (Commission on Civil Rights, 1982:16; Langan & Innes, 1986; Smith, 1983:89). While major changes occurred in the 1980s in police policy, many officers still cling to these traditional orientations (e.g., Ferraro, 1989).

Like many other institutions, government helps "bond people to the social order" (Gelles, 1983:157) by teaching them how to behave and penalizing those who ignore it. The traditional absence of popular and official concern for battered women allowed most offenders to avoid punishment. Although getting government to define battering as a public problem and to be more responsive to victims has been difficult, significant progress toward these ends has occurred. Chapters in this book that evaluate the work and effects of current interventions as well as other studies (e.g., Lein, 1986; Stark & Flitcraft, 1983) testify to this.

Pleck attributes this progress to social and political developments that stimulated the growth of the women's movement, notably the civil rights movement and more education and employment among women (1987). The women's movement has had an impact in many policy areas such as housing, job training, education, parks, and transportation (e.g., see Gelb & Gittell, 1986; Gottlieb, 1980; Masi, 1981) as well as on battering and other kinds of family violence.

Women's groups began establishing programs to help victims in the early 1970s. In 1971, the first hotline for battered women was created in St.Paul, Minnesota and the first shelters in the United States were set up in Pasadena, California. Women's groups also demanded action from government to protect victims and to punish offenders. Most of these demands were and still are directed at the police, the first responders and gatekeepers of the criminal justice system. Initially, many departments reacted to the demands by training officers to mediate what they viewed as family disputes. This let officers do their traditional peacekeeping job and look responsive without having to treat battering as a crime. Mediation led to fewer arrests (Bowker, 1982; Wylie, Basinger, Heinecke & Reuckert, 1976) and did not lower abuse rates (Bard, 1970; Pearce & Snortum, 1983).

As a result, demand for more action continued. Advocacy groups and private agencies did (and still are doing) everything they could to protect victims and to persuade public officials to define battering as a crime. Activists set up shelters, counseled victims and educated them about the justice system and their role in it, established anger control programs, and taught people about battering. In 1979, President Carter set up the Office of Domestic Violence to disseminate information about it. Studies appeared (e.g., Straus, Gelles & Steinmetz, 1980), as well as television dramas, movies and news reports showing that battering is neither rare nor limited to "problem" families.

Efforts to make battering a public problem were strengthened immeasurably by the findings of the Minneapolis domestic violence experiment (Sherman & Berk, 1984). Its research design called for a random use of three tactics in misdemeanor cases: arrest and temporary incarceration, mediation, and separating offenders and victims. After six months, men treated with the first tactic reoffended significantly less than men treated with the other tactics. More evidence of a deterrent effect for arrest has surfaced since (Berk & Newton, 1985; Steinman, 1989, 1990) as well as evidence to the contrary (Dunford, Huizinga & Elliot, 1989).

The Minneapolis experiment had a pivotal impact transforming battering into a public problem because it gave public officials a way to treat it. Like other networks that spread new policy ideas (Steel & Steger, 1988), national law enforcement networks helped publicize the experiment's findings and draw lessons from them. An Attorney General's Task Force cited the experiment, acknowledged the frequency and gravity of battering, and concluded that battering is a crime and that justice agencies should treat it as such (1984). Other networks like the Police Foundation and Crime Control Institute did the same thereby conferring the blessings of criminal justice opinion leaders on arrest as a proper response. Battering had evolved from a women's into a law-and-order issue (Pleck, 1987:182).

The impact of publicity about the Minneapolis experiment is reflected in the speed with which many police departments adopted policies after 1984 directing officers who find probable cause to arrest abusers. By 1986, an estimated 46 percent of the departments in cities of over 100,000 people had such policies, a big change compared to 10 percent in 1984 (Cohn & Sherman, 1987). Reports of such widespread adoptions (e.g., *Law Enforcement News*, 1987:1,13) probably had the same effect as reports on the experiment itself. In addition, national networks prompted adoptions by publicizing court decisions (e.g., *Thurman v. City of Torrington*, 1984) making police liable for not protecting victims. (Chapter 4 reports findings that raise questions about the extent of this liability.) Historically, the police have often adopted punitive policies to satisfy new community demands (Fogelson, 1977; S. Walker, 1977; Steel & Steger, 1988). Adopting arrest policies for battering is in this tradition.

Whether any policy response to battering produces benefits depends on whether it is designed properly and how it is implemented. In addition, getting results is often a function of whether treatments produce reinforcing effects. The rest of this chapter discusses the importance of coordination as a way to accomplish this.

GETTING RESULTS: SOME PROBLEMS

Now that battering is widely, albeit not universally, defined as a crime, more victims, offenders, and witnesses to it are coming into contact with a variety of public and private agencies. Most of these agencies are on the state and local levels, have different priorities, and use different skills and measures of success. They include law enforcement, prosecutors and defense counsels, pretrial diversion programs, courts, probation and corrections agencies, and legislatures as well as academics and private agencies that study battering, advocate and assess treatments, and offer services to victims and batterers. Federal agencies get involved too when they fund and disseminate the results of experimental interventions. State appellate and federal courts are also involved when they define victims' rights.

All these agencies and individuals, both public and private, are involved in treating aspects of battering. This section briefly discusses the problems that arise when many agencies and individuals work to achieve related goals. The widespread involvement of public agencies is a relatively new development but it has not introduced qualitatively new obstacles to effective treatment. Indeed, as the next section argues, government's involvement can produce real benefits.

A major problem in getting results is that the universe of public and private agencies involved in treating battering is fragmented. This has just begun to affect policy responses to battering because the weight of historical norms produced relatively uniform patterns of inaction in the past. More progress in getting more people to define battering as a crime will prompt more police action and inevitably reduce this uniformity. Interventions by different agencies (as measured by policies, priorities, budgets, and rank-and-file actions) will vary for a number of reasons.

One of the most important reasons is that most agencies have different responsibilities. Thus, prosecutors are supposed to get convictions while public defenders are supposed to protect defendants' rights. At the same time, police chiefs often manage larger administrative units with altogether different functions. Responsible for different jobs, many officials have an opportunity to set their own priorities and view their work as separate from and more important than the work of others. A contributing factor here is that so many officials are elected. Prosecutors, public defenders, and sheriffs are typically elected for four-year terms and can define their priorities according to what they think the public expects of them. Many officials who work for private agencies responsible to their own boards and funding sources can set their own priorities too.

Fragmentation is also a function of the fact that battering is a "mess" of definitions, explanations, and effects. A rational policy process produces and applies detailed, generally accepted problem definitions and policy responses. Our fragmented perspectives and definitions (see Chapter 2) and limited knowledge of battering and of the impacts of specific interventions do not allow this. What develop instead are competitions over procedures and definitions of success (Cole, 1988), even though everyone is committed to justice as a general goal and cooperates to some degree to process cases and guard their reputations (Steel & Steger, 1988:94). Chapter 10 offers an example of a competition over a procedure (should victims be subpoenaed to help prosecutors?) among agencies otherwise cooperating to stop battering. Competitions are also produced by overwork and the ambiguity of many laws and policies.

In addition, defining battering as a crime is change and change *per se* has diverse and sometimes divisive effects. Implementing change involves learning of, growing interested in, testing, and adopting new ways of thinking and acting (Burns & Stalker, 1961; Rogers, 1962). Until people take these steps and find change useful or proper, they may view it and those who promote it as threats. Some people are more apt to take these steps and to treat battering as a crime than others because of their training and positions.

For example, treating battering is *the* priority for those who work in men's anger control programs. The more progress therapists make with clients, the more job satisfaction and career success they enjoy. As a result, they are apt to greet change making battering a crime as a welcome sign that society shares their concerns, as a grant of more professional status, and as a harbinger of more support.

However, police officers may think defining battering as a crime is an unjustified repudiation of tradition. They may see efforts to push the enforcement of arrest policies as distractions from "real" police work and as threats to their discretion and personal styles of policing (Ferraro, 1989; Steinman, 1988). Wilson described this century's history of policing as the adoption of more and more policies to stop officers from doing what they consider "natural" (1968:279). He wrote that many officers consider this "a failure of confidence." Their resistance to it takes the form of ignoring policies (Bittner, 1974; Goldstein, 1977; Punch, 1983; Van Maanen, 1978) and can produce a "bifurcation of authority" within departments (Brown, 1981).

Pleck rightly explains many current efforts to treat battering as a crime as products of self-interest rather than of incidence rates or humanitarian motives (1987:5). Some officials may treat battering as a crime because they want a bigger caseload to justify a budget request or to be in step with national opinion leaders. Some police chiefs adopted arrest policies to protect themselves and their officers from liability suits. Whether many officials treat battering as a crime is a function of how they relate their interests, expertise, responsibilities, and traditions to local demands, expectations, and conditions.

GETTING RESULTS: POTENTIALS

Acknowledging the presence of different interests is a prerequisite to treating complex problems effectively. Policies that ignore these differences allow service providers with different responsibilities to focus on their own work without giving them an opportunity to learn about and appreciate others' contributions. This isolation makes treating complex problems more difficult, especially when it produces interventions with contradictory effects.

As a result, students of public policy often recommend coordinated efforts to treat complex problems. For example, finding current policy interventions "mired in self-indulgence" and defining all problems as interdisciplinary, one scholar called for people with different skills to make "creative interconnections" by not trying to agree on why they should work together (Cleveland, 1988:685). Appeals like this are based on rational assessments of how to make progress in a less than rational world. Those who make those assessments understand the difficulty of solving problems when different perspectives and fragmented interventions lead to contradictory problem definitions and policy preferences.

Many analysts have called for coordinated treatments of battering because of the problem's complexity and the many agencies concerned with it (e.g., Dobash & Dobash, 1979; Goolkasian, 1986; Lerman, 1986; Sonkin, Martin & Walker, 1985). They argue that coordination rationalizes effort by eliminating the counterproductive effects of "unpredictable, intermittent" treatments (L. Walker, 1984:137) and by exposing offenders to mutually reinforcing costs. These analysts believe that getting results, i.e., protecting victims and stopping abuse, requires service providers to resolve or ignore their differences and work together. Among other chapters in this book, Chapter 8 discusses the importance of coordinating all relevant components of state and local justice systems in order to use protection orders effectively.

Coordination is an attractive but difficult goal. It is attractive because it creates a greater potential for mutually supportive rather than contradictory effort. And it is difficult because it often requires more agreement, or toleration of disagreement, than is possible. For coordination to work, one of two things must happen. Either agencies and individuals must agree to change their goals or priorities or some must be able to coerce others into accepting goals and priorities that are not their own (Pressman & Wildavsky, 1974:133-134). The latter possibility is remote in a fragmented response system. And the former is difficult when events and their consequences are perceived and assessed differently.

Uncritical reactions to the Minneapolis experiment underscore the need for coordination and show why achieving it is difficult (Binder & Meeker, 1988). Many police chiefs adopted arrest policies without considering the effects of the policies on other agencies and victims. Even if arrest is the best police response, it may not be the best community response if it leads to fewer calls for service, more people on welfare, and dysfunctional caseloads for other agencies. However, from their perspectives, why should chiefs put scarce time and resources into working with others if they think they can lower battering rates themselves? And why should other agencies mind this if they want to avoid collaborations that pressure them to change their routines?

While coordination is unquestionably a difficult goal, it is not an impossible one. The organization of the criminal justice system ensures that some coordinated effort will occur. Justice agencies must work together to some degree to process cases and to protect their reputations. Dutton has reported evidence that this is happening with battering as much as with other kinds of offenses. He found that batterers tend to experience post-arrest sanctions at about the same rate as other offenders (Dutton, 1987).

Beyond this, there is evidence that more coordination is possible and useful. For example, police officers tend to value arrest policies more when they see that arresting offenders produces prosecution and other sanctions (Berk et al., 1982; Jaffe et al., 1986). Moreover, police and prosecutors who know about and value each other's support tend to make more arrests and prosecute more offenders (Gamach, Edleson & Schock, 1988). Chapter 5 seconds this finding and Chapter 7 discusses, among other things, the benefits of arresting offenders and giving them therapeutic treatments. Chapter 10 discusses the strategies that some communities use to produce coordination and Chapter 11 reports evidence that coordination among criminal justice agencies transforms arrest from a correlate of more violence into a correlate of less violence. And Chapter 7 discusses, among other things, the benefits of arresting offenders and giving them therapeutic treatments.

Most of this book's contributors speak directly or indirectly to the benefits of shared information and coordinated planning, service delivery, and oversight. Special effort to initiate and sustain these types of coordination will be especially necessary as long as battering's status as a public problem is not generally accepted.

CONCLUSION

Many current responses to battering exemplify what a student of the policy process called "speculative augmentation" (Jones, 1975:176). This occurs when public officials face rising popular concern about a problem but do not know the policies people will accept. Their uncertainty leads them to announce goals and to make policies that promise more than government's expert and administrative capacities can deliver.

Adopting arrest policies is an example of speculative augmentation. These policies must be attractive to police chiefs who worry about public opinion and feel caught between proponents of traditional views, many of whom are their own officers, and victim advocates who base their demands for change on rising incidence rates, the severity of victim injuries, and publicity about the Minneapolis experiment. An obvious step for chiefs who are worried about what to do is to fall back on a response they know—arrest—regardless of whether it is tied to temporary incarceration.

However, arrest is far from a panacea even when it is linked with temporary incarceration. The Minneapolis experiment helped make battering a crime and legitimated treating it with public resources, especially legal sanctions. While these sanctions may have an ameliorative effect, they are unlikely to work with all offenders just as therapeutic services are unlikely to help all victims. The Omaha replication of the experiment (Dunford et al., 1989) and conversations with researchers conducting other replications report that Sherman and Berk's findings are not generalizable. This news is probably least surprising to those who work in shelters and men's anger control programs who understand battering's complexity as a social phenomenon and the difficulties of treating it. This shows the limitations imposed by inadequate knowledge and helps explain why the policy process is incremental.

It is an awareness of the limited utility of isolated interventions that leads most of the contributors to this volume to argue for coordinated interventions. For example, Tony Bouza makes a deeply felt appeal for it based on his law enforcement experience. That this theme emerges is not a surprise given the many perspectives, values, types of expertise, institutional loyalties, and goals of those whose work is somehow related to treating battering.

Given the need for coordination, the decisions of criminal justice policymakers to define battering as a crime and to take action against it are significant. There are problems and potentials when government, of which these policymakers are a part, gets involved. Yet, to a large degree, the problems have always existed. People have always disagreed about how to define and measure battering or any public problem. However, the potentials created by government involvement are new, especially regarding coordination. Although it works imperfectly, the standard criminal justice process of arrest, prosecution, trial, and punishment imposes a degree of coordination that private agencies often cannot match. Government can also require offenders to participate in public or private therapeutic programs and, because it typically has more budget resources than private agencies, can fund those that cooperate with it and stimulate more coordinated action.

Finally, although even our coordinated interventions are more "speculative" than we want them to be and we cannot end battering now, there is no reason why our goals should not outstrip our means. To stop battering is an important goal and well-considered efforts to achieve it equip us to accomplish more. Representing diverse disciplines, this book's contributors offer the latest evaluations of how most types of today's interventions are working. Future progress depends on whether society pays attention to them and others like them.

REFERENCES

Attorney General's Task Force on Family Violence (1984). *Final Report.* Washington, DC: U.S. Department of Justice.

Ball, P.G. & E. Wyman (1977-1978). "Battered Wives and Powerlessness: What Can Counselors Do?" *Victimology*, 2:545-552.

Bard, M. (1970). *Training Police as Specialists in Family Crisis Intervention.* Washington, DC: U.S. Department of Justice.

Berk, R.A., S.F. Berk, P.J. Newton & D.R. Loseke (1984). "Cops on Call: Summoning the Police to the Scene of Spousal Violence." *Law and Society Review*, 18:479-498.

Berk, R.A. & P.J. Newton (1985). "Does Arrest Really Deter Wife Battery? An Effort to Replicate the Findings of the Minneapolis Spouse Abuse Experiment." *American Sociological Review*, 50:253-262.

Berk, R.A., D. Rauma, D.R. Loseke & S.R. Berk (1982). "Throwing the Cops Back Out: The Decline of a Local Program to Make the Criminal Justice System More Responsive to Incidents of Domestic Violence." *Social Science Research*, 11:245-279.

Berk, S. & D.R. Loseke (1981). "'Handling' Family Violence: Situational Determinants of Police Arrest in Domestic Disturbances." *Law and Society Review*, 15:317-346.

Binder, A. & J.W. Meeker (1988). "Experiments as Reforms." *Journal of Criminal Justice*, 16:347-358.

Bittner, E. (1974). "Esprit de Corps and the Code of Secrecy." In J. Goldsmith & S. Goldsmith (eds.) *The Police Community*, pp. 237-246. Pacific Palisades, CA: Palisades Publishers.

Bowker, L.H. (1982). "Police Services to Battered Women: Bad or Not So Bad?" *Criminal Justice and Behavior*, 9:476-494.

Brown, M.K. (1981). *Working the Street: Police Discretion and the Dilemmas of Reform.* New York: Russell Sage Foundation.

Bureau of Justice Statistics Bulletin (1984). "The Severity of Crime." Washington, DC: U.S. Department of Justice.

Burns, T. & G.M. Stalker (1961). *The Management of Innovation.* London: Tavistock Publications.

Cleveland, H. (1988). "Theses of a New Reformation: The Social Fallout of Science 300 Years After Newton." *Public Administration Review*, 48:681-686.

Cohn, E.G. & L.W. Sherman (1987). "Police Policy on Domestic Violence." Paper presented at annual meeting of the Academy of Criminal Justice Sciences, St. Louis, Missouri.

Cole, G.F. (1988). "The Paradigm Change in Criminal Justice: The Contribution of Political Science." *Journal of Contemporary Criminal Justice*, 4:49-56.

Commission on Civil Rights (1982). *Under the Rule of Thumb: Battered Women and the Administration of Justice*. Washington, DC: U.S. Commission on Civil Rights.

Dobash, R.E. & R. Dobash (1979). *Violence Against Wives*. New York: Free Press.

Dunford, F.W., D. Huizinga & D.S. Elliott (1989). *The Omaha Domestic Violence Police Experiment: Final Report*. Washington, DC: National Institute of Justice.

Dunn, W.A. (1981). *Public Policy Analysis: An Introduction*. Englewood Cliffs, NJ: Prentice-Hall.

Dutton, D.G. (1987). "The Criminal Justice Response to Wife Assault." *Law and Human Behavior*, 11:189-206.

Ferraro, K.J. (1989). "Policing Woman Battering." *Social Problems*, 36:61-74.

Ferraro, K.J. & J.M. Johnson (1983). "How Women Experience Battering: The Process of Victimization." *Social Problems*, 30:325-335.

Field, M. & H. Field (1973). "Marital Violence and the Criminal Process: Neither Justice nor Peace." *Social Service Review*, 42:221-240.

Finkelhor, D. (1983). "Common Features of Family Abuse." In D. Finkelhor, R.J. Gelles, G.T. Hotaling & M. Straus (eds.) *The Dark Side of Families*, pp. 17-28. Beverly Hills, CA: Sage Publications.

Fogelson, R. (1977). *Big City Police*. Cambridge, MA: Harvard Press.

Gamache, D.J., J.L. Edleson & M.D. Schock (1988). "Coordinated Police, Judicial, and Social Service Response to Woman Battering: A Multiple-Baseline Evaluation Across Three Communities." In G.T. Hotaling, D. Finkelhor, J.T. Kirkpatrick & M.A. Straus (eds.) *Coping with Family Violence: Research and Policy Perspectives*, pp. 193-209. Beverly Hills, CA: Sage Publications.

Gelb, J. & M. Gittell (1986). "Seeking Equality: The Role of Activist Women in Cities." In J.K. Boles (ed.) *The Egalitarian City*, pp. 93-109. New York: Praeger Publishers.

Gelles, R.J. (1983). "An Exchange/Social Control Theory." In D. Finkelhor, R.J. Gelles, G.T. Hotaling & M. Straus (eds.) *The Dark Side of Families*, pp. 151-165. Beverly Hills, CA: Sage Publications.

Gerth, H.H. & C.W. Mills (trans. and eds.) (1958). *From Max Weber: Essays in Sociology*. New York: Oxford University Press.

Goldstein, H. (1977). *Policing a Free Society*. Cambridge, MA: Ballinger Publishing.

Goolkasian, G. (1986) *Confronting Domestic Violence: A Guide for Criminal Justice Agencies*. Washington, DC: National Institute for Justice.

Gottlieb, N. (1980). *Alternative Services for Women*. New York: Columbia University Press.

Jaffe, P., D. Wolfe, A. Telford & G. Austin (1986). "The Impact of Police Charges in Incidents of Wife Abuse." *Journal of Family Violence*, 1:37-49.

Jones, C.O. (1975). *Clean Air: The Policies and Politics of Pollution Control*. Pittsburgh, PA: University of Pittsburgh Press.

Langan, P. & C.A. Innes (1986). *Bureau of Justice Statistics Special Report: Preventing Domestic Violence Against Women*. Washington, DC: U.S. Department of Justice.

Law Enforcement News (1987). "Roughening Up: Spouse Abuse Arrests Grow." 13 (March 10, 1987):1,13.

Lein, L. (1986). "The Changing Role of the Family." In M. Lystad (ed.) *Violence in the Home*, pp. 32-50. New York: Brunner/Mazel.

Lerman, L.G. (1986). "Prosecution of Wife Beaters: Institutional Obstacles and Innovations." In M. Lystad (ed.) *Violence in the Home: Interdisciplinary Perspectives*, pp. 250-295. New York: Brunner/Mazel.

Lindblom, C.E. (1980). *The Policy-Making Process*. 2nd edition. Englewood Cliffs, NJ: Prentice-Hall.

Martin, D. (1976). *Battered Wives*. San Francisco: Glide Publications.

_____ (1985). "Domestic Violence: A Sociological Perspective." In D.J. Sonkin, D. Martin & L. Walker (eds.) *The Male Batterer: A Treatment Approach*, pp. 1-32. New York: Springer Publishing.

Masi, D.A. (1981). *Organizing for Women*. Lexington, MA: Lexington Books.

Pearce, J. & J. Snortum (1983). "Police Effectiveness in Handling Disturbance Calls." *Criminal Justice and Behavior*, 10:71-92.

Pleck, E. (1987). *Domestic Tyranny: The Making of Social Policy Against Family Violence from Colonial Times to the Present.* New York: Oxford University Press.

Pressman, J.L. & Aaron B. Wildavsky (1974). *Implementation.* Berkeley, CA: University of California Press.

Punch, M. (1983). "Officers and Men: Occupational Culture, InterRank Antagonism, and the Investigation of Corruption." In M. Punch (ed.) *Control in the Police Organization*, pp. 227-250. Cambridge, MA: MIT Press.

Rogers, E.M. (1962). *Diffusion of Innovations.* New York: Free Press.

Rossi, P.H., E. Waite, C.E. Bose & R.E. Berk (1974) "The Seriousness of Crimes: Normative Structure and Individual Differences." *American Sociological Review*, 39:224-237.

Roy, M. (1977). "A Current Survey of 150 Cases." In M. Roy (ed.) *Battered Women*, pp. 25-44. New York: Van Nostrand Reinhold.

Sherman, L.W. (1980). "Causes of Police Behavior: The Current State of Quantitative Research." *Journal of Research in Crime and Delinquency*, 17:69-100.

Sherman, L.W. & R.A. Berk (1984). "The Specific Deterrent Effects of Arrest for Domestic Assault." *American Sociological Review*, 49:261-272.

Simon, H.A. (1955). "A Behavioral Model of Rational Choice." *Quarterly Journal of Economics*, 69:99-118.

Smith, B.E. (1983). *Non-Stranger Violence: The Criminal Court's Response.* Washington, DC: National Institute of Justice.

Sonkin, D.J., D. Martin & L. Walker (1985). *The Male Batterer: A Treatment Approach.* New York: Springer Publishing.

Spelman, W. & J.E. Eck (1987). *Research in Brief: Problem-Oriented Policing.* Washington, DC: National Institute of Justice.

Stark, E. & A. Flitcraft (1983). "Social Knowledge, Social Policy, and the Abuse of Women: The Case Against Patriarchal Benevolence." In D. Finkelhor, R.J. Gelles, G.T. Hotaling & M. Straus (eds.) *The Dark Side of Families*, pp. 330-348. Beverly Hills, CA: Sage Publications.

Steel, B.S. & M.A.E. Steger (1988). "Crime: Due Process Liberalism Versus Law-and-Order Conservatism." In R. Tatalovich & B.W. Daynes (eds.) *Social Regulatory Policy: Moral Controversies in American Politics*, pp. 74-110. Boulder, CO: Westview Press.

Steinman, M. (1988). "Anticipating Rank and File Police Reactions to Arrest Policies Regarding Spouse Abuse." *Criminal Justice Research Bulletin*, Vol. 4. Sam Houston State University.

_____ (1989). "The Effects of Police Responses on Spouse Abuse." *American Journal of Police*, 8:1-19.

_____ (1990). "Lowering Recidivism Among Men Who Batter Women." *Journal of Police Science and Administration*, 17(2):124-132.

Straus, M.A., R.J. Gelles & S.K. Steinmetz (1980). *Behind Closed Doors: Violence in the American Family*. Garden City, NY: Anchor Books.

Thurman v. City of Torrington, 595 F. Supp. 1521 (D. Conn. 1984).

Van Maanen, J. (1978). "Kinsmen in Repose: Occupational Perspectives of Patrolmen." In P.K. Manning & J. Van Maanen (eds.) *Policing: A View from the Streets*, pp. 115-128. Santa Monica, CA: Goodyear Publishing.

VanFossen, B.E. (1979). "Intersexual Violence in Monroe County, New York." *Victimology*, 4:299-304.

Walker, L. (1977). "Battered Women and Learned Helplessness." *Victimology*, 2:525-534.

_____ (1979). *The Battered Woman*. New York: Harper & Row.

_____ (1984). *The Battered Woman Syndrome*. New York: Springer Publishing.

Walker, S. (1977). *A Critical History of Police Reform*. Lexington, MA: Lexington Books.

Wilson, J.W. (1968). *Varieties of Police Behavior*. Cambridge, MA: Harvard University Press.

Wylie, P.B., L.F. Basinger, C.L. Heinecke & J.A. Reuckert (1976). *An Approach to Evaluating a Police Program of Family Crisis Interventions in Six Demonstration Cities-Final Report*. (Abstract) Washington, DC: National Criminal Justice Reference Service.

2

Conceptualization and Measurement of Battering: Implications for Public Policy*

Murray A. Straus
University of New Hampshire

INTRODUCTION

The purpose of this chapter is to identify some of the many ways in which "battering" or "abuse" of a partner in a married or cohabiting relationship have been conceptualized and measured and to illustrate the consequences of these differences. The consequences include tremendous differences in incidence rates, differences in findings on etiology, and differences in policy intended to reduce physical assaults on women by their partners. For example, some authors emphasize the occurrence of injuries as part of the definition of abuse (Breines & Gordon, 1983; Frieze & Browne, 1989), whereas others base it on whether an attack has occurred (Straus, 1979, 1990), regardless of whether the attack produced an injury. Incidence rates using attack as the criterion may be twenty times higher than those based on injury because, contrary to popular impressions, most physical assaults do not result in injury. Differences in

* This paper is a publication of the Family Violence Research Program of the Family Research Laboratory, University of New Hampshire, Durham, NH 03824. A program description and publications list will be sent on request. The work of the Family Research Laboratory has been supported by grants from several organizations, including the National Institute of Mental Health grants (R01MH40027 and T32MH15161), National Science Foundation (grant SES8520232), and the University of New Hampshire.

etiology are illustrated by data on gender differences. If injury is part of the definition and measurement, it is primarily a male crime; if attack is the criterion of abuse, the rates are about equal for men and women (Straus, 1989).

THE CONCEPTS OF BATTERING AND ABUSE

The history of science is not always a record of progressive clarification of concepts and measures. In some cases, the passage of time brings instead, increased confusion. To a certain extent this seems to be the case with the concepts of "abuse," "wife beating," and "woman battering." The reasons are complex and space permits discussion of only three of them.

Expansion of the Definition

One reason for the current state of confusion stems from the expansion of standards of humane conduct to include not just physical assaults, but also a variety of other noxious behaviors between married or cohabiting partners. For example, using physical force to have sexual relations with a wife is now a criminal act in most states (Finkelhor & Yllo, 1985). Until the early 1980s, this was a husband's legal right. The concepts of "battering" and "abuse" are also coming to include verbal aggression and domineering behavior by husbands. This is based on the sound principle that "names" can hurt more than "sticks and stones."

The last 20 years have also produced measurement techniques to operationalize varying conceptions of battering and abuse. These range from a concentration on physical assault (the perspective of this chapter) to definitions which encompass any act which harms or has the potential for harming, economically, psychologically, or physically. Even when the conceptual focus is restricted to physical violence, it has been operationalized in different ways, as: (1) violent *acts* (Straus, 1974; Schulman, 1979; Straus, Gelles & Steinmetz, 1980), (2) *injuries* (Washburn & Frieze, 1981; Berk et al., 1983), (3) both violent *acts and injuries* (McLeod, 1983; Pagelow, 1984), and through a "*battering syndrome*" involving repetitive acts of physical violence and psychological harm (Walker, 1979, 1984).

This diversity accurately reflects a complex reality. All of these behaviors should be the focus of remedial policies and should therefore be the focus of careful research; but subsuming them under the general heading of "abuse" or "battering" has created conceptual confusion and probably has inhibited the development of theory and public policies to deal with each of these forms of maltreatment. For example, measures which operationalize the expanded perspective by including both physical and verbal assaults in the same score (e.g., Hudson & McIntosh, 1981) preclude estimating the extent of either because verbal and physical assaults are combined into one "abuse" score. Such an overall abuse measure also makes it impossible to compare the rate of "woman battering" with "street violence" and therefore hinders integrating family violence theory and research with criminological theory and research.

Normative Ambiguity

Confusion over the concepts of abuse and battering also occurs because of a lack of clear normative standards. On the one hand, a physical assault against a partner, if it involves an act that has a high probability of producing an injury such as kicking or attacks with objects, is typically seen as "criminal violence." On the other hand, there is a lack of consensus on whether "minor" violence, such as slapping and throwing things at a partner, should be similarly conceptualized. Slapping one's partner is clearly violent behavior, but the public is far from unanimous in believing that it is criminal to the same degree as slapping a neighbor. The reluctance to view "minor" violence *within the family* as a criminal assault has inhibited research on the links between family and non-family violence.

This reluctance reflects normative confusion over behavior in families which is clearly violent but not viewed as criminal because of the implicit cultural support that exists for this kind of behavior (Straus, 1980; Gelles, 1982). Part of the normative ambiguity arises from important ethical and practical problems connected with "criminalizing" behavior in the family which would be a crime if it took place between strangers (Straus & Lincoln, 1985). It is by no means clear whether families and society would be better off if the police, the courts, and the public adopted the principle that the same standards should be used to judge crime within the family as outside the family.

Crime is only one of many types of behavior for which there are different rules and expectations for the family compared to other groups or situations. These differences are part of what makes the family such a unique and important institution. For example, the family is concerned with "the whole person," not just some specific aspect of the person. An employer will be concerned about things which have to do with the quality of one's work whereas the family will be concerned with work performance as well as with its members' religious, political, and leisure patterns of behavior. The tendency to apply different standards to crime within the family is partly a reflection of the fact that what goes on in families and expectations about family relationships are different from other groups in many ways.

Caution in treating crime within the family the same way as crime between other persons also arises because the state has conflicting interests. On the one hand, there is the interest of the state in maintaining a "civil" society in which citizens can live without fear of victimization. This implies a commitment to vigorous action to prevent and punish crime. On the other hand, the state has an interest in encouraging and protecting the family as a social institution. Consequently, the family is subject to restrictions, protections, and exemptions which do not apply to other groups. The most obvious of these are the restrictions on terminating a family. Parents cannot abandon children and husbands and wives must secure permission to terminate a marriage. For the same reasons, the state is reluctant to take actions which, however justified on other grounds, might break up a family.

Finally, it can be argued that, even if the same norms about crime are applied within the family, there may be good reason for not involving the legal system in enforcing those norms. Even if they were willing to devote the time to the case, the police and the courts cannot be expected to understand the unique circumstances of each family and cannot be depended on to take actions which are in the best interest of either the person committing the crime or the family as a whole.

Acts Versus Injuries

Finally, confusion occurs because of a failing to differentiate adequately between conceptualizations and measures which focus on abusive *acts* versus those which focus on *injuries* resulting from those acts. The two are distinct, both legally and operationally.

The legal definition of assault focuses on acts rather than on injuries. As Marcus (1983) puts it: "Physical contact is not an element of the crime...;" or as the Uniform Crime Reports puts it: "Attempts are included [in the tabulation of aggravated assault] because it is not necessary that an injury result..." (U.S. Department of Justice, FBI, 1985:21). However, many family violence researchers believe that the criterion of assault is injury. Since minor violence, such as throwing something or slapping a partner, rarely causes an injury which needs medical attention (Stets & Straus, 1990), those who incorrectly define assault and violence by an outcome such as physical injury sometimes object to including so-called minor violence within the family as a criminal assault.

Some theories and operationalizations of battering focus on injured persons (usually battered women), whereas others focus on the assaults which may or may not produce an injury. The vast difference between these two conceptualizations and measures is indicated by the fact that physical assaults against female partners occur at a rate which is about 30 times greater than the rate of injuries requiring medical attention (Stets & Straus, 1990). Moreover, the etiology of the type of assault which results in injury may be different (Straus, 1990).

DEFINITIONS

The preceding discussion clarifies the need for precise conceptual and operational definitions. Unfortunately, there is a lack of consensus on what those definitions should be. However, some progress can be made by explicitly differentiating the concepts of *abuse*, *violence*, and *assault* and by indicating their relation to the concept of *aggression* as used in social psychology.

Abuse or battering, violence, and assault are all "evaluative" concepts because the central element in each is the identification and labeling of certain acts as morally wrong. Therefore, acts which are regarded as "abuse" in contemporary American society might not fall into that category in other societies or other historical periods. Husbands had the common law right to "physically chastise an errant wife" until the mid-nineteenth century (Calvert, 1974) and the level of physical punishment often used on children in the eighteenth century would be considered child abuse today (Radbill, 1987). Letters between John Wesley and his mother Susanna (referring to her child-rearing methods circa 1700) show that she was both a devoted mother and a stern disciplinarian who, in a different historical period, would run the risk of being reported for child abuse. Referring to her children, she said "When turned a year old (and some before), they were taught to fear the rod and to cry softly..." (from Miller & Swanson, 1958:10).

Abuse and Battering

Abuse and battering are the most general of the three concepts. They cover many types of harmful acts including verbal abuse or verbal battering, physical abuse, sexual abuse, and fiscal abuse. Intention to do harm is *not* necessary for a behavior to be classified as battering or abuse. For example, the term "sexual abuse" refers to acts that usually have the intention of sexual gratification rather than of hurting the child. Husbands who engage in domineering behavior do not necessarily do so out of a desire to demean their partners, though it may have this effect.

Violence

Violence is an act carried out with the intention, or perceived intention, of causing *physical* pain or injury to another person (Gelles & Straus, 1979). That a physical assault occurred is not sufficient to understand violence. Several other dimensions must also be considered and measured separately so that their causes, consequences, and joint effects can be investigated. Among these other dimensions are the seriousness of the assault (which can range from slapping to stabbing and shooting), whether a physical injury was produced (which can range from none to death), motivation (which might range from a concern for a person's safety, as when a child is spanked for going into the street, to hostility so intense that the death of the person is desired), whether the violence is normatively legitimate (as in the case of slapping a child) or illegitimate (as in the case of slapping a spouse), and which set of norms are applicable (legal, ethnic or class norms, couple norms, etc.). Violence thus defined is synonymous with the term "physical aggression" as used in social psychology (Bandura, 1973; Berkowitz, 1962).

Assault

The Uniform Crime Reporting system defines assault as the "Unlawful intentional inflicting or attempted inflicting, of injury upon the person of another" (U.S. Department of Justice, 1989). The legal concept of assault differs from the concept of violence because not all violence is unlawful. Some violent acts, in fact, are required by law—capital punishment, for example.

Since the focus of this chapter is illegal violence, it is preferable to use the term "assault" rather than "violence" because violence includes legally permissible acts. "Assault" is also preferable to "battering" and "abuse" because these terms are sometimes applied to verbal attacks on a partner or to a partner who is domineering. However, for stylistic variation and for consistency with usage in other chapters, the terms *battering* and *abuse* will sometimes be used and should be taken to mean a physical assault.

MEASUREMENT OF BATTERING AND ABUSE

By 1970, every state had adopted a compulsory child abuse reporting law. Year-by-year national statistics have been available since 1976. However, no official national statistics are regularly gathered on battered women or any other aspect of partner abuse except homicide (Straus, 1986). Nevertheless, considerable data are available. This section reviews the techniques used to obtain them.

Police Reports

The FBI does not publish data on assaults on women by their partners because the Uniform Crime Reporting System does not have a separate category for this type of assault. In the last few years, a few states began requiring police departments to keep a separate record of partner assaults. In most of these states, data are only available by inspecting the records of each police department. In a few states, the results are aggregated to produce statistics for the state. No compilation for all the states requiring such records has ever been produced.

Compilations of police reports would be extremely helpful, provided their limitations are understood. These limitations are illustrated by the national child abuse reporting system which has been in place since 1976. Child abuse and neglect reports have increased each year since 1976 by 10 to 15 percent. The sexual abuse part of this rate approximately doubled each year since 1976, resulting in a 2,077 percent increase from 1976 to 1985 (American Association For Protecting Children, 1987). It seems unlikely that this many more parents began to engage in sex with one of their children during that brief period. Rather, sexual abuse became a national issue and cases that were previously ignored or treated in some other way were increasingly reported to child welfare departments. Thus, the national child abuse reports are a valuable indicator of *interventions* but not of *incidence* (Straus & Gelles, 1986).

Year-by-year statistics on police calls for partner assault would provide valuable data on intervention trends. However, as in the case of child abuse reports, these data must be understood in the context of why some cases are reported to the police but most are not. Correlates of a greater probability of a police report include: (1) an injury, or imminent threat of injury, (2) the assailant is a male, and (3) a long history of previous assaults. These correlates make reported cases unrepresentative. As will be shown below, the typical partner assault case involves no injury serious enough to require medical attention, the assailant is as likely to be the woman as the man, and few or no previous assaults took place (Feld & Straus, 1989).

The Conflict Tactics Scales

The most widely used procedure to measure the occurrence of woman battering is probably the *Conflict Tactics Scales* or CTS (Straus, 1979; 1990). This instrument is intended to measure the incidence, prevalence, chronicity, and severity of physical assaults within the family. The CTS also measures two tactics used to deal with intra-family conflicts: Reasoning and Verbal aggression. (The instrument is described in detail in Straus, 1979, 1990. A manual for the CTS, which includes a bibliography of more than 200 references on the CTS, can be ordered from the author.)

The introduction to the Conflict Tactics Scales asks respondents to think of situations in the past year when they had a disagreement or were angry with a specified family member and to indicate how often they engaged in each of the acts included in the CTS. The 1985 version of the CTS (Form R) consisted of 20 items, including the following 9 on physical assaults against a partner in a married or cohabiting relationship: threw something at the partner; pushed, grabbed or shoved; slapped or spanked; kicked, bit or hit with a fist; hit or tried to hit with something; beat up the partner; choked the partner; threatened with knife or gun; used a knife or a gun.

The CTS has been employed by more than 40 investigators including Allen and Straus (1980), Cate et al. (1982), Dutton, 1988, Henton et al. (1983), Giles-Sims (1983, 1985), Hornung et al. (1981), Jouriles and O'Leary (1985), Jorgensen (1977), Straus (1974), Steinmetz (1977), Margolin (1988). Four studies have established that the CTS measures three factorially separate variables: reasoning, verbal aggression, and violence or physical aggression (Barling et al., 1987; Jorgensen, 1977; Schumm et al., 1982; Straus, 1979, 1990). The validity and reliability of the CTS and its independence from social desirability response set effects have been demonstrated in many studies (summarized in Straus, 1979, 1987).

The violent acts included in the CTS can be combined to form a number of different indexes. The following measures are used in this chapter:

Overall Violence. This measure indicates the percentage of partners who used *any* of the violent acts included in the CTS during the year covered by the study.

Severe Violence. This measure is restricted to acts that have a relatively high probability of causing an injury. Thus, kicking is classified as severe violence because kicking a partner has a much greater potential for producing an injury than an act of "minor violence" such as spanking or slapping. The acts making up the Severe Violence index are kicking, biting, punching, hitting with an object, beating up, choking, threatening with a knife or gun, and using a knife or gun.

The CTS has been widely used and widely criticized as an instrument to measure violence between partners (see Straus, 1990 for a summary of the criticisms). However, no satisfactory alternative has as yet been developed, as the following discussion of alternatives shows.

The National Crime Surveys

By far the largest and most thorough epidemiological survey of crime, including assaults, is the National Crime Survey (NCS). It is an annual survey of approximately 60,000 households conducted for the Department of Justice by the Bureau of the Census. By standards of contemporary survey research it ranks high on all counts. Unfortunately, the NCS does *not* provide a valid measure of the incidence of woman battering. The inadequacy of the NCS as a measure of *partner* assault can be seen from the fact that it produces an incidence rate of only two tenths of a percent (Gaquin, 1977-1978). By comparison, the CTS shows a rate of 16.1 percent, which is more than 50 times higher.

Why is the NCS rate is so low? The most likely reason is that the NCS is presented to respondents as a study of crime whereas the CTS is presented as a study of family problems. The difficulty with a "crime survey" as the context for determining incidence rates of woman battering is that most people think of being kicked by their partner as wrong but do not think of it as a "crime" in the legal sense. Thus, only a minute proportion of assaults by partners are reported.

In addition to drastically underestimating incidence rates, the special circumstances which lead the few people who do report domestic assaults to the NCS produce problems. The first circumstance which prompts reporting is the occurrence of an injury. This causes the NCS injury rate from domestic assaults to be extremely high. The second circumstance leading respondents to report domestic violence to a NCS interviewer is an assault is by a former partner. This results in statistics which appear to indicate that women are more vulnerable to assault by a former than a present partner. Both of these "findings" are erroneous.

Other Partner Abuse Interview Scales

Alford (1982) developed an instrument to measure "dispute styles" which he describes as "similar in some respects" to the CTS. This instrument has some useful features such as measuring the degree of intimacy of the relationship and the frequency of contact with the other person in the relationship. However, it confounds verbal aggression and physical aggression in a way that makes it impossible to determine an assault rate. The same problem applies to the "Index of Spouse Abuse" (Hudson & McIntosh, 1981).

Emergency Room Protocols

Many victims of woman battering go to hospital emergency rooms for treatment. However, the fact that an injury was intentional is usually not divulged. Moreover, even when it is divulged or there are indications of intentional injury, it tends to be ignored (Stark, Flitcraft, Zuckerman & Gray, 1981). Procedures have therefore been developed to identify battered women so more appropriate treatment and referral can be provided (McGrath et al., 1980). One such protocol was used to examine case records at Yale-New Haven hospital. It found that about 20 percent of female trauma cases were the result of intentional injuries (Stark et al., 1981). These findings indicate that emergency room protocols should be used more to provide treatment and referrals.

Emergency room protocols can also be used to identify cases for research, particularly in-depth analyses and longitudinal analyses. However, as noted earlier, only a small fraction of battered women are injured seriously enough to require medical attention. Thus, incidence rates based on them will seriously underestimate the prevalence of women battering. Nevertheless, if one is careful to indicate that the phenomenon being measured is "women who are beaten seriously enough to require medical treatment" and that this level of injury is rare even among severely assaulted women, these would be extremely useful data in any community.

Randomized Response Technique

This technique was first developed by Warner (1965) and later modified by others (Kolata, 1987; Tracy & Fox, 1986). In its most commonly used format, respondents are asked two unrelated questions, one sensitive and the other not, and then given some randomizing device (like flipping a coin) for deciding which question to answer. The researcher does not know which question the respondent is actually replying to but does know the overall odds that each question will be answered. If the researcher also knows the prevalence of the non-sensitive characteristic (because it is fixed in the population, like being born in September, or because it can be determined from other sources), then the prevalence of the sensitive characteristic can be readily calculated. This technique is attractive because the researcher can promise the respondent complete anonymity of response.

The technique has been used in regard to child abuse. Zdep and Rhodes (1976) estimated that 15 percent of a national probability sample of 2000 responded "yes" to the question, "Have you or your spouse ever *intentionally* used physical force on any of your children in an effort specifically meant to hurt or cause injury to that child?" Finkelhor and Lewis (1987) obtained estimates of 17 percent and 4 percent to split samples of 1313 in a national probability survey in response to the question "Have you ever sexually abused a child at any time in your life?". However, the divergence of their two estimates and the absence of associations with expected characteristics of sexual abusers led Finkelhor and Lewis to conclude that the estimates were probably invalid. Randomized response technique has not yet been used in a study of partner abuse but offers some intriguing possibilities. It must be refined in order to produce valid and reliable results.

INCIDENCE RATES

In view of the problems mentioned above, the rates of partner assault presented below are based on the Conflict Tactics Scales. The data are from the 1985 National Family Violence Survey (Gelles & Straus, 1988; Straus & Gelles, 1986, 1990). This is a survey of a nationally representative sample of 6,002 married and cohabiting couples interviewed in 1985. In approximately half the cases, the data were obtained from the wife or female partner. Husbands or male partners were the respondents for the other half of the couples.

Overview of Rates

The 1985 survey, like the parallel survey conducted a decade earlier (Straus, Gelles & Steinmetz, 1980) revealed that about 16 percent of the couples experienced a violent incident during the year and that over one-third experience one or more incidents of assault during the course of a marriage.

It has been argued that these findings indicate a relatively low assault rate (Scanzoni, 1978) because 16 percent means that 84 percent of the couples did not experience an assault. Moreover, the relevance of these assaults for public policy tends to be discounted because most of the incidents are "simple assaults" such as slapping, shoving, or throwing something at a partner, rather than "aggravated assaults" and, as indicated previously, there are implicit norms tolerating this level of family violence (Straus, 1976). However, there are grounds for regarding even these levels of minor violence as an important social problem and as central to understanding severely assaultive behavior.

First, over one-third of these incidents do involve severe assaults such as punching, kicking, and attacks with objects or weapons (Straus & Gelles, 1988). In addition, 16 percent is a "lower bound" estimate. The "true" annual incidence rate is probably much greater than 16 percent because it is almost certain that there was underreporting. Moreover, when an assault occurred, it was typically part of a repeated pattern. Two-thirds of the couples who experienced an assault reported more than one incident during the base year of this study.

Then too, even if one regards 16 percent as a low rate, a large number of people are still involved. If this rate is applied to the 54 million cohabiting couples in the United States in 1984 it yields an estimated 8.7 million assault victims (Straus & Gelles, 1988).

Furthermore, violence between partners tends to be transmitted from generation to generation (Hotaling & Sugarman, 1986; Straus, 1983) and is related to assaults and other crime outside the family (Hotaling & Straus, 1988). And finally, even though the bulk of the assaults which occur in marriage are minor, they could continue indefinitely and escalate into more severe assaults. A number of studies report such a pattern (Feld & Straus, 1989; Giles-Sims, 1983, 1985; Pagelow, 1981; Walker, 1979).

How Many Battered Women?

Before one can determine the number of beaten women, one must define what this term means. My own view is that any hitting makes a woman a beaten wife or partner just as any hitting of a secretary makes her a beaten employee. However, although the common law right of a husband to "physically chastise an errant wife" has not been recognized by the courts since the mid-nineteenth century (Calvert, 1974), the marriage license remains a *de facto* hitting license provided the assaults are not too severe or frequent (Straus, 1980).

Popular Conceptions Of Battered Women. Consistent with these implicit norms, the general public tends to think of a "battered woman" as one who is repeatedly and severely assaulted by her partner. This conceptualization apparently affects those who seek refuge in shelters for battered women because studies of two different shelters show an average frequency of about 60 assaults per year (Straus, 1990). This contrasts sharply with the average of "only" about six per year for women in the National Family Violence Survey almost none of whom had used a shelter.

Any Assault as the Criterion. Nevertheless, public standards concerning the frequency and severity of assault which are tolerated in marriage are slowly changing. For this reason, and because the occurrence of minor assaults increases the risk of more severe assaults (Feld & Straus, 1989), it is important to estimate the number of beaten women using the criterion of "even one" incident of minor violence, such as being slapped. This is given in the first row of Table 2.1. It shows that, if the criterion is set at any assault, over 6 million women are beaten every year in the United States. This is a "lower bound" estimate and the true figure easily could be double that.

Severe Assaults. The second row of Table 2.1 shows that if the criterion is a more severe assault than "just a slap" the figure drops by two-thirds. Using this criterion produces a lower bound estimate of 1.8 million women who experienced one or more dangerous assaults during the year, such as being kicked, punched, choked or attacked with an object or weapon.

For most people, however, a single punch or kick does not constitute a "beaten wife." Consequently, the remaining rows of Part A of Table 2.1 show the effect of using multiple assaults as the basis for estimating the number of beaten women. Setting the criterion at 3 or more assaults during the year results in an estimate of 600,000. Setting it at 5 or more produces an estimate of 450,000 cases and at 12 or more an estimate of 270,000 beaten women each year in the United States.

Table 2.1 Rates of partner assault and estimated number of cases by severity and chronicity of assault and source of data.

Type of Partner Violence	Rate per 1,000 couples*	Estimated Number Assaulted**
A. ANNUAL INCIDENCE OF ASSAULT ON WOMEN ESTIMATED FROM THE 1985 NATIONAL FAMILY VIOLENCE SURVEY**		
Any Assault on Female Partner	116.0	6,250,000
One or More Severe Assaults on Female Partner	34.0	1,800,000
3 or More Severe Assaults	11.0	600,000
5 or More Severe Assaults	9.0	450,000
12 or More Severe Assaults	5.0	270,000
Assault Resulting in Injury to Female Partner	3.5	189,000
B. ANNUAL INCIDENCE ESTIMATES FROM OTHER DATA SOURCES		
Domestic Disturbance Calls to New Jersey Police		643,000
National Crime Survey, 1973-76		125,000
C. ANNUAL INCIDENCE OF ASSAULT ON MEN ESTIMATED FROM THE 1985 NATIONAL FAMILY VIOLENCE SURVEY**		
Any Assault on Male Partner	124.0	6,800,000
One or More Severe Assaults on Male Partner	48.0	2,600,000
Assault Resulting in Injury to Male Partner	0.6	32,400

* The rates in Sections A and C differ from those in Straus and Gelles (1986) because the rates in that paper were computed in a way which enabled the 1985 rates to be compared with the more restricted sample and more restricted version of the Conflict Tactics Scale used in the 1975 study.

** The "Number Assaulted" in Sections A and C was calculated by multiplying the rates shown by the estimate of 54 million couples in the United States in 1984, as given in the 1986 Statistical Abstract of the United States.

The last row of Part A in Table 2.1 shows that when the criterion includes an injury which requires medical attention, the estimate drops to 189,000 or 1/33 of the number estimated on the basis of "any assault."

Estimate Based on Police Calls. The figure of 643,000 in the first row of Part B in Table 2.1 was calculated from data based on the first year of a New Jersey law requiring police departments to keep a separate record of domestic violence calls (*New York Times*, December 11, 1983, p. 56). The assumptions which had to be made to arrive at this estimate suggest it is probably an "upper bound" estimate.[1]

National Crime Survey. The second row of Part B gives the figures from the NCS. Over 70 percent of these cases involve an assault by a divorced or separated husband because, as explained earlier, assaults by a current partner are rarely considered a "crime" unless they produced a serious injury. This figure is therefore invalid as an estimate of the number of beaten women but is presented because NCS data are widely used.[2]

Trends

One of the purposes of the 1985 National Family Violence Survey was to compare rates of partner assault with the rates estimated from the first National Family Violence Survey conducted in 1975 (Straus, Gelles & Steinmetz, 1980). The overall rate of assaults by men declined slightly from 121 to 113 per thousand couples—a 6.6 percent decrease which is not significant. However, the rate of severe assaults decreased substantially from 38 to 30 per thousand—a 21 percent decrease which is almost significant ($t = 1.60$, $p. <.10$). On the other hand, the overall rate of assaults by women on their male partners increased slightly from 116 to 121 and the rate of severe assaults by women decreased slightly from 46 to 44 (Straus & Gelles, 1986).

Straus and Gelles' interpretation of these data hinges on comparisons of the rates of change in different types of family violence. The 1975-1985 comparison of child abuse rates revealed a statistically significant decrease. For assaults against partners, Straus and Gelles (1986) point out that only the change in the rate of severe assaults on women (which is the closest of the rates to "battered women") even approaches statistical significance. They argue that one of the reasons the rate of physical assaults on children and women changed more than the others is because, of the six types of family violence they studied, child abuse and wife beating were the only two which were the subject of major ameliorative efforts. Of these, child abuse has been the focus of the longest and most intense ameliorative effort and it showed the largest decrease. Woman battering, which showed the second largest decrease, was also the subject of a major campaign although not as long or as intense as the campaign against child abuse. Straus and Gelles suggest that the correspondence between the duration and intensity of ameliorative effort and the decrease in severe assaults on women reflects a real change during this decade rather than a chance fluctuation.[3]

SOME POLICY IMPLICATIONS OF DIFFERENCES IN CONCEPTUALIZATION AND MEASUREMENT

Statistics as Justification for Policy

In contemporary American society, statistics are used to inform, guide, and justify social policy. The belief in statistics is so great that when the public or a legislature wishes to act and there are no statistics, statistics must somehow be created to fill the vacuum. Unfortunately, these statistics are often biased toward supporting the proposed policy.

Creating and interpreting statistics, like other modes of communication, is not a mechanical process. Non-random error affects the process as shown by Allport and Postman's classic experiment on "The Basic Psychology of Rumor" (1945). Inevitable errors in transmitting information tend to distort it in a way that reflects the values and beliefs of society as well as those of individual communicators.

The process of creating the statistics to justify a policy is illustrated by the statistics used to support establishing the National Center for Missing and Exploited Children. The statistical centerpiece of a 1984 congressional hearing was the statement that "two million children disappear each year in the United States." Gerald Hotaling (personal communication, 1989) has traced the origins of this figure and found a process analogous to that found by Allport and Postman's research on the origin of wartime rumors. Each retelling of the story produced distortions which made the statistics fit the preexisting belief that many children are abducted. The starting point was a 1974 analysis of National Youth Survey data. This analysis did yield an estimate of 2 million children. However, 1.85 million of these were runaway children, not abducted children, leaving 160,000 non-runaway children. Moreover, the original figures were for a three-year period, leaving a one-year estimate of 53,333 who "disappeared" rather than 2 million. Finally, most of those who "disappeared" were abducted by former spouses or other relatives. Similar distortions operated to create the widely cited figure of 5,000 children kidnapped and murdered (*New York Times*, 1982). The true figure is probably in the range of 52-158 (Hotaling & Finkelhor, 1989).

The process which leads to an acceptance of false statistics can also lead to a rejection of statistics which contradict the intentions of a legislature or the thrust of a social movement. More realistic estimates of the number of kidnapped and murdered children were presented but ignored. Another example of statistics which are ignored because they contradict a prevailing opinion is discussed below: the research which shows that women assault their male partners at about the same rate as men assault their female partners.

Assaults by Women

Data from the 1985 National Family Violence Survey on the high rate of assaults by women on their male partners is in Table 2.1, Part C. Similar findings from the 1975 survey are reported in Straus, Gelles, and Steinmetz (1980) and in more than a dozen other studies such as Lane and Gwartney-Gibbs (1985), Laner and Thompson (1982), O'Leary, Barling, Arias, Rosenbaum, Malone, and Tyree (1987), and Steinmetz (1977-78). However, these data tend to be ignored or dismissed as biased and irrelevant. The most frequently mentioned reasons for dismissing these extremely robust findings are that they fail to take into account whether the assault was in self-defense and whether the assault resulted in an injury.

It is unlikely that the similarity of the wife-to-husband and husband-to-wife assault rates can be dismissed on the grounds that wife-to-husband assaults are acts of either self-defense or retaliation. In the 1985 survey, we asked who hit first. According to the men, they struck the first blow in 44 percent of the cases, the woman in 45 percent of the cases, and they could not remember in the remaining 11 percent of the cases. According to the women, the man struck the first blow in 53 percent of the cases, they did in 42 percent of the cases, and the remaining 5 percent of the women could not disentangle who hit first (Stets & Straus, 1990; see also Straus, 1980).

The second most frequent criticism of the National Family Violence Survey rates of assault by women is that assaults by men are more likely to cause physical injury and should therefore be the primary focus of public policy (Straus, 1977; Straus, Gelles & Steinmetz, 1980). To investigate this issue, the 1985 National Family Violence Survey included data on injury. These data were used to compute the injury adjusted rates which are on the last line in Parts A and C of Table 2.1.

The 1985 National Family Violence Survey found a physical injury rate of 3 percent for female victims and 0.5 percent for male victims (Stets and Straus, 1990a). Somewhat lower rates are reported by Brush (1989) for another large national sample—1.2 percent of women victims and 0.2 percent of men victims. The injury adjusted rate in Part A of Table 2.1 was computed by multiplying the assault rates in the first row of Part A by the higher of these two injury estimates (expressed as a proportion = .03). Similarly, the injury adjusted rate in Part C was obtained by multiplying by .005.

The resulting injury adjusted rates shown in Table 2.1 correspond more closely to police and NCS rates than to rates based only on whether an attack occurred. They result in a rate of domestic assaults by men that is almost six times greater than the rate of domestic assaults by women, thus bringing out an important aspect of domestic assault. On the other hand, there are several disadvantages to using rates based on injury (Straus, 1990b:79-83). Three will be mentioned.

One disadvantage is that the criterion of injury contradicts new domestic assault legislation and new police policies. These statutes and policies (for example, New Hampshire RSA 173-B) encourage arrest on the basis of attacks and do not require an observable injury.

Another disadvantage of injury as a criterion for domestic assault is that injury based rates omit the 97 percent of assaults by men which do not result in injury but which are nonetheless a serious social problem. Without an adjustment for injury, the National Family Violence Survey produces an estimate of over 6 million women assaulted by a male partner each year of which 1.8 million are "severe." If the injury adjusted rate is used, the estimate falls to 189,000 assaulted women per year. The figure of 1.8 million seriously assaulted women every year has been used in many legislative hearings and countless publications to indicate the prevalence of the problem. If that estimate was replaced by 189,000, it would under understate the extent of the problem and handicap efforts to educate the public and secure funding for shelters and other services. Fortunately, that is not necessary. Both estimates can be used since each highlights a different aspect of the problem.

A final limitation of using a rate based on injury is that it makes it too easy to ignore the fact that the attack rate, not the injury rate, is about the same for men and women. Although first priority does need to be given to ameliorating the plight of battered women, assaults by women are extremely important because they suggest policies which have profound implications for preventing assaults *against* women.

Let us assume that most of the assaults by women fall into the "slap the cad" genre and are not intended to, and do not, physically injure the husband (Greenblatt, 1983; Stets & Straus, 1990). The danger to women of such behavior is that it helps legitimize assaults by men. Sometimes this is immediate and severe retaliation. But regardless of whether that occurs, the fact that she slapped him provides the precedent and justification for him to hit her when she is being obstinate, "bitchy," or "not listening to reason" as he sees it. Unless women also forsake violence in their relationships with male partners and children, they are unlikely to be free of the risk of being assaulted. Women must insist as much on non-violence by their sisters as they rightfully insist on it by men. That is beginning to happen. After years of denial, shelters for battered women are confronting this problem. Almost all shelters now have policies designed to deal with the high rate of child abuse; some are also facing up to the problem of female-to-male violence. But primary prevention requires carrying this message to women in general.

This will not be easy to accomplish, in part because the cost of publicizing violence by women is that it may be used to justify male violence. The National Family Violence Survey data on assaults by women have, in fact, been used against battered women in court cases and to minimize the need for shelters for battered women. However, failing to educate women about their own violence is a major obstacle to reducing the rate of woman battering. There may be costs associated with acknowledging the fact of violence by women in the family; but the cost of denial and suppression is even greater. Rather than attempting to deny the existence of such violence (see Pleck et al., 1977 for an example of such denial and the reply by Steinmetz, 1978), a more productive solution is to confront the issue and work towards eliminating violence by women. The achievements of the 20-year effort to reduce child abuse and the 10-year effort to reduce woman battering (see Straus & Gelles, 1986) suggest this is a realistic goal.

Survey Data, Clinical Data, and Policy

The section on "How Many Battered Women" showed that the estimate can vary from 125,000 to over 6 million. But even this understates the degree to which the procedures used to obtain data on battered women affect rates and the utility of one's findings. This section focuses on two variations in measurement procedure: the extent to which frequency of assault is used as a criterion and use of "clinical" versus random samples.

Frequency of Assault. The 1985 National Family Violence survey found that women who were assaulted by their partners during the year of the survey experienced an average of 6 assaults during the year. Since the average number of assaults was so high, it seemed as though the survey had been successful in identifying a group of "battered women" and that an analysis of the experiences of these women could provide clues to the prevention and treatment of woman battering. On the other hand, there are a number of discrepancies between the findings of our surveys and findings based on police calls and shelter populations. These discrepancies raise questions about the validity of generalizing from the experiences of assaulted women in the survey to battered women in shelters and suggested the need for a direct comparison of the two groups.

Two studies which used the CTS with women in shelters were located. Giles-Sims (1983) interviewed 31 women at a shelter in Portland, Maine. These women reported an average of 68.7 assaults during the year preceding their shelter stay (p. 53). A second study by Okun (1986) is based on 300 women in a shelter in the Ann Arbor, Michigan area who reported an annualized frequency of 65 assaults. These averages of more than one assault per week are about 11 times greater than the 6 assaults per year experienced by the women in the National Family Violence Survey.[4] It seems plausible that, despite what seemed to be a very high average number of assaults experienced by the women in the national survey, the women in these two shelters had suffered a qualitatively as well as a quantitatively different experience.

Whatever the reason for much higher frequency of assault on shelter clients than on assaulted women in the National Family Violence Surveys, this difference may explain some of the discrepancies in research findings based on the two populations. One of the most controversial differences is the finding that women in the two national surveys had a high rate of assault on their partners and often hit first whereas studies of women in shelters show that they almost never assault their partners (Saunders, 1986). Perhaps this is because the shelter women were assaulted so frequently—an average of more than once a week—that they did not dare hit back.

The "Clinical Fallacy" and the "Representative Sample Fallacy." Sociologists sometimes use the term "clinical fallacy" to call attention to the fact that research based on "clinical" samples (i.e., samples of persons or families receiving assistance or treatment for a problem) may not be generalizable because those who seek or receive "treatment" are often not representative of the entire population with the problem. An extreme example of this fallacy is manifested in such statements as "Once abuse starts, it gets worse and more frequent over time" (leaflet published by the Domestic Violence Project, 1988) or, as Pagelow (1981:45) puts it, "One of the few things about which almost all researchers agree is that batterings escalate in frequency and intensity over time."

These statements are based on the experience of thousands of battered women who have received help from shelters. However, their experience cannot be generalized to all battered women because women whose partners stopped assaulting them are unlikely to seek help from a shelter. Of course, it could apply to all assaulted women but the longitudinal analysis reported in Feld and Straus (1989) shows that this is not the case.

The other side of the coin is a similar problem that I call the *representative sample fallacy.* This refers to the danger of trying to generalize from the characteristics and experiences of the total population who manifest a certain problem (such as assaults on a female partner) to populations receiving assistance for the problem (such as clients of battered women's shelters).

The representative sample fallacy refers to the assumption, implicit in most survey research, that a representative sample of the population is always superior to clinical samples. This assumption is unwarranted if persons in the general population who manifest the problem are different from a "clinical" population manifesting the problem. The preceding section on frequency of assault provides an example. Women in shelters experienced a frequency of assault that is so much greater than that experienced by assaulted women in the general population that it is reasonable to assume a qualitatively different experience for these two groups of women. As noted above, this difference could explain why studies based on women in shelters show that very few report assaulting their partner whereas survey findings reveal that women tend to assault their partners at about the same rate as men assault their partners and indeed often hit first. The survey findings are the basis for the recommendation that part of the effort to prevent wife battering should stress the importance of non-violence by women. However, for women who are assaulted more than once a week, this is not likely to be helpful in alleviating their immediate situation.

A similar situation exists in research on elder abuse and other types of deviant behavior. The characteristics associated with abuse of a representative sample of persons 65 and over in the Boston metropolitan area studied by Pillemer and Finkelhor (1987) differ in important ways from the characteristics associated with abuse cases known to the State Adult Protective Services departments reported by Steinmetz (1988). Pillemer and Finkelhor find that the victims tend to be men in their 70s who are assaulted by their wives whereas Steinmetz finds that victims tend to be older, widowed women. She suggests that the difference arises because the minor assaults by elderly women on their husbands rarely produce the type of injury that will bring a case to the attention of Adult Protective Services.

Criminologists point out that research on criminal behavior using samples of incarcerated persons is analogous to research on business using samples of businesses that have failed. In both cases, one learns about what produces failure and that is important. But it is also important to realize that the findings may not apply to the majority of criminals who are not apprehended and incarcerated nor to the majority of businesses which do not fail. Similarly, findings based on samples of successful criminals and successful business may not be useful in working with failed criminals (i.e., those in prison) and failed businesses because such studies do not provide evidence on the causes of failure.

In mental health research, discrepancies have been found between alcoholics identified among the general population and alcoholics in treatment samples, between those who attempt suicide and those who actually commit suicide, and between depression identified in the general population and in clinical samples. As in the case of assaulted women, the population classified as "alcoholic" or "depressed" in the surveys is much greater than the population being treated for these problems. Moreover, many of the social and psychological characteristics of persons in treatment for alcoholism and depression are quite different than the characteristics of the populations identified as alcoholic or depressed in community surveys (Room, 1980). For example, alcoholics in the general population tend to be young whereas alcoholics in treatment tend to be middle-aged or older.

Appropriate Generalization from Clinical and Representative Samples

This analysis does not mean that one type of sample is superior to another. It also does not necessarily mean that findings from a clinical sample are not applicable to a community sample or vice versa. Rather, it means that without a specific investigation, there is no way of knowing if the experiences of a representative sample of battered women apply to a police call sample or a treatment population of battering cases.

In the absence of such cross-validation, the appropriateness of a sample depends on the purpose for which information from it is used. On the one hand, findings based on a random sample of assaulted women may be misleading if the goal is to uncover relationships that can be the basis for counseling battered women in shelters. This requires knowledge based on the experiences of the population being assisted, regardless of whether their experience is representative of the total population. The experience of other populations may or may not be relevant.

On the other hand, findings based on a "treatment sample" do not necessarily apply to the community at large. The experience of women who have sought assistance from battered women's shelters may not be relevant for designing intervention in the larger community to prevent marital violence because, unless the program is based on information obtained from the experiences of a representative sample of the community, one cannot know if it fits their life circumstances. Community survey samples, such as the two National Family Violence Surveys, provide information about that population. This information indicates that there are a large number of women who are being battered but not to the point that drives a woman to a shelter. However, while their needs may be less acute, they are real. The assaulted women in the 1985 National Survey, for example, were attacked an average of 6 times during the year. Six assaults a year is only 1/11 of the 68 assaults per year experienced by women in shelters; but it indicates an urgent need for policies to end these assaults. Moreover, the fact that a representative sample was studied enables us to estimate that there are over 6 million such women in the United States. This makes the magnitude of the task clear.

NOTES

1 Eighteen thousand calls were recorded during the first nine months of the law. The estimate was obtained by multiplying this by 1.33 to obtain an annual figure of 23,940. Since there were an estimated 1,551,772 couples in New Jersey that year, this results in a rate of 1.54 percent (23,940/1,551,772 * 1 = 1.54. This rate was then multiplied by the 48,497,903 "spouse present" couples in the United States (.0154 * 48,497,903 = 748,202). The final step was to multiply by .86 to allow for the fact that 14 percent of the calls were instances of assaults by women on their sopuse (.14 * 748,202 = 643,453).

2 Several other factors affect estimates of the incidence of wife assault but, within the space of this chapter, only three can be noted. (1) Gender of the respondent: estimates based on interviews with male and female respondents are virtually identical for "minor violence" but, for severe violence, more women than men report committing such violence against their partners and being the victims of such violence. (2) The number of items in the instrument used to measure the assault rate: the more complete the list of assaultive acts used in the interview, the higher the rate (Straus, 1989). (3) Injury: if a physical injury is used as the criterion, the rates are much lower.

3 Straus and Gelles (1986) also document many other social changes during this decade that could have reduced the rate of child abuse and spouse abuse.

4 Although these figures are useful for comparing groups, they cannot be taken as literal descriptions of the actual number of assaults. It is unlikely that any of the assaulted spouses kept records such as a diary which would be needed for descriptively accurate statistics.

REFERENCES

Alford, R.D. (1982). "Intimacy and Disputing Styles within Kin and Nonkin Relationships." *Journal of Family Issues*, 3:361-374.

Allen, C.M. & M.A. Straus (1980). "Resources, Power, and Husband-Wife Violence." In M.A. Straus & G.T. Hotaling (eds.) *The Social Causes of Husband-Wife Violence.* Minneapolis, MN: University of Minnesota Press.

Allport, G.W. & L.J. Postman (1945). "The Basic Psychology of Rumor." In M.A. Straus & J.I. Nelson (eds.) *Sociological Analysis: An Empirical Approach Through Replication*, pp. 109-117. New York: Harper & Row.

American Association for Protecting Children (1987). *Highlights of Official Child Neglect and Abuse Reporting 1985*. Denver, CO: Author.

Bandura, A. (1973). *Aggression: A Social Learning Analysis.* Englewood Cliffs, NJ: Prentice-Hall.

Barling, J., K.D. O'Leary, E.N. Jouriles, D. Vivian & K.E. MacEwen (1987). "Factor Similarity of the Conflict Tactics Scales Across Samples, Spouses, and Sites: Issues and Implications." *Journal of Family Violence*, 2:37-55.

Berk, R.A., S.F. Berk, D.R. Loseke & D. Rauma (1983). "Mutual Combat and Other Family Violence Myths." In D. Finkelhor, R. Gelles, G. Hotaling & M. Straus (eds.) *Dark Side of Families: Current Family Violence Research.* Beverly Hills, CA: Sage Publications.

Berkowitz, L. (1962). *Aggression: A Social Psychological Analysis.* New York: McGraw-Hill.

Breines, W. & L. Gordon (1983). "Review Essay: The New Scholarship on Family Violence." *Signs: Journal of Women in Culture and Society*, 8:490-531.

Browne, A. (1987). *When Battered Women Kill.* New York: Free Press.

Brush, L.D. (1990). "Violent Acts and Injurious Outcomes in Married Couples: Methodological Issues in the National Survey of Families and Households." *Gender and Society*, 4:1, March, 56-67.

Calvert, R. (1974). "Criminal and Civil Liability in Husband-Wife Assaults." In S.K. Steinmetz & M.A. Straus (eds.) *Violence in the Family*, pp. 88-91. New York: Harper & Row.

Cate, R.M., J.M. Henton, K. Joval, F.S. Christopher & S. Lloyd (1982). "Premarital Abuse: A Social Psychological Perspective." *Journal of Family Issues*, 3:79-90.

Domestic Violence Project (1988). Ann Arbor, Michigan.

Dutton, D.G. (1988). *The Domestic Assault of Women: Psychological and Criminal Justice Perspectives.* Boston: Allyn and Bacon.

Feld, S.L. & M.A. Straus (1989). "Escalation and Desistance of Wife Assault in Marriage. *Criminology*, 27:141-161.

Finkelhor, D. & K. Yllo (1985). *License to Rape: Sexual Abuse of Wives.* New York: Holt, Rinehart & Winston.

Finkelhor, D. & I.A. Lewis (1988). "An Epidemiologic Approach to the Study of Child Molestation." In R. Prentky & V. Quinsey (eds.) *Human Sexual Aggression: Current Perspectives.* New York: The Annals of the New York Academy of Sciences.

Fox, J. & P. Tracy (1986). *Randomized Response: A Method for Sensitive Surveys.* Newbury Park, CA: Sage Publications.

Frieze, I.H. & A. Browne (1989). "Violence in Marriage." In L. Ohlin & M. Tonry (eds.) *Family Violence*, Chapter 11. Chicago: University of Chicago Press.

Gaquin, D.A. (1977-78). "Spouse Abuse: Data from the National Crime Survey." *Victimology*, 2:632-643.

Gelles, R.J. (1982). "Domestic Criminal Violence." In M.E. Wolfgang & N.A. Weinger (eds.) *Criminal Violence.* Newbury Park, CA: Sage Publications.

Gelles, R.J. & M.A. Straus (1979). "Determinants of Violence in the Family: Toward a Theoretical Integration." In W.R. Burr, R. Hill, F.I. Nye & I.L. Reiss (eds.) *Contemporary Theories About the Family*, pp. 549-581. New York: Free Press.

_____ (1987). "Is Violence Toward Children Increasing? A Comparison of 1975 and 1985 National Survey Rates." *Journal of Interpersonal Violence*, 2:212-222.

_____ (1988). *Intimate Violence.* New York: Simon & Schuster.

Giles-Sims, J. (1983). *Wife Battering: A Systems Theory Approach.* New York: Guilford Press.

Giles-Sims, J. (1985). "A Longitudinal Study of Battered Children of Battered Wives." *Family Relations*, 34:205-210.

Greenblat, C.S. (1983). "A Hit Is a Hit Is a Hit...Or Is It? Approval and Tolerance of the Use of Physical Force by Spouses." In D. Finkelhor, R.J. Gelles, G.T. Hotaling & M.A. Straus (eds.) *The Dark Side of Families.* Newbury Park, CA: Sage Publications.

Henton, J., R. Cate, J. Koval, S. Lloyd & S. Christopher (1983). "Romance and Violence in Dating Relationships." *Journal of Family Issues*, 4:467-482.

Hornung, C.A., B.C. McCullough & T. Sugimoto (1981). "Status Relationships in Marriage: Risk Factors in Spouse Abuse." *Journal of Marriage and the Family*, 43:675-692.

Hotaling, G.T. & D. Finkelhor (1989). "Stranger Abduction Homicides of Children." *Juvenile Justice Bulletin,* Office of Juvenile Justice and Delinquency Prevention. Washington, DC: U.S. Department of Justice.

_____ (in press). "Estimating the Number of Stranger Abduction Homicides of Children: A Review of Available Evidence." *The Journal of Criminal Justice.*

Hotaling, G.T. & M.A. Straus (1989). "Intra-family Violence and Crime and Violence Outside the Family." In L. Ohlin & M. Tonry (eds.) *Family Violence.* Chicago: University of Chicago Press.

Hotaling, G.T. & D.B. Sugarman (1986). "An Analysis of Risk Markers in Husband to Wife Violence: The Current State of Knowledge." *Violence and Victims,* 1:101-124.

Hudson, W.W. & S.R. McIntosh (1981). "The Assessment of Spouse Abuse: Two Quantifiable Divisions." *Journal of Marriage and the Family,* 43:873-885.

Jorgensen, S.R. (1977). "Societal Class Heterogamy, Status Striving, and Perception of Marital Conflict: A Partial Replication and Revision of Pearlin's Contingency Hypothesis." *Journal of Marriage and the Family,* 39:653-689.

Jouriles, E.N. & K.D. O'Leary (1985). "Interspousal Reliability of Reports of Marital Violence." *Journal of Consulting and Clinical Psychology,* 53:419-421.

Lane, K.E. & P.A. Gwartney-Gibbs (1985). "Violence in the Context of Dating and Sex." *Journal of Family Issues,* 6:45-59.

Laner, M.R. & J. Thompson (1982). "Abuse and Aggression in Courting Couples." *Deviant Behavior: An Interdisciplinary Journal,* 3:229-244.

Marcus, P. (1983). "Assault and Battery." In S.H. Kadish (ed.) *Encyclopedia of Crime and Justice* (Vol. 1). New York: Free Press.

Margolin, G. (1988). "Interpersonal and Intrapersonal Factors Associated with Marital Violence." In G.T. Hotaling, D. Finkelhor, J.T. Kirkpatrick & M.A. Straus (eds.) *Family Abuse and Its Consequences: New Directions in Research.* Newbury Park, CA: Sage Publications.

McGrath, P.E., P.S. Schultz & P. O'Dea Culhane (1980). *The Development and Implementation of a Hospital Protocol for the Identification and Treatment of Battered Women.* Monograph series. Rockville, MD: National Clearinghouse on Domestic Violence.

McLeod, M. (1983). "Victim Non-Cooperation in the Prosecution of Domestic Assault." *Criminology,* 21:395-416.

Miller, D.R. & G.E. Swanson (1958). *The Changing American Parent*. New York: John Wiley & Sons, Inc.

New York Times (1982). "Child Abductions A Rising Concern." December 5:A7.

O'Leary, K.D., J. Barling, I. Arias, A. Rosenbaum, J. Malone & A. Tyree (1989). "Prevalence and Stability of Spousal Aggression." *Journal of Consulting & Clinical Psychology*, 57(2):263-268.

Okun, L. (1986). *Woman Abuse: Facts Replacing Myths*. Albany, NY: State University of New York Press.

Pagelow, M.D. (1981). *Woman-Battering: Victims and Their Experiences*. Newbury Park, CA: Sage Publications.

_____ (1984). *Family Violence*. New York: Praeger Publishers.

Pillemer, K. & D. Finkelhor (1988). "The Prevalence of Elder Abuse: A Random Sample Survey." *The Gerontological Society of America*, 28(1):51-57.

Plass, P. & M.A. Straus (1987). *Intra-family Homicide in the United States: Incidence Rates, Trends, and Differences by Region, Race and Gender*. Paper presented at the Third National Family Violence Research Conference, University of New Hampshire, Family Research Laboratory, Durham, New Hampshire.

Pleck, E., J.H. Pleck, M. Grossman & P.B. Bart (1977). "The Battered Data Syndrome: A Comment on Steinmetz' Article." *Victimology: An International Journal*, 2:680-683.

Radbill, S.X. (1987). "Children in a World of Violence: A History of Child Abuse." In R.E. Helfer & R.S. Kempe (eds.) *The Battered Child*. Chicago: University of Chicago Press.

Saunders, D.G. (1986). "When Battered Women Use Violence: Husband-Abuse or Self-Defense?" *Violence and Victims*, 1:47-60.

Scanzoni, J. (1978). *Sex Roles, Women's Work, and Marital Conflict*. Lexington, MA: Lexington Books.

Schulman, M.A. (1979). *A Survey of Spousal Violence Against Women in Kentucky* (Study No. 792701). Washington, DC: Law Enforcement Assistance Administration, U.S. Government Printing Office.

Schumm, W.R., M.J. Martin, S.R. Bollman & A.P. Jurich (1982). "Classifying Family Violence: Whither the Woozle?" *Journal of Family Issues*, 3:319-340.

Stark, E., A. Flitcraft, D. Zuckerman, A. Grey, J. Robinson & W. Frazier (1981). *Wife Abuse in the Medical Setting: An Introduction to Health Personnel* (Monograph Series #7). Washington, DC: National Clearinghouse on Domestic Violence.

Steinmetz, S.K. (1977). *The Cycle of Violence: Assertive, Aggressive, and Abusive Family Interaction.* New York: Praeger Publishers.

_____ (1977-1978). "The Battered Husband Syndrome." *Victimology*, 2(3-4):499-509.

_____ (1978). "Services to Battered Women: Our Greatest Need: A Reply to Field and Kirchner." *Victimology: An International Journal*, 3:222-226.

_____ (1988). *Duty Bound: Elder Abuse and Family Care.* Newbury Park, CA: Sage Publications.

Stets, J.E. & M.A. Straus (1990). "The Marriage License as a Hitting License: A Comparison of Dating, Cohabiting, and Married Couples." In M.A. Straus & R.J. Gelles (eds.) *Physical Violence In American Families: Risk Factors And Adaptations to Violence in 8,145 Families.* New Brunswick, NJ: Transaction Books.

_____ (1990). "Gender Differences in Reporting Marital Violence and its Medical and Psychological Consequences." In M.A. Straus & R.J. Gelles (eds.) *Physical Violence In American Families: Risk Factors And Adaptations to Violence in 8,145 Families.* New Brunswick, NJ: Transaction Books.

Straus, M.A. (1974). "Leveling, Civility, and Violence in the Family." *Journal of Marriage and the Family*, 36:13-29, plus addendum in August 1974 issue.

_____ (1977). "A Sociological Perspective on the Prevention and Treatment of Wife-Beating." In Maria Roy (ed.) *Battered Women.* New York: Van Nostrand Reinhold.

_____ (1979). "Measuring Intrafamily Conflict and Violence: The Conflict Tactics (CT) Scale." *Journal of Marriage and the Family*, 41:75-88.

_____ (1980). "The Marriage License as a Hitting License: Evidence from Popular Culture, Law, and Social Science." In M.A. Straus & G.T. Hotaling (eds.) *The Social Causes of Husband-Wife Violence.* Minneapolis: University of Minnesota Press.

_____ (1980). "Victims and Aggressors in Marital Violence." *American Behavioral Scientist*, 23:681-704.

_____ (1983). "Ordinary Violence, Child Abuse, and Wife-beating: What Do They Have in Common?" In D. Finkelhor, R.J. Gelles, G.T. Hotaling & M.A. Straus (eds.) *The*

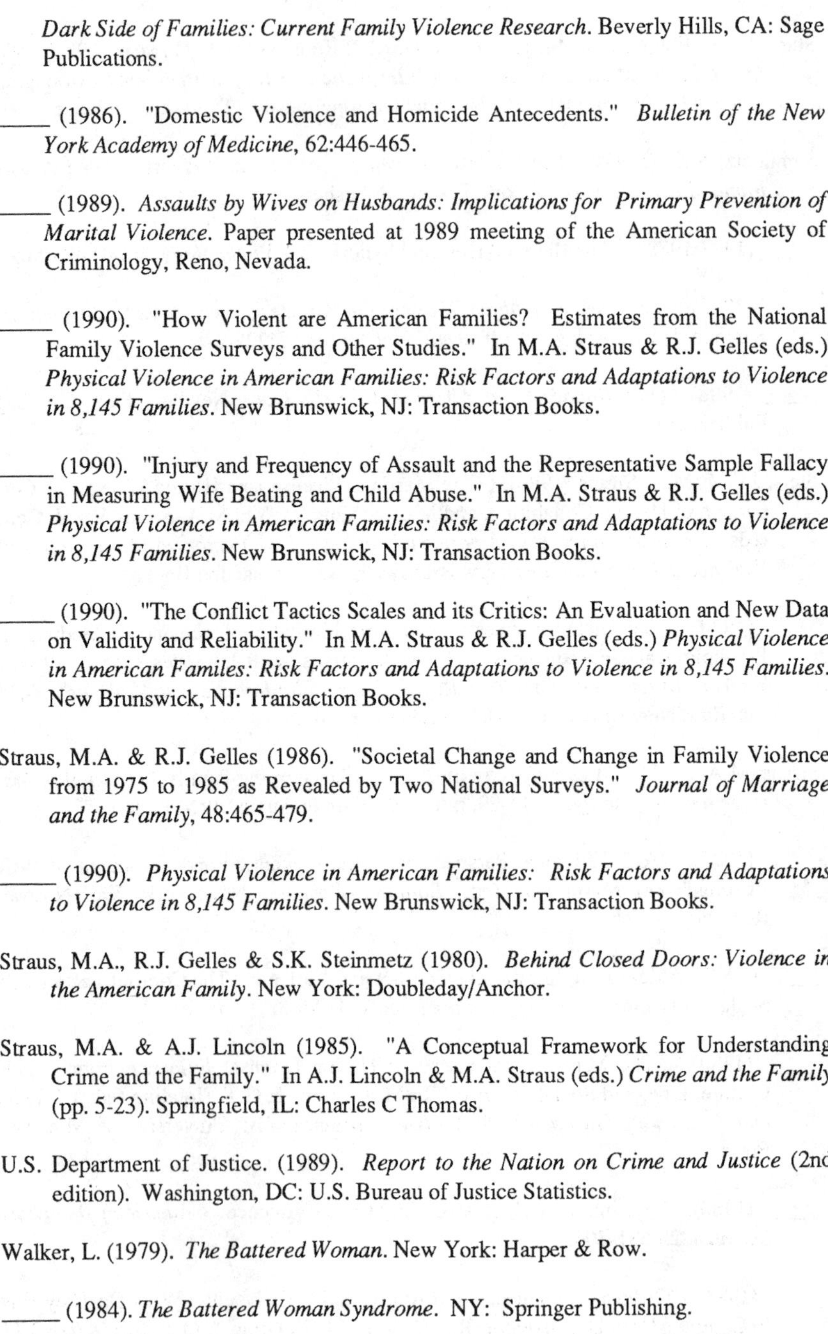

Dark Side of Families: Current Family Violence Research. Beverly Hills, CA: Sage Publications.

_____ (1986). "Domestic Violence and Homicide Antecedents." *Bulletin of the New York Academy of Medicine*, 62:446-465.

_____ (1989). *Assaults by Wives on Husbands: Implications for Primary Prevention of Marital Violence*. Paper presented at 1989 meeting of the American Society of Criminology, Reno, Nevada.

_____ (1990). "How Violent are American Families? Estimates from the National Family Violence Surveys and Other Studies." In M.A. Straus & R.J. Gelles (eds.) *Physical Violence in American Families: Risk Factors and Adaptations to Violence in 8,145 Families*. New Brunswick, NJ: Transaction Books.

_____ (1990). "Injury and Frequency of Assault and the Representative Sample Fallacy in Measuring Wife Beating and Child Abuse." In M.A. Straus & R.J. Gelles (eds.) *Physical Violence in American Families: Risk Factors and Adaptations to Violence in 8,145 Families*. New Brunswick, NJ: Transaction Books.

_____ (1990). "The Conflict Tactics Scales and its Critics: An Evaluation and New Data on Validity and Reliability." In M.A. Straus & R.J. Gelles (eds.) *Physical Violence in American Familes: Risk Factors and Adaptations to Violence in 8,145 Families*. New Brunswick, NJ: Transaction Books.

Straus, M.A. & R.J. Gelles (1986). "Societal Change and Change in Family Violence from 1975 to 1985 as Revealed by Two National Surveys." *Journal of Marriage and the Family*, 48:465-479.

_____ (1990). *Physical Violence in American Families: Risk Factors and Adaptations to Violence in 8,145 Families*. New Brunswick, NJ: Transaction Books.

Straus, M.A., R.J. Gelles & S.K. Steinmetz (1980). *Behind Closed Doors: Violence in the American Family*. New York: Doubleday/Anchor.

Straus, M.A. & A.J. Lincoln (1985). "A Conceptual Framework for Understanding Crime and the Family." In A.J. Lincoln & M.A. Straus (eds.) *Crime and the Family* (pp. 5-23). Springfield, IL: Charles C Thomas.

U.S. Department of Justice. (1989). *Report to the Nation on Crime and Justice* (2nd edition). Washington, DC: U.S. Bureau of Justice Statistics.

Walker, L. (1979). *The Battered Woman*. New York: Harper & Row.

_____ (1984). *The Battered Woman Syndrome*. NY: Springer Publishing.

Warner, S. (1965). "Randomized Response: A Survey Technique for Eliminating Evasive Answer Bias." *Journal of the American Statistical Association*, 60:63-69.

Washburn, C. & I.H. Frieze (1981). *Methodological Issues in Studying Battered Women.* Paper presented at the First National Conference for Family Violence Researchers, Durham, New Hampshire.

Zdep, S.M. & I.N. Rhodes (1976). "Making the Randomized Response Technique Work." *Public Opinion Quarterly*, 40:531-537.

3

Police-Preferred Arrest Policies

J. David Hirschel
University of North Carolina—Charlotte

Ira Hutchison
University of North Carolina—Charlotte

INTRODUCTION

During the past decade there has been a nationwide movement toward adopting arrest as the preferred law enforcement response to woman battering. This chapter will examine what a "preferred arrest policy" means. The term is neither clear nor uniformly understood. Ambiguity can breed intra-departmental confusion, misleading interpretations of change, and conflicts between police departments and others involved in treating battering.

Nationally, several different terms are used to denote police policies that either suggest or require arrest. While nuances may differentiate between such terms as "preferred," "presumptive," and "proarrest," the terms are taken to have a similar core meaning, namely that arrest is suggested in certain circumstances. For the sake of consistency, "preferred arrest" will be the term used in this chapter. Similarly, the term "mandatory" will be used to signify a policy that requires arrest whether that policy is described as "mandatory," "required," or given another synonymous label.

Interestingly, police departments themselves seem to shy away from using these terms. The common approach appears to be to tell officers that they "should" (suggestive) or "shall/must" (mandatory) arrest in certain stated circumstances. A review by the present authors of the policies of 20 police departments with preferred arrest policies revealed, for example, that only two departments used the terms "preferred," "presumptive," or "proarrest" to denote suggestive arrest policies.

In this chapter, we will explore issues and ambiguities surrounding preferred arrest policies. For example, to what extent have police departments adopted them? Has the adoption of preferred arrest policies been a result of departmental initiative or legislative mandate? What exactly does it mean in theory to have a preferred arrest policy? What does it mean in practice? How do officers react to these new policies which radically alter the traditional law enforcement response to battering? We then describe some exploratory research to help clarify the situations in which such policies apply.

The chapter concludes by identifying significant impediments to a uniform interpretation and implementation of preferred arrest policies. Little attention has been paid to whether arrest is a viable police response in domestic situations. It is often taken for granted that arrest is a straightforward, easily implemented response. However, responding officers must find grounds to conclude that a crime was committed to make an arrest.

A twofold approach is used to answer the questions raised here. First, an intensive literature review examines current research on these issues. Second, original survey data help answer questions unresolved in the literature. These data come from two sources: police departments with preferred arrest policies and women's advocates operating in the same jurisdictions. The objective in surveying these two populations is to obtain a balanced view of preferred arrest policies.

THE PREFERRED ARREST MOVEMENT

There are many vexing issues involving the meaning, implementation, and effects of preferred arrest. However, there is no disputing the current trend toward preferred arrest policy. As detailed elsewhere in this book, the law enforcement response to women battering evolved from a long period of complacency, to a short period in which crisis intervention was emphasized, to the present period of an orientation toward arrest. The past five years have seen a major increase in the number of police departments which now apply arrest policies. To a large extent, this is attributable to changes that have taken place in state statutes. Lerman (1983:44) observed that "twenty-seven of the recent state laws on domestic violence expand(ed) police power to arrest in domestic abuse cases.". Ferraro notes that, as of 1986, six states had passed laws requiring arrest with a positive determination of probable cause and the presence of the offender on the scene (1989:61). By 1988, there were ten states with such laws (Victim Services Agency, 1988:3). It is important, however, to note that such statutory provisions are often limited by conditional requirements that must be satisfied before they can be invoked. Thus, some state laws require the existence of a visible injury and/or the lapse of a short period of time between the commission of the offense and the arrival of the police. Moreover, it may be estimated that, subject to jurisdictional variation, about half of all offenders leave the scene before police arrive (Hirschel & Hutchison, 1987:11).

Preferred arrest policies are far more common than mandatory policies. A study by the Crime Control Institute (Sherman & Cohn, 1989; *Law Enforcement News*, 1987) investigated arrest policies in cities with populations of over 100,000 people. This research, based on telephone surveys conducted in 1984, 1985, and 1986 identified 78 cities in 27 states which had adopted preferred arrest policies by 1986. This represented a fourfold increase from the number of departments with such policies in 1984. The trend is, therefore, indisputable. However, the study did not include police departments in cities with populations of less than 100,000 people so it is not possible to determine the extent to which the large city trend is being replicated in less populous areas.

In general, the literature does not deal with whether police departments have adopted these arrest policies on their own initiative or as a result of changes in state law. It is clear that a number of factors have prompted police departments to change their policies. The same forces that have operated on state legislatures have also influenced police departments. Foremost among these have been various women's groups, including the National Coalition against Domestic Violence, state chapters of this organization, and local coalitions which have formed to alter existing policies and practices.

While it is difficult to unravel the different factors that have motivated police departments to adopt arrest policies, it is important to gauge the extent to which departments have willingly adopted them. This is important because the orientations of top administrators might reasonably be expected to influence rank-and-file enforcement of the policies. Available information suggests that, by and large, police departments have not played a lead role in adopting arrest policies and have occasionally been very reluctant to do so. For example, Arizona's legislature passed a law in 1980 that expanded police arrest powers and prohibited officers from citing and releasing domestic violence offenders. However, the law had "very little impact on law enforcement" (Ferraro, 1989:62). According to Ferraro, it was only when faced with the possibility of more legislation mandating arrest that the chief of the Phoenix police department adopted a presumptive arrest policy for his department and promised that he would encourage other Arizona police chiefs to do the same (1989:63). A similar reluctance among police departments to change their policies to conform with new statutory provisions has been noted by Miller (1979:16) in Oregon, Bell (1985:532) in Ohio, and Buzawa (1988:174-175) in New Hampshire.

Ambiguities About Preferred Arrest

There is perhaps no area of literature or policy more muddled about the meanings of specific words than that describing the trend toward the greater utilization of arrest policy regarding battering. There are at least three potential sources of confusion and inconsistency. First, as noted earlier, there is inconsistency concerning the name of the policy itself, i.e., preferred, proarrest, presumptive, mandatory, and required. Second, there is wide variation in conditional requirements which must be met before the policy is applied. For example, in some states offenses must have taken place within a specified period of time (e.g., in Washington State within the preceding four hours (Ferguson, 1987:9)) and probable cause is treated inconsistently both across and within jurisdictions. Third, the nature of the victim-offender's relationship may disqualify a particular domestic situation from a policy's coverage. For example, state laws and police policy sometimes do not call for the same response for cohabiting couples and married couples. Even when law or policy treats these two types of relationship equivalently, police practice does not necessarily do so. Thus, to note that a particular police department or some number of departments have a preferred arrest policy may tell us little more than that some kind of policy exists.

The terminology itself, as noted above, implies a dichotomy of sorts: those policies which are preferred (proarrest or presumptive) versus those which are mandatory/required. The former officially authorize an element of officer discretion in defining and deciding how to handle situations. This exposes preferred policies to criticisms that responding officers can be influenced by personal or historical aversions to arrest and that only more severe or blatant cases result in arrest. On the other hand, mandatory policies have an absolute quality. However, each situation must still be defined by the responding officer as falling under the requirements of the policy mandating arrest. While there appear to be clear-cut differences between preferred and mandatory arrest policies, the differences may often be more illusory than real.

Nevertheless, terminology is important because it affects interpretation and practice. Sherman and Berk conclude in their seminal article:

> ...we favor a presumption of arrest; an arrest should be made unless there are good, clear reasons why an arrest would be counterproductive. We do not, however, favor requiring arrests in all misdemeanor domestic assault cases. Even if our findings were replicated in a number of jurisdictions, there is a good chance that arrest works far better for some kinds of offenders than others and in some kinds of situations better than others. We feel it best to leave police a loophole to capitalize on that variation. Equally important, it is widely recognized that discretion is inherent in police work. Simply to impose a requirement of arrest, irrespective of the features of the immediate situation, is to invite circumvention (1984:270).

The implication of this conclusion is that even states or departments with mandatory arrest policies cannot depend on such policies being uniformly followed. The element of discretion retained in the preferred arrest policies does permit, for better or worse, wide officer latitude in enforcing them. Unfortunately, there is no literature which clearly addresses intra-department variations in enforcing preferred arrest policies.

The conditional requirements necessary for implementing a particular policy, whether preferred or mandatory, also are diverse. All states delineate probable cause and misdemeanor criteria. As a result, concluding that two departments in different states have similar policies because each specifies preferred arrest may be erroneous because of state-to-state differences. Moreover, many departments have mandatory arrest policies in cases of "serious injury," but preferred arrest policies in cases of "minor injury." Responding officers must apply these distinctions themselves. In addition, while the terms mandatory arrest and required arrest appear to leave little room for variation, there may still be conditional requirements not apparent to those outside a specific legal system. Furthermore, mandatory arrest provisions may be rather limited in scope and encompass, for example, only situations involving violations of protection orders.

Finally, policy trends toward either preferred or mandatory arrest adoptions do not necessarily protect all victims. It is known that cohabiting victims call police disproportionately more often than married victims (Hutchison, Hirschel & Pesackis, 1988:14). However, in at least some states, non-married couples are not covered by preferred arrest policies (Ferraro, 1989).

Enforcing Preferred Arrest Policies

While there is agreement that the way in which department policies are written affects their enforcement, there is no consensus about their optimum form. As Steinman notes (1988), Goolkasian stresses the need for "detailed, written policies and procedures" (1986:21), while Bayley argues that "structural forms are undoubtedly much less important in shaping accountability than political ethos and the character of regimes" (1983:33) and Skolnick suggests that detailed policies may actually encourage the use of police discretion since the promulgation of rules is often interpreted as enabling (1967:235).

The success of formal policies depends on the support of both command and line personnel. The impact of negative attitudes among police chiefs regarding the use of arrest in battering cases is clearly demonstrated by Buzawa's (1988) research in New Hampshire. She found that a lack of support by chiefs was associated with low enrollments in the voluntary state-administered training program, the absence of written departmental policies, low or non-existent arrest rates for battering incidents, and a feeling among officers that responding to abuse calls was usually a waste of time (Buzawa, 1988:175-178). In one jurisdiction, the chief even went so far as to say that "he could not recall a 'genuine' call for domestic violence in his numerous years as an administrator" and as a consequence "did not highly value the role of police intervention in this area" (Buzawa, 1988:175).

Another issue relates to the need for complementary changes in both the criminal justice system and social support services. While there is little apparent disagreement over the desirability of strengthening law and police policy as it applies to women battering, the lack or inadequacy of secondary support services undermines the utility of police action. Hemmons (1981), for example, decries the impotence of law unless it is backed up by support services. Such services might be particularly important for those who are outside the modal American family, such as cohabiting couples.

In some jurisdictions, police departments have adopted preferred arrest policies without working with other agencies. In other jurisdictions, adoptions have been part of a coordinated community response. Thus far, it is the latter departments that have reported positive results with their new policies. Gamache et al. (1988) report that after the introduction of community intervention projects in three Minnesota communities there were increases in both arrest and successful prosecution rates, while similar results are recorded by Steinman (1988:2) in Lincoln, Nebraska, by Ferguson (1987:9) and Goolkasian (1986:37-38) in Seattle, by Pence (1983:257-258) in Duluth, and by Burris and Jaffe (1983:312) in London, Ontario. After noting that police policies in these jurisdictions are coordinated with community-wide support, Steinman suggests that "this is probably not the case in most communities where departments have adopted arrest policies" (1988:2). Thus, in Phoenix for example, Ferraro found that the move to a presumptive arrest policy "represented only one minor change in an extensive city and county criminal justice system" and that the "police were not supported in their policy shift by correlative changes in other parts of the system" (1989:63).

In addition, most cities that have been closely studied are fairly small with relatively modest crime and battering rates. Thus, the three Minnesota communities studied by Gamache et al. range from 15,000 to 36,000 inhabitants and recorded five or less battering arrests a month per community during the research period (1988:195,201). Duluth, meanwhile, which has received considerable national attention for its Domestic Abuse Intervention Project that coordinates the efforts of nine law enforcement, criminal justice, and human service agencies, has a population of under 100,000 and recorded only some ten arrests a month during the research period reported by Pence (1983:258-259). All this suggests that post-arrest coordination can be more easily achieved in smaller communities with relatively modest crime and battering rates.

A problem emerges in interpreting higher arrest rates when information about the number of battering calls eligible for arrest under a new policy is unknown. It is impossible to distinguish real change from apparent change without this information. In the only available in-depth study of officer response to a new preferred arrest policy, Ferraro (1989) provides a fascinating study of the Phoenix police department. Despite the fact that Arizona passed legislation regarding arrest policy in 1980, little actual change occurred until 1984 when the Phoenix department finally adopted a preferred arrest policy. According to department figures, there was an initial doubling of the arrest rate from 33 percent to 67 percent in the second month after the policy was adopted. The following month, however, the rate fell to 52 percent, and then to 42 percent in the subsequent month. Although it is imperative to interpret Ferraro's research with caution due to both the limited duration of her study and the small sample (n=69), her findings are illuminating. Based on ride-along observational data, she reports that in spite of the new policy, arrests were made in only 18 percent of the battering incidents to which her research team responded. It is worth noting that this percentage, based on investigated incidents, provides a far different picture than the simple "doubling" of the arrest rate indicated by police department figures. A problem was that officer interpretations of probable cause employed "a level of evidence high enough for felony arrests" (Ferraro, 1989:64).

This brief review of Ferraro's work does not do justice to her analysis of the complexities of the situation. After noting wide variation in both specific characteristics of incidents as well as police handling of them she concludes that:

> Officers were free to guess how much importance they should attach to a policy that drastically altered their traditional approach to domestic violence. No explicit incentives were offered for compliance, and no penalties were attached to evasion of the new policy....these data indicate that each case is evaluated in terms of its relationship to a web of considerations, including legal, ideological, practical and political issues (Ferraro, 1989:72).

The analogy to a web is most appropriate. Given officers' opportunities to interpret both policy and case circumstances and lack of command support for the policy, there is no reason to expect officers to disavow their traditional reluctance to arrest.

Police officers are accustomed to making their own decisions on the street and are traditionally opposed to policies that limit their discretion. In his survey of Minneapolis officers conducted after the Sherman and Berk experiment, Steinman found a strong indication of independent mindedness, with 99 of 100 respondents voicing the belief that they "should make their own decisions about problems that arise on duty," 77 reporting that they "usually do what they think necessary even if they expect supervisors to disagree," and 43 declaring that "they should use their own standards of police work even when department procedures prohibit them from doing so" (1988:2). On the other hand, data from Duluth indicate that a mandatory arrest policy has led to a reduction in officer injury (Pence, 1989). Such an effect could be a selling point with some officers.

Research indicates that certain factors are associated with positive attitudes toward preferred arrest policies. Not surprisingly, an officer's general orientation toward battering is likely to affect his/her attitude toward preferred arrest policies (Ferraro, 1989:66-67; Homant & Kennedy, 1985; Berk & Loseke, 1981:320-321; Walter, 1981). Thus, if an officer considers battering to be a private matter, the officer is likely to be against a preferred arrest policy. In addition, female officers tend to be more supportive than male officers of arrest policies. Perhaps as more women enter police work there will be a shift in police responses. Homant and Kennedy's (1985) study, based on self-reported perceptions, suggests that policewomen see themselves (relative to policemen) as more understanding of abuse situations and more involved. Homant and Kennedy are careful to note, however, that gender accounted for only a small proportion of the differential involvement. They also note that it is naturally impossible to obtain comparative samples of policemen and policewomen. It seems reasonable to assume that policewomen and policemen would not generally react to abuse the same when males are primarily the offenders and females are overwhelmingly the victims. Kennedy and Homant (1985) bound some corroboration of this in a sample of shelter residents who rated policewomen more positively than male officers. Though Ferraro (1989) found negative attitudes on the part of both male and female officers toward the new Phoenix preferred arrest policy, "negative evaluations were more extreme" among male officers (p. 68).

Another influence on police attitudes is training. Studies have found training positively associated with both officer perception and citizen evaluation of officer handling of abuse calls (Pearce & Snortum, 1983), improved officer attitudes about handling battering cases (Buchanon & Perry, 1985), and officer willingness to arrest batterers (Buzawa, 1982:421-422). Interestingly, no association was found by Jaffe et al. (1986) between evaluations of arrest policies and years of service and experience in answering calls for service. As noted earlier, however, such factors as attitude and training have yet to be evaluated systematically for their effect on enforcement.

POLICE AND ADVOCATE PERCEPTIONS OF PREFERRED ARREST POLICY

Although current trends are clearly toward preferred arrest policy, the issues raised above indicate that this term is both conceptually and operationally nebulous. In order to obtain a clearer picture of what adopting such a policy means, the authors undertook an exploratory study of current policy in 26 cities. The goal was to determine the conditions under which an offender should be arrested according to formal policy. While it is not possible to identify or contrast actual rates or changes in arrest rates in these cities, it is possible to identify the variable conditions under which policy calls for the arrest of an offender.

Methodology

Data were collected from a nonrepresentative sample of police departments with preferred arrest policies in order to identify what preferred arrest policy means as policy in them. Additionally, data were collected from particular women's advocate groups to obtain an external assessment of police policies in the same jurisdictions. This parallel effort was designed to validate police policy statements.

The most current list of police departments with preferred arrest policies is provided by Sherman (*Law Enforcement News*, 1987). Based on research conducted through the Crime Control Institute, Sherman concluded that there were 78 police departments which had adopted preferred arrest policies by 1986 in cities of over 100,000 people. Utilizing the 27 states in which these departments are located as a sampling universe, one city in each state was selected using sequential criteria. First, cities were excluded in which National Institute of Justice funded replications of the Minneapolis experiment were being conducted. Since Atlanta was the only city in Georgia included in Sherman's list, applying this criterion reduced the sampling universe to 26 states.* In states with only one city listed, that city was selected. In states with more than one city listed, the largest city was excluded (e.g., New York City and Los Angeles) to avoid multiple policies and regulations. After excluding such cities, the selection procedure ordinarily excluded capital cities on the presumption that they might receive disproportionate state government attention and be less representative. In those states where more than one city still remained, the city was selected which had the most battering-related services, as documented in the handbook of the National Coalition Against Domestic Violence (1986). This was done because the police departments in these cities were likely to be the focus of more demands for aggressive enforcement.

This process resulted in the selection of 26 cities. A brief questionnaire was devised and sent to the police chief in each, to be completed by him or his

---

* The 26 states are Arizona, California, Colorado, Connecticut, Florida, Illinois, Indiana, Iowa, Kentucky, Massachusetts, Michigan, Minnesota, Missouri, Nebraska, Nevada, New Jersey, New York, Ohio, Oklahoma, Oregon, Pennsylvania, Tennessee, Texas, Virginia, Washington, and Wisconsin.

designate. The questionnaire presented a variety of situations (such as "victim receives minor injury") and asked respondents to identify which of several alternative responses would most likely be made in each *according to existing department policy.* Alternative responses included: arrest is required, arrest is preferred, separation is preferred, advice/mediation is preferred, officer follows own discretion, and no official policy applies in the stated situation. Additional questions solicited data on the length of time current policies have been in effect, any anticipated changes in policy, and police perceptions of external evaluations of current policy.

External evaluations were conducted through phone interviews in which comparable questions were asked of community sources. The community sources utilized consisted of women's advocate organizations.

The generic term "advocate" encompasses political activists, shelter personnel, intervention agents, and so forth. The National Directory of Domestic Violence Programs (National Coalition Against Domestic Violence, 1986) was used to identify advocates in targeted communities. Within our sample of 26 cities, there are a variety of program titles: crisis centers, support services, shelters, YWCA programs, domestic violence programs, and prevention centers. They offer such services as shelters, 24-hour hotlines, counseling and advocacy, and counseling for children.

The authors assume that key personnel in these agencies, those who responded to the telephone survey, must know about official police policy in their areas to be effective advocates for victims. Advocate respondents tended to be agency administrators, supervisors, or directors and most considered themselves very well informed about police policy. Indeed, these respondents often reported a working relationship with local police. In many cases, this relationship appeared to be mutually respectful and cooperative; in other cases, respondents appeared to believe that officers were not complying with formal policy. The most positive comments emerged from advocates in cities having a domestic violence unit in their police departments. Undoubtedly the existence of such units has both practical and symbolic benefits. Practically, advocates must find it logistically easier to work with a specialized team than with a diffuse department. Symbolically, advocates may take the existence of such units as a commitment by local police to do everything within their authority to help victims.

Unfortunately, there is no way to validate advocate responses. That is, advocate responses were taken at face value. It is possible that a hostile advocate might deliberately distort the policy and procedures of a local police department. There was, however, no evidence of this. It is the authors' perception that advocates responding to this survey were well-intentioned and had a lot of information about the police and judicial systems in their areas.

Results: Police Responses

Questionnaires were mailed at the beginning of May, 1989, to the police chiefs of the 26 departments. Four weeks later a second wave of surveys was sent to the 8 departments that had not responded. A total of 25 completed questionnaires were received from the 26 departments for a response rate of 96.2 percent.

All the responding departments provided, as requested, contact persons so that follow-up inquires could be made. Only 3 departments would not provide copies of their formal policies. Twenty included copies of their policies with their responses to the questionnaire. Two, which were in the process of updating their policies, said they would send copies when they became available.

Written department guidelines specifying the conditions under which arrest is preferred in battering cases existed in 21 (84%) departments; 19 (76%) had written guidelines specifying conditions under which arrest is mandatory. Twenty-two (88%) of the departments indicated that there were no differences in guidelines for handling calls that involved cohabiting and married couples. The three departments with such differences were in states that gave police broader warrantless arrest powers when dealing with married couples. In one of these states, however, the law has recently been amended to remove this distinction.

The 25 departments had their present policies in effect for varying amounts of time with changes in state law and fine tuning of previous policy accounting for the most recent modifications. All the departments appear to have had a preferred arrest policy for at least two years. Prior to this time they generally had less formal policies which allowed far greater officer discretion. Five departments indicated it was likely that their present policies would change because of recent statutory changes (2 departments), as part of a general revision of general orders (2 departments), and because of a move toward a "more proarrest" policy (1 department).

As discussed earlier, the meaning of "preferred arrest policy" is unclear. To clarify this issue, contact persons were asked a number of questions to relate department policy to a variety of situations. Their responses are presented in Table 3.1.

As reported in Table 3.1, all the departments have a policy which either mandates arrest or shows a preference for arrest in the following circumstances: (i) when the suspect has inflicted serious injury on the victim, such as broken bones or loss of consciousness; (ii) when the suspect has inflicted minor injuries on the victim, such as scratches and bruises; (iii) when the suspect has threatened the victim with a deadly weapon like a gun or knife; and (iv), more generally, when it is clear that there is probable cause to believe that a crime was committed. Twenty-three (92%) departments have a mandatory arrest policy in cases of serious injury, 18 (72%) have one in cases of minor injury, and 17 (68%) when probable cause clearly exists and where there is a threat with a deadly weapon.

Table 3.1 Police Official Descriptions of Arrest Policies in Percentages

	Alternative Police Responses*					
	Arrest Required	Arrest Preferred	Advising Preferred	Separating Preferred	Officer Discretion	Other
Serious injury	92.0	8.0				
Minor injury	72.0	28.0				
Threat with deadly weapon	68.0	32.0				
Verbal threat	28.0	16.0	4.0		36.0	16.0
Property damage**	32.0	16.0	4.0		28.0	16.0
Probable cause clearly exists	68.0	32.0				
Uncertainty as to probable cause		32.0	16.0	8.0	32.0	12.0

*n=25 police departments
**One department did not respond to this question

Department policies are more varied in cases that involve property damage or verbal threats and when there is uncertainty whether probable cause exists. While 8 (32%) departments have a mandatory and 4 (16%) a preferred arrest policy in cases where the suspect has damaged property, 7 (28%) leave it to the officers' discretion, 1 (4%) prefers to have the couple advised, and the remaining 4 (16%) employ a variety of measures. One department, for example, informs the victim how to obtain a protection court order. Another department arrests the offender if there is an emergency protection order in effect stating that he is not to damage property, but otherwise advises the victim and recommends obtaining a warrant if appropriate. For some departments, the response varied depending on who owned the damaged property.

A similar variation in policies exists when the suspect has verbally threatened the victim. While 7 (28%) departments have mandatory and 4 (16%) preferred arrest policies, 1 (4%) prefers to have the couple advised, 9 (36%) leave it to the officers' discretion, and 4 (16%) utilize a variety of responses, such as allowing responding officers to choose between advising and separating the couple.

In cases of uncertainty regarding probable cause, none of the departments have a policy of mandatory arrest. However, 8 (32%) have a preferred arrest policy, while 4 (16%) prefer to advise the couple, 2 (8%) to separate the couple, 8 (32%) leave it to the officers' discretion, and 3 (12%) employ other measures.

Responses to questions gauging police perceptions of external satisfaction with department policies revealed that respondents believe the public and those who work with victims (e.g., shelter personnel and women's support groups) are generally pleased with those policies. No department reported that its public is dissatisfied with current policy. Nine (36%) reported that the public was "highly satisfied," 13 (52%) that the public was "satisfied," 2 indicated mixed public feelings, and another did not respond.

Some negative department perceptions of advocate group satisfaction were expected. While 11 (44%) departments reported that advocates were "highly satisfied" and 10 (40%) that they were "satisfied" with police policy, 1 (4%) believed that advocate groups had mixed feelings and 3 (12%) that advocates were "dissatisfied." This perceived dissatisfaction may originate in police beliefs that advocate expectations are higher than police can satisfy. An explanatory note written by one police official stated that "support groups and agencies would like to see a mandatory arrest policy." Another police respondent remarked that while advocate groups may be satisfied with official police policy, they are "perhaps not as satisfied with its implementation in the field."

These data offer a picture of what it means for some police departments to have a preferred arrest policy regarding battering. However, the data do not tell us what such policies mean in practice. To find out, police respondents were asked whether their departments had data available on the numbers of battering calls and arrests made annually. Ten (40%) departments indicated they collected both types of data. One department did not respond. To obtain these data, telephone calls were made to the contact persons in these 11 police departments and 9 of them supplied the data. However, most of the data did not permit meaningful analysis since comparable call for service, offense report, and arrest data were either not available or were only available for a year or two. Indeed, only one department had comparable data for periods before and after its adoption of the preferred arrest policy.[1]

Results: Advocate Responses

Advocate respondents were successfully contacted in 25 (96.2%) of the 26 target cities. In cities with more than one listed advocate group, additional sources were contacted; respondents who considered themselves most familiar with police policy were interviewed.

Advocates were asked to indicate on a 4-point scale how familiar they were with the "local police department's official policies regarding spouse abuse." If a potential respondent indicated that she was only "somewhat familiar" or "not at all familiar" with local policy, she was asked to direct the interviewer to someone more informed. About two-thirds (64%) of the advocate respondents indicated they were "very familiar" and one-third indicated that they were "familiar" with local policy. No attempt was made to secure random or representative sources of assessment among advocate groups; the effort deliberately targeted well-informed advocates.

Based on responses from advocates in 25 cities, a large majority (88%) believe that local police policy is a preferred arrest policy, i.e., is "basically one which shows a preference for arresting offenders when the legal criteria for making arrests are satisfied." However, as shown in Table 3.2, advocate perceptions are conditional and much more variable than police reports of their own policies.

Table 3.2 Advocate Perception of Police Policy in Percentages*

	Arrest Required	Arrest Preferred	Advising Preferred	Separating Preferred	Officer Discretion	Other
Serious injury	88.0	8.0			4.0	
Minor injury	52.0	16.0	8.0	4.0	16.0	4.0
Threat with deadly weapon	68.0	16.0	8.0		8.0	
Verbal threat	8.0	8.0	40.0	12.0	28.0	4.0
Property damage	28.0	28.0	12.0	4.0	24.0	
Probable cause clearly exists	64.0	16.0	4.0	4.0	12.0	
Uncertainty as to probable cause	8.0	32.0	32.0	8.0	16.0	4.0

*n=25 advocate groups

Advocates reported that arrest is most likely to occur in cases where there is serious injury (96% combined mandatory and preferred arrest), threat with a deadly weapon (84%), clear probable cause (80%), or minor injury (68%). In each of these situations, advocates believe that police policy is most likely to be mandatory arrest with preferred arrest a distant second possibility. In addition, advocates believe that mandatory/preferred arrest is relatively less common when there is property damage (56%), uncertainty about probable cause (40%), and verbal threats (16%). While these data are not too dissimilar from data reported by the police, they do reflect a belief among advocates that non-arrest is the operational policy in situations which lack definitive grounds for arrest.

The 25 advocates show more dissatisfaction with policy implementation than with policy. Forty percent of them believe that local advocate groups are "dissatisfied" or "highly dissatisfied" with department policy; however, 60 percent fall into these two dissatisfaction categories when asked how police officers are "actually carrying out such policies." None of the advocate respondents reported advocate groups as being highly satisfied with the way police policy was actually being implemented. The most favorable were the 3 (12%) advocates who reported high satisfaction with policy itself and satisfaction with the implementation; another 6 (24%) were satisfied with both policy and its implementation. The modal response among the 25 advocates came from the 8 (32%) who said that they perceived dissatisfaction with both policy and its implementation among advocates in their communities. There are two ways of viewing these data. On the one hand, only 2 (8%) reported that advocate groups were highly dissatisfied with both policy and implementation. On the other hand, in these cities which were identified as having strong preferred arrest policies, the majority of advocate respondents (60%) reported dissatisfaction with either actual police policy, or its implementation, or both. The primary problem according to advocate respondents in our survey is the inconsistent application of existing policy.

These data on advocate group perceptions may be misleading since they do not reflect a city-by-city matched comparison with police reports. When such comparisons are made, much more variation emerges between police and advocate reports. The following data and discussion are based on 24 cities where both police and advocates were interviewed. The data in Table 3.3 indicate some of the variation between police reports and advocate perceptions.

As Table 3.3 reports, it is only in cases of serious injury that there is near total consensus about police policy, with 20 of the 23 (87%) comparisons of advocates and police agreeing that official policy requires the arrest of offenders. Beyond this one situation, there is almost as much dissension as consensus about police policy. In cases of threat with a deadly weapon, 12 cities have policies which require arrest, as confirmed by both advocates and police, and two cities have a confirmed preferred arrest policy. However, in 9 cities a deadly weapons threat is not clearly a mandatory arrest situation with police and advocates reporting different police responses. Even when probable cause is clear, only 12 cities produce police-advocate agreement that arrest is mandatory or preferred. There are as many cities (5) where police say arrest is required but advocates say something less stringent is official policy as there are cities where advocates say arrest is required but police report something less.

Table 3.3 Police Policy as Reported by Police and Matched-City Advocate Groups

	Police-Advocate Agreement Arrest Required	Police-Advocate Agreement Arrest Preferred	Police: Arrest Required Advocate: Arrest Preferred	Police: Arrest Preferred Advocate: Arrest Required	Police: Arrest Required or Preferred Advocate: Arrest Not Required Nor Preferred	Police: Arrest Not Required Nor Preferred Advocate: Arrest Required or Preferred	Police-Advocate Agreement on Response Other Than Required or Preferred Arrest	Police-Advocate Disagreement on Response Other Than Required or Preferred Arrest
Serious injury	20	1	2		1			
Minor injury	11	2	1	2		8		
Threat with deadly weapon	12	2	2	4	4			
Verbal threat	2		2		6		3	11
Property damage	2		3		5	8		4
Probable cause clearly exists	11	1	2	5	5			
Uncertainty as to probable cause		1		1	5	8	2	6

a. Based on 24 cities for which data obtained from both police department and an advocate group in the same city. "Agreement" means that both police and matched advocate group report official police policy identically. Advocate responses all refer to their perceptions of police policy, not to what they either might want or believe is actually implemented.

b. Example: Both police and advocates say that police policy is "officer discretion" in this situation.

c. Example: Police report that separation is official policy, advocates report that advising is official policy in this situation.

d. Does not total 24 due to missing data.

Finally, it is important to note that the apparently high level of agreement reflected in the last column in Table 3.3 is really illusory. Due to space limitations, individual tables for each situation could not be presented. Given 6 potential police responses, 36 possible combinations of police and advocate reports are possible. The apparent agreement, for example, on situations where probable cause is uncertain (n=20) actually reflects 12 different combinations of responses, e.g., police report that advising is the preferred policy but advocates report that officer discretion is the preferred policy. It is difficult to determine how much of this apparent dissension is real and how much is due to interpretation. Certainly, there is no reason to think that in ambiguous situations both police and advocates as separate collectives would perceive policy the same way. Nor is there reason to think individual police officers interpret policy the same way in ambiguous situations. However, the category "officer discretion" is itself an inclusive and therefore ambiguous category and could incorporate one or more of the other alternatives for all respondents.

DISCUSSION

We have examined the movement toward arrest as the preferred response to woman battering. We have also observed the lack of clarity inherent in the term "preferred arrest policy." The empirical research reported here was designed to elucidate what it means in theory and in practice for a police department to have a preferred arrest policy regarding battering.

As discussed earlier, the terms used to describe police policies are themselves problematic. A variety of terms is used to refer to policies that we have chosen to label as "preferred" or as "mandatory." We have construed the term "preferred arrest policy" to connote a policy that raises a presumption that an offender will be arrested if certain criteria are met. A "mandatory arrest policy," on the other hand, is one that requires the arrest of offenders, provided again that certain baseline criteria are satisfied. It is interesting that police departments themselves rarely use such terminology, preferring to give officers guidelines by using such words as "should" (suggestive) or "shall/must" (mandatory).

In theory, the process of issuing guidelines and having officers apply them seems rather mechanistic. However, one must not forget the discretion retained by individual officers even when dealing with a "mandatory" policy. Responding officers must always determine how the facts of particular cases relate to the criteria set out by official policy.

As a result, it is mistaken to consider the enforcement of arrest policies without considering the specific conditions in which they are enforced and officer interpretations of them. In this study, we have explored what it means for a police department to have a preferred arrest policy. As our results have indicated, preferred arrest policies apply in situations where probable cause to believe a crime was committed clearly exists and where a victim has suffered visible injury or an offender has threatened her with a deadly weapon. Only in a minority of departments do preferred arrest policies apply when there have been verbal threats or property damage. Thus, officers must encounter fairly serious situations before they enforce preferred arrest policies. Interestingly, few departments employed a different policy for dealing with cohabiting, as opposed to married couples.

Although police departments may operate as relatively closed systems, they are subject to a variety of external forces. Internal definitions of police policy are always shaped by such external forces as state laws, local politics, and community pressures. While state law alone establishes the legal boundaries for responding to battering, policy is implemented locally.

It is no surprise, then, that differences of opinion exist about the definition and implementation of policy among police personnel and such external groups as womens' advocates. Even definitive and unambiguous policy language, such as "shall arrest," is open to interpretation. It is simply impossible to identify and describe in policy statements the diversity of situations which police encounter.

Moreover, police and advocate groups are operating from different historical perspectives and prejudices. Police have a traditional antipathy to arrest while advocate groups believe the law should punish offenders. Advocate groups rarely see both sides of specific situations since they usually have little interaction with batterers. Even if abuse has stopped by the time police arrive, police are still in a better position to make an objective assessment of most situations. Since 75 percent of the calls for police service regarding abuse do not involve a crime, as defined by state law (see, e.g., Hirschel & Hutchison, 1987:11), police are frequently legally constrained from doing anything, much less making an arrest.

There are objective and subjective opportunities to interpret police policy differently. Different interpretations are unavoidable and reflect differences in purpose among police and advocacy systems. Are these differences significant for a community? In general, we found that although differences between police and advocacy group perceptions of police policy tend to be minor, the climate of interaction between the police and the larger community and advocacy groups is important. In a negative climate, it is likely that police will feel unfairly hounded for not doing more. In turn, advocacy groups may come to perceive police antagonistically and not work cooperatively with them for the benefit of victims. In a more positive climate, we speculate that existing differences will be sore points but will not abort cooperative interaction between police and advocates. Given differences of purpose, it is unrealistic to expect different groups to operate with the same day-to-day understandings of specific situations. It is difficult enough to persuade individuals within the same organization to share a common purpose and cooperate. Cutting across organizational lines magnifies these differences. Interagency cooperation requires individuals (i.e., police officers and advocates) to focus more on shared goals (reducing battering) than on their differences.

The implementation of preferred arrest policies is affected by a wide range of factors. State laws and department guidelines provide a framework within which implementation occurs. The ways they are interpreted and applied are influenced by factors both external and internal to a police department. For example, the political climate in a jurisdiction may affect the degree to which officers enforce arrest policy. A community conscious of the plight of battered women and with vigorous advocate groups is likely to demand more of its police department than one that does not possess these attributes. The significance a community attaches to the problem of battering is also likely to affect the amount of resources the community is willing to allocate to combat this problem. Without adequate resources, police departments are going to be hard pressed to implement preferred arrest policies fully. The additional arrests that accompany preferred arrest policies require additional police time for booking and processing arrested suspects. While extra time goes to these activities, other matters requiring police attention must be put on hold.

The responses of other criminal justice and social support systems are likewise important. We have noted elsewhere that preferred arrest policies have been more vigorously pursued and more successfully implemented when they have been part of a coordinated community response (see the studies conducted by Gamache et al. (1988), Steinman (1988), Ferguson (1987), Goolkasian (1986), Pence (1983), and Burris and Jaffe (1983) discussed above). Police departments and their officers do not operate in a vacuum. If they observe that their actions are not receiving the support of the rest of the criminal justice system, they are likely to desist from undertaking those actions. Thus, if they are actively pursuing a preferred arrest policy, but see that magistrates are reluctant to endorse their actions by finding probable cause, or that the District Attorney is not prosecuting offenders they have arrested, they are likely to stop making arrests because arresting offenders serves no purpose.

In order to be implemented effectively, preferred arrest policies must have the support of both command and line personnel. Buzawa (1988) has clearly demonstrated how such policies are undermined by a lack of support from the top. Police chiefs must encourage their officers to make arrests and see that adequate resources are allocated for this objective. This means that low priority response codes must not be given to calls for service that involve battering.

A major obstacle to an effective implementation of preferred arrest policies is the traditional rank and file officer opposition to policies that limit their discretion. Since officers like to make their own decisions, they are likely, at least initially, to have a negative reaction to such policies. Since implementing arrest policies is dependent on officer definitions of the situations they encounter, officers retain the ability to circumvent them. Recall that Ferraro found that officers' implementation of a preferred arrest policy in Phoenix interpreted probable cause in terms of "a level of evidence high enough for felony arrests" (1989:64). In order to counteract the impact of negative officer reactions to a new policy, departments must conduct rigorous training programs. These programs should seek to instill more positive attitudes both toward the plight of victims and the policies themselves. Once in the field, officers should be monitored so that circumvention of policy can be detected. If possible, incentives for compliance should also be instituted.

CONCLUSION

There are many reasons why preferred arrest policies must not be viewed as a panacea to resolve the problem of battering. First, as noted earlier, a great many calls for police service do not involve situations which state law defines in criminal terms. Thus, many officers respond to calls at which they are not legally empowered to make arrests. And, unless major legal changes are made, this will remain the case for the future. Second, many cities with preferred arrest policies require that the abuser be present when police arrive in order to make an arrest; otherwise the victim must swear out a warrant. Since offenders have left the scene in half the cases before police arrive, an on-the-scene arrest is not an option in many cases. Third, the movement toward preferred arrest policies was fueled by the findings of a single experiment. It remains to be seen whether replications of it will produce the same results. If they find that police action is not related to less recidivism, state and local policymakers may be tempted to consider whether arresting batterers is worth the cost. This is certain to be a major issue. Fourth, arrest now means widely varying outcomes in different communities. In one community, arrest may mean an hour at the jail; in another, arrest may mean a weekend. In short, there is little empirical evidence available which shows the effects of arrest with varying terms of incarceration. Fifth, arrest as a preferred response tends to overlook the fact that many abusers have been arrested before, for battering and/or for other crimes. It is naive to expect that arrest and incarceration will have a deterrent impact on many or most of them.

Finally, it is myopic to think that isolated police action can have a long-term impact on the basic problem. Other authors have noted the degree to which many forms of family violence are endemic to American society. We believe that long-term progress on them will only come when we treat their causes rather than their symptoms.

NOTES

1 Analysis of these data revealed great increases both in the number of reported cases and the percentage of those cases that resulted in arrest. While the three years prior to implementation of preferred arrest policy yielded an average of 841 reported cases, 32.4 percent of which resulted in arrest, the four years after implementation saw an average of 3,237 reported cases, 74.3 percent of which resulted in arrest. Whether these trends will be replicated in the other jurisdictions will not be known until more fully developed reporting systems have been in operation for a number of years.

REFERENCES

Bard, M. (1970). *Training Police as Specialists in Family Crisis Intervention.* Washington, DC: U.S. Department of Justice.

Bayley, D.H. (1983). "Knowledge of the Police." In M. Punch (ed.) *Control in the Police Organization*, pp. 18-35. Cambridge, MA: MIT Press.

Bell, D. (1985) "Domestic Violence: Victimization, Police Intervention, and Disposition." *Journal of Criminal Justice*, 13(6):525-534.

Berk, R., S. Berk, P. Newton & D. Loseke (1984). "Cops on Call: Summoning the Police to the Scene of Spousal Violence." *Law and Society Review* 18(3):479-498.

Berk, S. & D.R. Loseke (1981). "Handling Family Violence: Situational Determinants of Police Arrest in Domestic Disturbances." *Law and Society Review*, 15:317-346.

Buchanon, D. & P. Perry (1985). "Attitudes of Police Recruits Toward Domestic Disturbances: An Evaluation of Family Crisis Intervention Training." *Journal of Criminal Justice*, 13(6):561-572.

Buel, S.M. (1988). "Mandatory Arrests for Domestic Violence." *Harvard Women's Law Journal*, 11:213-226.

Burris, C.A. & P. Jaffe (1983). "Wife Abuse as a Crime: The Impact of Police Laying Charges." *Canadian Journal of Criminology*, 25(3):309-318.

Buzawa, E.S. (1982). "Police Officer Response to Domestic Violence Legislation in Michigan." *Journal of Police Science and Administration*, 415-424.

_____ (1988). "Explaining Variations in Police Response to Domestic Violence: A Case Study in Detroit and New England." In G.T. Hotaling, D. Finkelhor, J.T. Kirkpatrick & M.A. Straus (eds.) *Coping with Family Violence*, pp. 169-182. Beverly Hills: Sage Publications.

Dobash, R.E. & R.P. Dobash (1971). "Love, Honour and Obey: Institutional Ideologies and the Struggle for Battered Women." *Contemporary Crisis*, 1(4):403-415.

Dolan, R., J. Hendricks & S.M. Meagher (1986). "Police Practices and Attitudes Toward Domestic Violence." *Journal of Police Science and Administration*, 14(3):187-192.

Erez, E. (1986). "Intimacy, Violence and the Police." *Human Relations*, 39(3):265-281.

Ferguson, H. (1987). "Mandating Arrests for Domestic Violence." *FBI Law Enforcement Bulletin*, 56(4):6-11.

Ferraro, K.J. (1989). "Policing Woman Battering." *Social Problems*, 36(1):61-74.

Finn, J. (1986). "The Relationship Between Sex Role Attitudes and Attitudes Supporting Marital Violence." *Sex Roles*, 14(5-6):235-244.

Gamache, D.J., J.L. Edleson & M.D. Schock (1988). "Coordinated Police, Judicial, and Social Service Response to Woman Battering: A Multiple-Baseline Evaluation Across Three Communities." In G.T. Hotaling, D. Finkelhor, J.T. Kirkpatrick & M.A. Straus (eds.) *Coping with Family Violence*, pp. 193-209. Beverly Hills: Sage Publications.

Glick, P.C. & G.B. Spanier (1980). "Married and Unmarried Cohabitation in the United States." *Journal of Marriage and the Family*, 42(1):19-30.

Goolkasian, G.A. (1986). *Confronting Domestic Violence: A Guide for Criminal Justice Agencies*. Washington, DC: U.S. Department of Justice.

Hemmons, W.M. (1981). "The Need for Domestic Violence Laws with Adequate Legal and Social Support Services." *Journal of Divorce*, 4(3):49-61.

Hirschel, J.D. & I.W. Hutchison (1987). *Experimental Research on Police Response to Spouse Assault: The Charlotte Project*. Paper presented at the annual meeting of the American Society of Criminology: Montreal, Canada.

Homant, R.J. (1985). "The Police and Spouse Abuse: A Review of Recent Findings." *Police Studies*, 8(3):163-172.

Homant, R.J. & D. Kennedy (1985). "Police Perceptions of Spouse Abuse: A Comparison of Male and Female Officers." *Journal of Criminal Justice*, 13(1):29-47.

Humphreys, J.C. & W.O. Humphreys (1985). "Mandatory Arrest: A Means of Primary and Secondary Prevention of Abuse of Female Partners." *Victimology*, 10:267-280.

Hutchison, I.W., J.D. Hirschel & C.E. Pesackis (1988). *Domestic Variation in Domestic Violence Calls to Police*. Paper presented at the annual meeting of the Southern Sociological Association: Nashville, Tennessee.

Jaffe, P., D. Wolfe, A. Telford & G. Austin (1986). "The Impact of Police Charges in Incidents of Wife Abuse." *Journal of Family Violence*, 1(1):37-49.

Kennedy, D.B. & R.J Homant (1983). "Attitudes of Abused Women Toward Male and Female Police Officers." *Criminal Justice and Behavior*, 10(4):391-405.

Law Enforcement News. "Roughening Up: Spouse Abuse Arrests Grow." (March 10, 1987), 13:1,13.

Lerman, L.G. (1982). "Expansion of Arrest Power: A Key to Effective Intervention." *Vermont Law Review*, 7:59-70.

Lerman, L.G., L. Landis & S. Goldzweig (1983). "State Legislation on Domestic Violence." In J.J. Costa (ed.) *Abuse of Women: Legislation, Reporting, and Prevention*. Lexington, MA: D.C. Heath.

Miller, M.G. (1979). *Domestic Violence in Oregon*. Salem, OR: Governor's Commission for Women, State of Oregon Executive Department.

National Coalition against Domestic Violence (1986). *1986 National Directory of Domestic Violence Programs: A Guide to Community Shelter, Safe Home, and Service Programs*. Washington, DC: Author.

Pearce, J. & J. Snortum (1983). "Police Effectiveness in Handling Disturbance Calls: An Evaluation of Crisis Interventiom Training." *Criminal Justice and Behavior*, 10(1):71-92.

Pence, E. (1983). "The Duluth Domestic Abuse Intervention Project." *Hamline Law Review*, 6:247-275.

_____ (1989). Public presentation April 19, 1989. Charlotte, North Carolina.

Sherman, L.W. & R.A. Berk (1984). "The Specific Deterrent Effects of Arrest for Domestic Assault." *American Sociological Review*, 49:261-272.

Sherman, L.W. & E.G. Cohn (1989). "The Impact of Research on Legal Policy: The Minneapolis Domestic Violence Experiment." *Law and Society Review*, 23(1):117-144.

Skolnick, J.H. (1967). *Justice Without Trial*. New York: John Wiley.

Spanier, G. (1983). "Married and Unmarried Cohabitation in the United States: 1980." *Journal of Marriage and the Family*, 45(2):277-288.

Steinman, M. (1988). "Anticipating Rank and File Police Reactions to Arrest Policies Regarding Spouse Abuse." *Criminal Justice Research Bulletin*, 4(3):1-5.

Victim Services Agency (1988). *The Law Enforcement Response to Family Violence: A State by State Guide to Family Violence Legislation.* New York: Author.

Walter, J. (1981). "Police in the Middle: A Study of Small City Police Intervention in Domestic Disputes." *Journal of Police Science Administration*, 9:243-260.

Wharton, C.S. (1986). "'The Burning Bed': The Media's (Re)constructions of a Social Problem." Paper presented at the meetings of the Southern Sociological Society.

Worden, R.E. & A.A. Pollitz (1984). "Police Arrests in Domestic Disturbances: A Further Look." *Law and Society Review*, 18(1):105-119.

4

Predicting Domestic Homicide: Prior Police Contact and Gun Threats*

Lawrence W. Sherman
University of Maryland

Janell D. Schmidt
Crime Control Institute

Dennis Rogan
Crime Control Institute

Christine DeRiso
Montgomery County, Maryland Police Department

INTRODUCTION

Can police predict individual cases of domestic homicide? For most of police history, the very idea was preposterous. Homicide was viewed as an act of God, a tragedy no one could foresee. But the advent of computers and police research raised our hopes and expectations. If we could predict the volcanic explosion of Mount St. Helens, then perhaps we could predict a homicide in an

* We wish to thank the Law Firms of Kirk Wines, Seattle, and Touchstone, Bernays, Johnstone Beall and Smith of Dallas for supporting this analysis of data collected under Grant # 86IJCXKO43 from the National Institute of Justice to the Crime Control Institute, the "Milwaukee Domestic Violence Experiment." Points of view or opinions expressed in this publication are those of the authors, and do not necessarily reflect those of the U.S. Department of Justice. We also wish to thank the Milwaukee Police Department for their cooperation in the data collection, particularly Captain Dean Collins and Lieutenant Anthony Bacich, as well as Patrick R. Gartin and Danee Gaines of Crime Control Institute for their screening of the hotline files. Please address all correspondence to Lawrence W. Sherman, Crime Control Institute, 1063 Thomas Jefferson St., N.W., Washington, DC 20007. Tel. 202-337-2700.

ongoing domestic relationship. Over the last fifteen years, in fact, several findings have supported the hope for a domestic homicide "early warning system."

One of those findings, from the 1977 Police Foundation publication of domestic homicide research done in Kansas City, is among the most cited results in the entire domestic violence literature. The study reported that in about 90 percent of the cases, police had responded to at least one call for service at the address of the domestic homicide victim or suspect in the two years preceding the homicide, and to five or more calls in about 50 percent of the cases (Breedlove et al., 1977:23). Similar findings were reported for domestic aggravated assault. Wilson (1977:iv) concluded from these results that, at least in Kansas City, "the police can obtain some early warning of assaults and homicides," since "any given homicide arrest is likely to be the culmination of a series of police interventions."

A follow-up study conducted by the Kansas City Police Department under a National Institute of Mental Health grant reached a similar conclusion about assaults, if not homicides: "The premise that we may have some kind of 'early warning system' embedded in the relationship of disturbances and assaults is substantiated" (Meyer & Lorimor, 1977:V-2). The evidence for this conclusion was that among all 16,994 Computer-Aided Dispatch (CAD) records of disturbance calls in 1976 (including non-domestic disturbances), Kansas City police had only one call that year at the addresses of 12,093 calls (71.2%). Another 23 percent of the calls were dispatched to addresses with 2 to 4 calls, 5.2 percent (891) were dispatched to addresses with 5 to 8 calls that year, and 1.5 percent (250) were dispatched to addresses with 9 or more calls (the exact distribution, with numbers of addresses at each call level, was not displayed).

These data are consistent with subsequent results of repeat call analysis restricted to domestic disturbance calls in Boston and Minneapolis. In Boston, Pierce, Spaar and Briggs (1984) found that 9 percent of apartments reporting any calls for "family trouble" over a five-year period accounted for about 28 percent of all such calls (no base number of all apartments in the city was reported). In Minneapolis over a one-year period for buildings—and not apartments as in Boston—9.1 percent of the addresses with any domestic calls accounted for 39.5 percent of all domestic calls, while 9 percent of all addresses accounted for 100 percent of all domestic disturbance calls (see Table 4.1, derived from Sherman, Gartin & Buerger, 1989:41).

The Minneapolis analysis of crime "hot spot" addresses also found that domestic calls had the greatest concentration by address of any of six types of calls examined (including robbery, auto theft, burglary, assault, and criminal sexual conduct). Compared to the number of addresses at which domestic calls would be expected to occur without any repeat call addresses, the actual number of addresses with domestic calls was 59 percent lower than expected due to repeat calls—the largest reduction among call types examined (Sherman, Buerger

& Gartin, 1989:39). Table 4.1 also shows that the building addresses at which domestic disturbance calls occur are highly predictable, with better than two-thirds accuracy of predicting an additional call at some time within the year once there have already been three such calls.

Table 4.1 Distribution of Domestic Disturbance Calls by Building Address in Minneapolis (December 15, 1985 - December 15, 1986)

Call Level	Total Addresses	Calls	% Calls	Cumulative % Calls*	Cumulative % Addresses*	Cumulative % Addresses w/Calls	Conditional Problem of More Calls
0	105,158	0	0	0	99.91	0	8.5%
1	5,519	5,519	22.1	99.8	8.47	99.9	43.9%
2	1,790	3,580	14.4	77.7	3.73	43.8	58.5%
3	866	2,598	10.4	63.3	2.17	25.6	65.8%
4	468	1,872	7.5	52.9	1.42	16.8	71.9%
5	293	1,465	5.9	45.4	1.01	12.1	75.5%
6	208	1,248	5.0	39.5	0.76	9.1	76.9%
7	156	1,092	4.4	34.5	0.58	7.0	77.6%
8	97	776	3.1	30.1	0.44	5.4	82.0%
9	86	774	3.1	27.0	0.36	4.4	80.5%
10	56	560	2.2	23.9	0.29	3.5	84.3%
11	41	451	1.8	21.7	0.25	2.9	86.4%
12	48	576	2.3	19.9	0.22	2.5	81.5%
13	33	429	1.7	17.6	0.18	2.1	84.4%
14	18	252	1.0	15.9	0.16	1.8	89.9%
15	161	3,736	14.9	14.9	0.14	1.6	—
Total:	115,000	24,928	99.8**			99.91**	

$x^2 = 34,423$ df = 14 $p = .0001$ $\bar{X} = .217$

* in reverse order of cumulation

** does not total 100% due to rounding error

Taken in conjunction with the Kansas City homicide findings, these data have suggested a pattern of escalating frequency of police interventions in domestic violence which might describe a high risk profile for homicide. The findings raised the possibility of proactive police interventions for preventing domestic homicide, a major contributor to all forms of homicide. Depending on how domestic relationships are defined, they can account for anywhere from 8 percent to 21 percent of all murders nationally (FBI, 1985), and even more in specific cities.

The hopes for prediction and prevention were further intensified by evidence that arrests in misdemeanor battering cases in Minneapolis had a deterrent effect on the prevalence of subsequent misdemeanor violence in the same victim-offender relationships (Sherman & Berk, 1984; Sherman & Cohn, 1989), which led to proposals for experiments in police intervention with households recording high rates of repeat domestic disturbance calls (Sherman, 1987). It also appears to have led to increased expectations about police ability to prevent homicide through arrest, about which the Minneapolis experiment offered absolutely no evidence. Nonetheless, both the Kansas City study (Breedlove et al., 1977) and the Minneapolis experiment (Sherman & Berk, 1984) have been cited in lawsuits brought against police departments for their failure to prevent domestic homicides and serious injuries.

Closer examination of the research, however encouraging it may be, raises several issues complicating any attempt to predict—let alone prevent—domestic homicide. This essay examines those issues and presents new data from Milwaukee on several of the key points. We conclude with an assessment of unexplored questions and future prospects for predicting domestic homicide.

LIMITATIONS OF EXISTING DATA

The findings reviewed above have several limitations for predicting domestic homicides: units of analysis, sample sizes and selection, and heterogeneity of behavior measured.

Units of Analysis

The research to date has confused the criminology of places with the criminology of people. The prediction of domestic homicide would normally require advance identification of the people involved: the victim and the offender or, at least, two persons who will fill one or the other of those roles. None of the findings cited above measures the prior behavior of the persons involved in the homicide. All of them involve police CAD records of police cars dispatched to events at certain locations, without any record of the identities of the individuals involved. Even if we set aside the substantial error problems in linking the occurrence of events to the addresses indicated in the CAD records (Sherman et al., 1989:34-36), there are major problems with presuming that events at certain places necessarily involve certain people.

The first Kansas City study was somewhat sensitive to this issue, and therefore decided to omit homicides occurring in "apartment buildings with many tenants" (Breedlove et al., 1977:23). This exclusion implies, however, that two- and three-family houses, not uncommon in Kansas City, were left in the analysis. The question then becomes "What percentage of the prior calls involved one of the parties involved in the subsequent homicide?" Given the nameless CAD data, there was no way to tell.

Even in a sample of nothing but single-family homes, or (as in Boston) apartment-specific data on domestic disturbance calls, it is still highly speculative to assume that prior calls involved the later homicide participants reportedly residing at the address. The majority of repeat calls appear to come from underclass households. Our observations suggest that such households are both large in number and fluid in membership, with fairly frequent turnover. On any given day, the population of such households can vary, including several generations of immediate family, extended family, friends and lovers. If the mean household size is more than three adults, then there is at least a one-third chance that a prior domestic disturbance call did not involve the later homicide participant who led to the search for calls at the address. With more adults in the home, the odds of a false linkage to the later homicide increase.

Moreover, police are often unable to determine the exact location of residence for homicide victims and offenders for a two-year period. With the apparently high residential mobility in underclass housing in some cities, it becomes difficult even for the principals to recall where they have resided, let alone for police to verify that recollection.

At most, then, all the Kansas City study may have shown is that the homicide participants reside in the kinds of buildings that have high prevalence and incidence of police calls dispatched for disturbances. All the Boston and Minneapolis follow-up studies may suggest is that certain households or buildings have a predictably high likelihood of recurrence of domestic disturbance calls. Neither of these implications may connect to individuals at all. They suggest, more plausibly, that the social ecology of the building is associated with a high rate of calls to police. But this may be far too general for predicting domestic homicides among specific couples, and perhaps even at specific locations.

Most important is the postdictive nature of the study, for either unit of analysis. Because the study was retrospective, it was unable to say (predictively) what percentage of buildings with repeat calls for disturbances experience a domestic homicide in a given period. All it did was to work backwards from the homicides to the prior calls. If the number of buildings with repeat calls is far greater than the number of domestic homicides, then the fact that such homicides emerge from high-call buildings has little predictive value. But to test that possibility, we must first know how many homicides the analyses were based upon.

Sample Sizes and Selection

It is striking that the published version of the Kansas City study, apparently based on 1970-71 homicides (Police Foundation, 1977:5), did not report the exact numbers of homicides included in the analysis. We can, however, estimate the number based on the report's claim that about one-third of the 1970-71 homicides were "specifically" domestic, excluding friends and relatives (Police Foundation, 1977:11). The 1970 Uniform Crime Report homicide total for Kansas City was 120, and 103 for 1971. This suggests that the entire analysis of prior calls for service was based on a sample of *at most* 73 domestic homicides, before exclusions for "many" tenant buildings. How many remained after those exclusions is impossible to say, but it could well be less than 50. If the many-tenant buildings are the most likely buildings to experience domestic homicide, then this exclusion rule could have deleted half of the sample of 73 homicides or more.

The small number of homicides suggests several things. One is that there are probably far more *buildings* with a high frequency of domestic calls than there are domestic *homicides.* In Minneapolis, for example, a city of half the population size, there were 1,197 buildings with 5 or more disturbance calls in 1986. If we assume there were twice as many buildings with that many calls in Kansas City, with no more than one homicide in any one building over two years, we have a predictive ratio of only 73 homicides in 2,394, or only 3 percent of high risk buildings with a homicide. Predicting domestic homicide on the basis of five or more calls would therefore lead to a 97 percent false positive rate, and that is only at the level of buildings. If we multiply the number of buildings by the number of couples in them, the false positive rate would substantially exceed 99 percent. When cases (and buildings) deleted for multiple tenancy are taken into account, the error rate could be even higher. A small sample is also more prone to instability of estimates. Put another way, small samples pose a greater risk that the results are not generalizable to other time periods.

Both issues can be illustrated more clearly with the Minneapolis data, which cover all but two weeks of 1986. Minneapolis police reported 44 homicides in 1986, of which we may estimate that about 33 percent, or 13, were domestic. Table 4.1 shows that there were 161 addresses with 15 or more domestic disturbance calls in that year, and 1,197 addresses with 5 or more domestic calls. Even if all of the domestic homicides occurred at the high-risk buildings, they would still afflict only 8 percent of the 15 or more call buildings and 1 percent of the 5 or more call buildings. Knowing the prior number of domestic calls at an address may thus provide little increase in our ability to predict where domestic homicides will occur, even if it does narrow it down to about 1,000 buildings. Attempts to intervene for prevention of those homicides would clearly produce substantial over-prediction.

These prediction errors are compounded by the instability of estimates. Let us suppose that all 13 of the domestic homicides happened at the addresses with the highest rankings of any addresses in the city for domestic disturbance calls. Even then the sample size poses problems. What would hypothetically appear as a perfect correlation between call frequency and homicides could be a mere chance result for that single year, unlikely to recur for tens or hundreds of years.

Heterogeneity of Behavior

A call for service to a domestic disturbance embraces a wide range of behavior. Observations suggest the majority involve no physical violence, being limited to high volume words and perhaps property damage. The majority of violent incidents are quite minor, with few visible injuries. At the far end of the distribution, some involve threats to kill, pointing of guns, and actual attempts to kill with serious injuries.

The "escalating violence" hypothesis would suggest that the risk of homicide grows with the level of seriousness of the prior violence. Predicting homicide from prior police contacts, under this theory, would require distinguishing prior episodes as to level of seriousness. This hypothesis might even suggest greater predictive power from a single event of gun-pointing than from many calls for non-violent disturbances, or disturbances with only minor violence.

None of the findings reported so far, however, distinguish prior police contacts by level of seriousness. The closest finding is the Kansas City study's analysis of threats in a non-random sample of 324 disturbance calls, comprising 5 percent of all disturbance calls in May-September, 1973, in the East Patrol Division. This analysis found, predictively, that if threats were made during an incident, some force was actually used in that incident in about half the cases. Postdictively, where force was used, threats had been made in about 80 percent of the cases (Police Foundation, 1977:19). This finding is limited to the disturbances which the reporting officers encountered, and entailed no follow-up or connection to risks of harm in subsequent events involving the same persons or places.

In sum, the "early warning system" of escalating frequency of disturbance calls is plagued by at least three problems. One is confusion of units of analysis, with a speculative link between addresses and individuals. A second is an unknown, and presumably quite small, sample of domestic homicides in relation to a presumably large population of addresses with high numbers of repeat domestic calls. A third problem is the wide range of seriousness of behavior lumped together under the common label of "disturbance," without distinguishing the small proportion of serious injury or threats from the vast numbers of mere shouting matches.

Given these limitations, it would appear inappropriate to base public policy in general, or civil liability in particular, on the premise of police ability to predict or prevent domestic homicides. At the very least, there is a clear need for more data, which we report in this chapter.

PREDICTING DOMESTIC HOMICIDE IN MILWAUKEE

The Data

Several of the problems described above can be overcome with data from the Milwaukee Domestic Violence Experiment (Sherman et al., 1990), one of the six replications of the Minneapolis Domestic Violence Experiment (Sherman & Berk, 1984) funded by the National Institute of Justice. These data offer:

* 15,537 Police Reports of Domestic Battery citywide from April 7, 1987 to February 8, 1989, including 110 gun threat incidents (hard copy only).
* Computer-readable reports on all 1,112 couples included in the 1200 cases randomly assigned (with repeats) to receive different police interventions in misdemeanor battery situations covering the period May 1, 1986 to February 8, 1989.
* Offense reports on all 33 domestic homicides in Milwaukee from April 7, 1987 to February 8, 1989.

The police reports of domestic battery are not offense reports, but rather records of the city's domestic violence "hotline" generated by police calls to a battered women's shelter. The calls were to be made whenever police encountered a situation in which there was probable cause to believe that a domestic battery or violation of a restraining order (misdemeanors), aggravated battery (felony), or other domestic violence situation had occurred. This reporting policy was adopted May 1, 1986 in conjunction with the city's mandatory arrest policy for misdemeanor domestic battery. Battery was defined as including acts resulting in non-visible injuries, including slapping and shoving. The threshold for counting violent events was therefore quite low, and probably lower than that in Kansas City in the early 1970s.

Under the policy, police were ordered to call the hotline *whether or not the offender was present, and whether or not they were therefore making an arrest.*

This reporting procedure was a marked diversion from prior practice in Milwaukee and most cities, in which police rarely made a record of misdemeanor domestic batteries unless they were making an arrest as well. Even if they had only created these records upon making an arrest, however, the high volume of arrests alone would have created a sensitive indicator of domestic battery. Over the period of the experiment, arrests for domestic violence exceeded 5,000 per year, in a city of 600,000 people. In contrast, Washington D.C., a city of roughly equal size, reportedly made several hundred arrests each year for the same offense. The mandatory arrest policy in Milwaukee, in fact, may have created the most comprehensive police record to date of individual-level data on minor domestic violence.

Under the funding for the experiment, only the "hotline" records on the 1,112 experimental couples could be rendered computer-readable. We retained the hard copy on all hotlines citywide, however, in order to extract those hotlines naming the individuals in the study. This allowed research associate Christine DeRiso to undertake a subsequent manual search of the full hard copy files for the names of any of the victims or offenders in the 33 domestic homicides occurring during the experimental period and its six-month follow-up. This search was comparable to the Breedlove et al. (1977) postdictive search of CAD data in Kansas City for records of police calls for service at the addresses of the victims and offenders in domestic homicides. The homicide records were obtained by reviewing the offense report on every homicide in the city during the surveillance period on all hotlines. We relied on our own determination of what constituted a domestic relationship based on our review of the circumstances of the homicide. We did not rely on any preexisting police categories in making that decision.

This search also provided the numerator for the ratio of domestic gun threats to homicides. The denominator came from the manual review of the 15,537 hotline records, in which we searched for several indications of a threat to commit homicide, usually backed up by the use or pointing of a gun:

1. a gun was actually used to harm the victim,
2. a Reckless Use of Weapon, Disorderly Conduct While Armed, or Strong Arm Robbery charge was filed by police and the record noted that the suspect threatened to kill the victim,
3. the felony charge of Injury by Conduct Regardless of Life, or of Endangering Safety by Conduct Regardless of Life was filed, even though no specific weapon was listed,
4. the victim told police the offender had threatened homicide.

The search revealed a total of 108 couples with at least one incident fitting the categories defined above. Both the homicide reports and subsequent hotline sheets were searched for any evidence of injury subsequent to the initial homicide threat hotlines.

There are two limitations in the Milwaukee data. One is that there are only 33 domestic homicides in the study period, which could raise some of the instability problems discussed above. The other is that there are no records of police calls for service to the addresses of the victims and offenders. This gap is caused by the lack of a CAD system in Milwaukee at the time of the data collection. In this report, then, we are unable to link the criminology of places to the criminology of persons. We can, however, test two claims about domestic homicide predictions implied by the prior research.

Claims Tested

The first claim we test is that homicides are more likely to occur at the extreme end of a distribution of repeated events of less serious violence, or the "escalating violence" theory of prediction. The second claim is that serious threats of gun use, including gun pointing, suggest an escalated risk of domestic homicide.

"Escalating Violence" and Domestic Homicide

Under the "escalating violence" theory of domestic homicide prediction, the risk of homicide should increase with the number of repeated events of lesser violence. Homicide should be most likely among those couples with the highest volumes of prior violence and lowest among those with no record of prior violence.

One difficulty in testing that claim is the rarity of homicide at any risk level, even in a study population of over 2,000 people. At the 1988 Milwaukee homicide rate of 13.5 homicides per 100,000, the expected odds of one homicide in that population over a two-year period would be only .5798—if the population had the same homicide risk as the population in general. But this risk analysis neglects three points. First, the experimental population was approximately 75 percent black, while the city is only about 25 percent black. Second, underclass blacks have higher homicide risks than whites in general. Third, we would expect that a sample of people with at least one prior police record of violence, regardless of race, would have a higher risk of homicide than the population of the city in general. For all these reasons, we would expect the risk of a homicide in the study population to be at least greater than one incident over the study period, and perhaps much higher.

There were, however, no homicides among these couples during the 22-month surveillance period, with a mean follow-up period of 15.8 months from the first hotline report to the end of the surveillance period. This finding would be more compelling if the expected number of homicides had been higher, with a larger sample size or a longer follow-up period. Nonetheless, it is striking how many cases of high volume repeat batteries there are in the population, with no homicide in over 3,000 person-years observed. Consider the "five or more" calls threshold for 50 percent of the Kansas City homicides as a benchmark for high-risk couples, for example. Table 4.2 shows that 70 couples had five or more domestic violence hotline calls during the surveillance period, all without homicides.

Table 4.2 Truncated Poisson Probability Distribution for Observed/Expected Cases and Incidents of Domestic Violence (May 1, 1986 - February 2, 1989)

No. of Crimes	No. of Cases	Observed Incidents	Expected Incidents	Cum. % of Cases	Cum. % of Incidents	Conditional Probability
1	651	651	290	1.0000	1.0000	41.45
2	241	482	460	0.4146	0.6890	47.72
3	89	267	487	0.1978	0.4587	59.54
4	61	244	387	0.1178	0.3311	53.43
5	36	180	246	0.0629	0.2145	48.57
6	14	84	130	0.0306	0.1285	58.82
7	5	35	59	0.0180	0.0884	75.00
8	5	40	24	0.0135	0.0717	66.67
9	3	27	8	0.0090	0.0526	70.00
10	2	20	3	0.0063	0.0397	71.45
11	2	22	1	0.0045	0.0301	60.00
12	2	24	0	0.0027	0.0196	33.00
13	0	0	0	0.0008	0.0008	
14	0	0	0	0.0008	0.0008	
15	0	0	0	0.0008	0.0008	
16	0	0	0	0.0008	0.0008	
17	1	17	0	0.0008	0.0008	

n = 1,112 (cases) n = 2,093 (incidents) Theta = 3.177
df = 16 Chi-Square = 92.86 p < .0001

Time at Risk from Entering Sample:

Days from First Hotline Until February 8, 1989

Mean Days = 429.02 Minimum = 184 Standard Deviance = 148.69
Median Days = 427 Maximum = 673 Variance = 22,108

Table 4.2 also shows that the concentration of repeat violence among couples is substantial. Indeed, with the conditional probability of recurrence exceeding 50 percent at 3 or more hotlines, the repetition of domestic violence among couples in Milwaukee is only slightly less predictable than the repetition of domestic disturbances among addresses in Minneapolis. As Table 4.1 shows, the odds of repeat calls to Minneapolis addresses exceed 50 percent at 2 or more calls. The chi-square test in Table 4.2 indicates the distribution of repeat couple violence clearly deviates from a model expected by chance. That is, the data violate the truncated Poisson model of frequencies of cases at each number of incidents ("truncated" because there are no zero incident cases in the sample). This means that the concentration of repeat cases at the high end of the scale of frequency is far greater than would occur by chance, producing an extreme end group at unusually high probabilities of recurrence. The fact that those high probabilities of less serious violence did not translate into a homicide suggests that such repetition alone is not predictive of extreme violence.

Table 4.2 alone, of course, does not completely disprove the "escalating violence" theory of domestic homicide prediction. It can be viewed as a "case control" population of couples involved in domestic violence, even at high rates, but which had no homicides (although that is not how the sample was selected, in contrast to usual case control samples). Even with the data in Table 4.2, the escalating violence claim could be supportable. The necessary evidence would be even higher frequencies of prior violence among the couples in which homicide does occur. The escalating violence claim is simply that mean frequency levels of prior violence are higher among homicide cases than among non-homicide cases.

As Table 4.3 shows, the Milwaukee data do not support the escalating violence claim. Rather than having higher mean frequency of prior battery, the 33 domestic homicides during that time period actually had much lower frequencies. Table 4.2 is restricted entirely to same-couple data, with no inclusion of parties entering other couple relationships or switching roles. The comparable mean number of prior domestic batteries, then, is 0.3 for the homicides, and 1.88 for the case control sample of 1,112 non-homicide couples. The mean prior violence level for the non-homicide couples is over six times greater than it is for the homicide couples—in direct contradiction to the escalating violence hypothesis.

These findings must be presented with suitable caution. Both the low expected number of homicides in the experimental (case-control) sample and the small number of actual homicides in the city during that period may make these estimates unstable. Somewhat different results might be found with more data. But the differences in mean rates of prior hotlines are so great that they are statistically significant ($t = -2.106$, $p = 0.035$), despite the extreme skewness of the distribution.

Table 4.3 Prior Records of Domestic Battery Among Participants in 33 Domestic Homicides in Milwaukee (April 7, 1987 - February 8, 1989)

Relationship		Cases		Incidents
		n	%	n
Same Suspect, Same Victim		1	3	2
Same Suspect, Different Victim		4	12	6
Different Suspect, Same Victim		1	3	1
n = 33	Total:	6	18	9

Given the virtually complete absence of prior violence among the actual homicide cases, it would have been impossible for police (or anyone) to have predicted those homicides based on prior police records of violence. Even worse for the escalating violence claim, it appears from these data that the highest rates of prior violence had a lower risk of domestic homicide.

The Death Rate from Gun Threats

The second claim we examine is that overt threats involving guns create an elevated risk of homicide. This claim addresses the heterogeneity issue described above. It is also especially relevant to civil litigation. One multi-million dollar suit against a police department has already been settled after it was proven police had knowledge of one prior gun-pointing incident. Police had not arrested the suspect when the offense was reported the day after it occurred; some weeks later, the gun-pointing incident was followed by a homicide. The claim was that the gun-pointing threat made the subsequent homicide "reasonably foreseeable," or predictable.

In trying to place a domestic gun threat in the context of a risk level, we are hampered by the relatively low frequency of gun threats. On the other hand, our sample of 110 gun pointings and threats is far bigger than the sample used in the Kansas City study (Breedlove et al., 1977) to suggest an early warning for domestic homicides by place of occurrence. Moreover, our sample is, to our knowledge, the first reported group of gun threats followed by extensive measurement of subsequent violence. Figure 4.1 shows the results.

Figure 4.1 Prior Batteries, Gun Incidents and Subsequent Gun Use Among Same Couples in Milwaukee (April 7, 1987 - February 8, 1989)

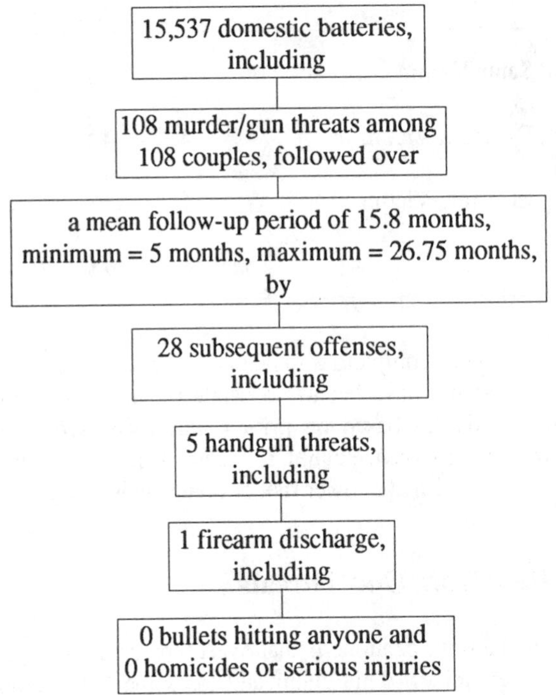

With a base of 15,537 domestic violence incidents and 108 threats or gun pointing incidents, the rate of subsequent domestic homicide in the 15.8 month mean follow-up period was zero. Only two events were recorded on hotlines with these same couples after these 108 serious "warnings." One was a second verbal threat of homicide. The other was a threat with a knife followed by the victim being struck with a phone.

To double-check the risks of subsequent shootings, we searched the index cards of all offense reports by victim names and examined every offense report for serious injury or gunshot wounds. Five victims did report an additional incident in which the suspect threatened them with a handgun, but none of them were injured. In the most serious of the five, the suspect actually fired a gun through a door and a window, but did not appear to aim for the victim who was untouched. Fifteen other victims reported various additional offenses, but the only injury was a stab wound to the shoulder suffered by one victim.

One argument might be that the risk levels in Figure 4.1 are based on the policy of mandatory arrest for minor domestic battery in Milwaukee. That is, some might argue that the risk level is lower than it would ordinarily be if police do not make arrests for such incidents. Table 4.4 suggests that this premise is at least partially false. While a majority of the threat cases did result in arrest at the scene, over one-third of them did not. There was no difference in rate of shootings following either the arrest or non-arrest cases. At the very least, the Milwaukee risk of shooting following a domestic gun/death threat in the follow-up period is less than 1 in 42, or under 2.4 percent. How much less, no one can say.

Table 4.4 Disposition at Scene of Milwaukee Domestic Murder/Gun Threats

n = 110

Suspect On-Scene	Suspect Arrested		n	%
yes	yes		57	52
yes	no		1	1
no	no		40	36
no	yes		6	5
missing	yes		2	2
no	missing		3	3
missing	no		1	1
		Total	110	100
		Total Arrested:	65	59
		Total Not Arrested:	42	38
		Total Missing:	3	4

These data suggest that *gun-pointing and death threats are poor predictors of subsequent domestic shootings.* Victims involved in such events have a less than one percent chance of a subsequent shooting incident within a more than one-year follow-up period. Thus, even if police compiled a "threat data bank," as Sherman (1983) has suggested, its value (if any) would be limited to investigations. It would produce far too many false positives to have much preventive value.

A larger sample might provide more precise estimates of the actual homicide risk levels associated with death threat or gun-pointing incidents: 1 in 200, 1 in 500, 1 in 10,000, etc. These data suggest that the odds must exceed at least 1 in 108. The data do not show that such incidents have no predictive power. Such incidents could, for example, *hypothetically* increase the risk of domestic shootings from 1 in 12,000 to 1 in 1,000; the data are not inconsistent with such a possibility. But even if that was true, it is very hard for police to make practical use of data showing a couple is in a 1 in 1,000 homicide risk category, or the under 1 in 110 risk level we have demonstrated for Milwaukee.

CONCLUSION

These findings suggest several implications for both the prediction of violence and police attempts to prevent it.

Prediction

The ability to predict misdemeanor domestic calls and minor batteries is far greater than the ability to predict domestic homicide or serious injury. Police can clearly identify

* *buildings* which have high predictability of recurrent domestic *disturbances*, and
* *couples* who have high predictability of recurrent minor domestic *battery*.

We have no direct data on police ability to predict buildings where domestic battery will occur, but we can presume that they are the same buildings with recurrent domestic disturbances.

What police clearly cannot do is to predict, with a reasonable level of accuracy, either the buildings or the couples in which domestic homicides will occur, at least not in Milwaukee. This is not surprising, given the extreme rarity of the events and the general difficulty of predicting any rare event. But it is disappointing, given the great hopes that the Kansas City research had held out for many years.

Moreover, police cannot even predict the couples likely to have more minor batteries, or the places likely to have more domestic calls, without a substantial rate of false positives. The best prediction Milwaukee police could make about repeat batteries over an almost three-year period, for example, is that couples with 7 or more hotlines will have another one during that time period. This prediction will be wrong in 1 out of 4 cases. While this error rate is low for purposes of scientific analysis, it is extremely high for any practical purposes. Depending upon the intrusiveness of any prevention measure suggested, it could be fiscally or ethically unacceptable to impose a measure which turns out to be unnecessary in such a large proportion of the cases.

This distinction between theoretical and practical purposes of prediction is not unimportant. It suggests that no matter how well we may advance criminological theory in our ability to predict homicide, it will have little practical value until the error rate of predictions can be reduced to a socially and legally acceptable level.

We can imagine, for example, a more effective approach to prediction which might use multiple variables simultaneously, or which might focus on individuals rather than on couples. It might examine calls for service at specific addresses in conjunction with prior offenses of individuals ranked by offense seriousness. A prediction model might also include situational variables from prior incidents, such as the presence of alcohol or evidence of any drug dealing. A more detailed case-control approach, beginning with an extensive review of each homicide investigation or interviews with persons who knew the victim or offender, might reveal even more variables of some predictive value. As Farrington and Tarling (1985:15) observe, the best predictors are not necessarily those which are conveniently available in official records. A wide variety of approaches could still be tried to see if domestic homicides can be predicted with at least as much accuracy as minor domestic batteries, despite the much greater rarity of homicides.

Whether that line of research could lead to a low rate of error in predictions about individual couples, however, seems doubtful, given the evidence reviewed here. It would also imply a much more costly data system for police to maintain. Bivariate models, such as those examined in this chapter, are rather simplistic by criminological standards. But they are often the only feasible approach for a large organization to employ on vast quantities of records maintained in data base, rather than analytic, files. Moreover, the "escalating violence" thesis is not just based on the convenience of existing records systems. Rather, the records directly reflect the theory that homicide is preceded by increasingly frequent violence—the theory falsified by the Milwaukee data in this chapter.

Regardless of the potential of alternative approaches, we must clearly reject the currently prevailing "escalating violence" theory. There is no "early warning system," or any linear increase in police reports of violence, preceding domestic homicide. The data suggest that there is no difference in the homicide risks of couples who have come to police attention and those who have not, at least in Milwaukee. And since the Milwaukee data concern persons rather than places, predictions rather than post-hoc review, and prior actual violence rather than calls for service, they offer far more compelling evidence than the Kansas City data.

These findings, however disappointing, are at least good news for police departments being sued for negligent failure to prevent domestic homicide. Such lawsuits are only legally possible if homicide is "reasonably foreseeable," or predictable. The premise that such homicides are predictable on the basis of prior occurrences of domestic battery has been clearly falsified in the Milwaukee case, at least for this time period. The premise that homicide is predictable from gunpointing or a death threat is also falsified, although with somewhat less clarity. Very small differences in risk of homicide may vary according to the police action taken in the prior contact. The Milwaukee data, for example, may show a lower risk of injury after gunpointing than one would find in other cities because of the preponderance of arrests in such cases in Milwaukee. Nonetheless, two facts stand out:

* There was no difference in the risk of serious injury or homicide between cases in which there had and had not been an arrest.
* There were at least 42 cases of such incidents in which no subsequent shooting or homicide resulted.

Both of these findings falsify the claims that homicide is almost certain, or even likely, to follow from a death threat or gun-pointing incident. To hold police liable for negligence in acting on such threats, in the context of massive amounts of other information and demands for service, seems to go beyond the evidence about the foreseeability of the injury.

Prevention

The inability to predict domestic homicides also relieves us of the burden of a very difficult policy question. Even if we were able to predict domestic homicide, what could we do about it? What strategies and tactics of prevention would be both acceptable and effective?

After two 1989 domestic homicide cases in Suffolk County, New York, some observers implied that police should have provided something approaching bodyguard protection. Both homicides were committed by estranged males who had been barred from further contact with the victim by a court order of protection. The implication of self-enforcement that protection orders imply creates a special outrage when homicides occur. But the order itself is, of course, worthless against a determined murderer, absent police bodyguard protection. Such bodyguard services would be extremely costly and virtually unprecedented. Even if taxpayers were willing to provide such services, it is not clear how effective they would be. As the assassinations of 1 out of every 10 U.S. presidents suggests, even extensive bodyguard services have a high failure rate.

Offender-oriented strategies of homicide prevention might be less costly, but there is little police can do without breaking the law and violating the Constitution. The best hope would be for sentencing guidelines requiring the longest sentence possible for a conviction on any charge which might be pending against an offender predicted to be at high risk of committing domestic homicide.

Short of protecting the potential victim or incarcerating the potential offender, it is hard to see what prevention steps could be taken after completing an accurate prediction. Warning the victim is an obvious step, but may have little value. Helping the victim to flee to an undisclosed location might work in the short run, but would again entail great expense. Predicting couples likely to produce a homicide is not only impossible with current data, it also seems to have questionable value for prevention.

The major option police do have is whether to make arrests for minor domestic violence, something which varies widely in practice (Sherman & Cohn, 1989). Whether arrest reduces future violence is a question addressed in six replications of the Minneapolis experiment on that issue. None of the seven experiments, however, have sufficient numbers of cases to provide an adequate test of the effects of arrest on future homicide. The rarity of homicides would require tens of thousands of cases randomized to arrest or non-arrest in order to determine the effect of arrest upon homicide.

A more fruitful approach to both prediction and prevention of homicide in general, and perhaps even domestic homicide, would be to focus on the locations of homicides, rather than the individuals involved. Places as the unit of analysis generally provide greater predictive power than do persons (Sherman, 1989). They also provide more feasible options for prevention. Sixteen of Milwaukee's first 100 homicides in 1989, for example, have occurred inside or in front of taverns. While there are about 1,000 taverns (and some 200,000 total addresses) in Milwaukee, it may be possible to use prior call data to predict which taverns are likely to have homicides. The obvious preventive measure, given accurate prediction, would be to revoke the liquor license and incapacitate the dangerous place from producing the predicted homicide. Whether a similar strategy could be employed in predicting which residential addresses will have domestic homicides, however, seems much less likely, if not implausible.

Place-oriented strategies also offer greater tolerance for false positives, or errors in predictions. To close a bar unnecessarily is an unfortunate imposition on commerce; to incarcerate some person due to a false prediction is a gross imposition on liberty. Both errors are bad, but communities may be willing to accept a higher rate of error with impositions on commerce. If homicides can truly be prevented, the errors to commerce may be a price worth paying.

Identification of risk factors always entails over-prediction to some degree. Consider, for example, heart-bypass surgery or total mastectomies, neither of which are always necessary. Patients who agree to them are willing to accept the risk of false positives, as against the risk of a false negative. Society incurs costs for annual mammographies of women in the higher risk older age groups. The issue is therefore not simply over-prediction, but the expected return in exchange for prediction error. In the case of tavern homicide, the return could well justify the error rate. In the case of domestic homicide, the return would be much smaller.

This chapter suggests that predictions of domestic homicide based on prior police contacts with couples have a false positive error rate of over 99 percent. Moreover, it suggests that there is no known preventive treatment which could be over-applied, even if police or the courts would be willing to tolerate such a high rate of error. Unlike surgery or medical screening procedures, then, there is little to be gained from police intervention, even if we were willing to pay the price of 99 percent error. There is even less to be gained for society in holding police liable for negligence in predicting something that is now unpredictable, and failing to prevent something which is still unpreventable.

REFERENCES

Blumstein, A., J. Cohen, J. Roth & C.A. Visher (1986). *Criminal Careers and "Career Criminals."* Washington, DC: National Academy Press.

Breedlove, R.K., J.W. Kennish, D.M. Sandker & R.K. Sawtell (1977). "Domestic Violence and the Police: Kansas City." In *Domestic Violence and the Police: Studies in Detroit and Kansas City*, pp. 22-33. Washington, DC: Police Foundation.

Farrington, D.P. & R. Tarling (1985). "Criminological Prediction: An Introduction." In David P. Farrington and Roger Tarling (eds.) *Prediction in Criminology*, pp. 2-33. Albany: SUNY Press.

Federal Bureau of Investigation (FBI) (1985). *Crime in the United States, 1984*. Washington, DC: U.S. Government Printing Office.

Meyer, J.K. & T.D. Lorimor (1977). "Police Intervention Data and Domestic Violence: Exploratory Development and Validation of Prediction Models." Report Prepared under grant #Ro1MH27918 from National Institute of Mental Health to Kansas City, Missouri, Police Department.

Pierce, G.L., S.A. Spaar & L.R. Briggs IV (1984). "The Character of Police Work: Implications for the Delivery of Services." Center for Applied Social Research, Northeastern University.

Police Foundation (1977). *Domestic Violence and the Police: Studies in Detroit and Kansas City*. Washington, DC: Police Foundation.

Sherman, L.W. (1983). "Police in the Laboratory of Criminal Justice." In K.R. Feinberg (ed.) *Violent Crime in America*, pp. 26-43. Washington, DC: National Policy Exchange.

_____ (1987). "Preventing Serious Domestic Violence: A RECAP (Repeat Call Address Policing) Experiment." Proposal submitted by the Crime Control Institute to the National Institute of Justice.

_____ (1989). *The Hotspots of Crime and Criminal Careers of Places*. 1989 Gwynne Nettler Lecture, University of Alberta.

Sherman, L.W. & R.A. Berk (1984). "The Specific Deterrent Effects of Arrest for Domestic Assault." *American Sociological Review*, 49:261-272.

Sherman, L.W. & E.G. Cohn (1989). "The Impact of Research On Legal Policy: The Minneapolis Domestic Violence Experiment." *Law and Society Review*, 23:117-144.

Sherman, L.W., P.R. Gartin & M.E. Buerger (1989). "Hot Spots of Predatory Crime: Routine Activities and the Criminology of Place." *Criminology*, 27:27-55.

Sherman, L.W., J.D. Schmidt, P.R. Gartin, D. Rogan, D. Collins, A. Bacich & E.G. Cohn (1990). "Effects of On-Scene Arrest on Subsequent Domestic Violence: A Randomized Field Experiment." Washington, DC: Crime Control Institute.

Wilson, J.Q. (1977). "Foreword." In *Domestic Violence: Studies in Detroit and Kansas City*, pp. iii-vi. Washington, DC: Police Foundation.

5

Prosecuting Woman Abuse*

Naomi R. Cahn
Georgetown University Law Center
Lisa G. Lerman
The Catholic University of America

INTRODUCTION

Only a few writers have examined the role and the impact of prosecutors[1] in stopping woman abuse[2] (Goolkasian, 1986; Lerman, 1981; Schmidt & Steury, 1988; Waits, 1985). Most of the research done on criminal justice system responses to woman abuse has been on the police.

Why? Most law enforcement agencies do not initiate reforms or put additional resources into treating woman abuse without external pressure. Reforms in this area are most often initiated by victim advocates working in shelters and legal services offices. These efforts are supported by shoestring funding and overworked staff consumed by the immediate service needs of their clients. Since the resources available to generate institutional reform are paltry, advocates focus on institutions whose assistance is most immediately needed by battered women.

As a result, in many communities, advocates start by trying to change police practices and do not discover how many barriers to the prosecution of batterers exist until the police begin making arrests. Given this, one would expect to find more consideration of prosecution policy in communities where police have been persuaded to treat woman abuse as a crime or where police and prosecutors have worked together to change criminal justice system responses.

In the District of Columbia, for example, primary attention in the early 1980s was focused on the improvement of the civil protection order law and the

---

* The authors appreciate the research assistance of Joseph Holohan.

response of the clerks and judges who handled protection orders. (The civil protection law was amended in 1982 to create a private right of action for victims and to expand the relief available.) In more recent years, primary attention has shifted to the police. In 1988, the police department issued a new directive calling for arrests in woman abuse cases. However, advocates' work is far from over because the directive has yet to be implemented effectively (Baker, Cahn & Sands, 1989). Once the police begin to enforce it, there should be more arrests and this will put pressure on the prosecutor's office to begin filing charges in more cases.

The failure of prosecutors to pursue criminal charges aggressively in woman abuse domestic violence cases is an historical problem. Prosecutors have always had a great deal of discretion in deciding which cases to pursue. Until the late 1970s, prosecutors commonly viewed battering cases as inappropriate for criminal prosecution (Fromson, 1978). There was a general consensus among prosecutors that woman abuse cases were mostly minor disputes and that they were impossible to prosecute because the women dropped the charges (Fromson, 1978; Meier, 1987; Woods, 1981). Often, prosecutors viewed woman abuse as a private family matter or they believed that victims precipitated the violence by provoking batterers. The preferred policy was nonintervention. Even if a case was accepted by the prosecutor's office, it often was diverted to mediation or another non-criminal resolution.

During the intervening 15 years, prosecutors in a number of communities have taken the emergence of woman abuse seriously as a major crime problem and have developed procedures that allow them to prosecute batterers successfully. In other places, however, prosecutors still argue that most abuse cases are minor, undeserving of their attention, and/or that the women always drop the charges because they do not want their husbands to go to jail, so there is no point in prosecuting these cases (Ellis, 1984). As one District of Columbia prosecutor explained about a failure to pursue charges in a case that resulted in the victim's death, "It's just one of those horrible, bizarre things ...You deal with a thousand of these kinds of cases and 999 of them turn out as you expect them to: just a domestic problem" (Meier, 1987).

Because they represent the government in pressing charges against abusers, prosecutors have an important role to play in communicating to abusers that society will punish them for their behavior. Prosecutors who do not bring charges discourage the police from making arrests. The police see no point in initiating cases if there is no follow-through (Ellis, 1984).

Prosecuting woman abuse should be a priority for three reasons:

(1) Prosecution is the formal expression of social norms. If we want woman abuse to stop, we must prosecute those who abuse women. If we do not prosecute them, we give them tacit permis-

sion to continue. Increased intervention could have a significant impact on one of the most serious crime problems in the United States. Woman abuse results in more injuries that require medical treatment than rape, car accidents, and muggings combined (National Woman Abuse Prevention Project, 1988). Approximately one-quarter of all homicides and serious assaults are domestic violence (Sherman, 1985). There were approximately 2.1 million victims of it per year between 1978 and 1982 (Langan & Innes, 1986).

(2) Unless there is prosecution following arrest, law enforcement is a fiction. Only the prosecutor and the judge may exercise continuing authority over a defendant once he has been arrested.

(3) Woman abuse is a particularly dangerous form of violent crime. In no other category of violent crime does one find the offender going home to live with the victim. The violence is often serious and usually chronic. Absent intervention, the same woman will often be assaulted again by the same man. Data from the National Crime Survey showed that within the six-month period following a battering incident, approximately 32 percent of the victims experienced more violence (Langan & Innes, 1986).

WHAT WE KNOW ABOUT PROSECUTING WOMAN ABUSE

Over the past 15 years, some state legislatures have adopted measures to improve the response of the justice system to woman abuse by allowing innovations in prosecutors' handling of abuse cases (California Penal Code, 1989). In addition, many prosecutors have adopted new policies on their own. These policies have modified various stages of the prosecution process, beginning with simplified procedures for filing complaints that make the prosecutor, rather than the victim, responsible for filing charges, and including specialized training for personnel, psychological support for victims, and alternative options for sentencing.

Where they have been implemented, these new programs have led to more prosecutions of batterers. One of the primary reasons for this success is that reformed procedures and training give victims more support. Without it, victims often ask that charges be dropped or otherwise do not help prosecutors. Victims may not cooperate for many reasons, such as intimidation by the abuser with whom they often must live during the prosecution process, ignorance of the criminal justice system, continued attachment to the abuser, and delays and inconvenience in waiting for trial. New prosecutorial approaches produce more victim cooperation and prosecutions by seeking to neutralize or counter such reasons.

The most effective programs are based on a recognition that violence against women is criminal behavior and should be treated seriously by prosecutors (City of Alexandria, Virginia Domestic Violence Intervention Project, 1988; Mickish & Schoen, 1988). This includes a belief that abusers must be forced to take responsibility for their actions (Mickish & Schoen, 1988). These programs focus the court's attention on abusers while supporting victims (Pence, 1983) by recognizing their particular needs (Lerman, 1981). They consider victim goals, which may be to continue a relationship with an abuser, while using the criminal process to stop the abuse.

This section discusses how different prosecutors have implemented innovations at critical stages of the process to increase the number of charges pursued. The first concerns increasing the pool of victims brought to the attention of prosecutors and making filing decisions. The second ensures that prosecutors take responsibility for pursuing cases and the third seeks victim cooperation with the prosecutors. The fourth establishes special programs for prosecution. The fifth develops options for post-charge diversion and sentencing and the last concerns other creative approaches.

Our discussion is far from a comprehensive listing of all programs in all jurisdictions. Instead, it is a sampling of different innovations that prosecutors have implemented. Most of the programs are variations on two or three models. Though few prosecutors keep good data on their cases, they consistently report higher rates of victim cooperation and higher rates of convictions and guilty pleas using some of the following procedures.

Case Intake: Identification of Abuse Cases and the Filing Decision

Before they can file charges against abusers, prosecutors must identify victims. In many places, however, most abuse cases are never brought to the attention of prosecutors (Goolkasian, 1986). This is because victims are most likely to contact the police for help before pursuing other actions. The police have the power to stop the violence by removing the abuser. Unless the abuser is arrested or a charge is filed, however, the victim may not seek or receive further help from the criminal justice system.

Because the police are generally a victim's first and only contact with the criminal justice system, some prosecutors have developed cooperative programs with the police to identify abuse cases and facilitate prosecutorial involvement. These cases need special attention because of the close relationship between offender and victim and the continuing access of the offender to the victim. Some prosecutors have found it helpful to identify these cases as soon as they come to the attention of the police. Methods of identification include requiring officers who respond to incidents to fill out special forms and refer victims to special domestic violence workers; another directs that all police incident reports on abuse cases be referred to prosecutors for appropriate action. By reviewing these reports, prosecutors can identify abuse cases in which arrests were not made and interview victims to determine whether to prosecute. These practices can increase the number of cases in which charges are filed.

In Denver, the police use a special case summary that was developed in conjunction with the city attorney's office. It includes such useful information as whether there is an existing restraining order (Goolkasian, 1986). An interagency protocol in Orleans County, Vermont, sets out the responsibilities of the police, prosecutors, and a cooperating victims' shelter. The police are required to complete a "State's Attorneys Domestic Violence Incident Report" with information about the victim and perpetrator, the nature of the complaint, whether the complaint was verified, and how the victim can be contacted. In Bellevue, Washington, the police identify abuse cases and file reports on them with prosecutors (Bellevue Police Department, 1984). Washington state law requires that, where there is probable cause to believe that an offense has been committed, officers transmit domestic violence offense reports to prosecutors within 10 days of when reports are made, unless the cases are under investigation (Washington Code, 1989).

Some jurisdictions require that police indicate on general incident reports whether calls involve abuse (Goolkasian, 1986). For example, in St. Joseph County, Indiana all police responses to abuse incidents must be reported to prosecutors (Hile, 1988). At that time, prosecutors may send information to victims under plain cover (so that abusers will be less likely to notice) that informs them of their options, police officers may file formal complaints, or the victims themselves may file complaints. In the majority of cases brought to the attention of the prosecutors, charges are filed. Police reports in Alexandria, Virginia are labeled with the actual offense with a notation if abuse was involved. The reports are screened on a daily basis so a caseworker from Alexandria's domestic violence project can contact the victim and support her through criminal proceedings (City of Alexandria Domestic Violence Intervention Project, 1988).

Once they have identified abuse cases, in the absence of special programs, many prosecutors appear to apply stricter standards in determining whether to file charges in them than in other cases (Lerman, 1981). Many prosecutors discourage victims from filing charges, often indicating to victims that violence between intimates is not worthy of the prosecutor's office. Some prosecutors interview women to see whether they feel any ambivalence about filing charges; others file criminal complaints only when the injury is so egregious that it would be unconscionable not to do so (Lerman, 1981). In general felony cases, prosecutors do not file charges because of the victim's unwillingness or unavailability to testify in approximately 5 percent of the cases (Spohn, Gruhl & Welch, 1987); in abuse cases, this is the reason commonly given by prosecutors for failing to file charges (Lerman, 1984). In fact, victim cooperation appears to be significantly affected by the attitudes and conduct of prosecutors (Lerman, 1981; Pensworth, 1989). If prosecutors really want abuse cases to proceed, the rate of case attrition usually goes way down (Meier, 1987).

To overcome traditional perceptions of victim ambivalence and other obstacles to pursuing criminal charges, some offices have adopted objective criteria to decide when to file. In San Francisco, the Misdemeanor and Felony Prosecution Protocols require prosecutors to consider the facts of each case in conjunction with the following criteria in determining whether to issue a warrant: "extent or seriousness of the injuries," "use of a deadly weapon," "defendant's prior criminal history" and "past history of violence," and, in felony cases, the "potential lethality of" the situation (San Francisco District Attorney's Office, 1982 & 1985). The Protocols direct that where the factual support exists, a charge should be filed even if the victim has not yet been contacted. Within its first year, San Francisco's Family Violence Project (which also includes victim advocacy and other programs, discussed infra) resulted in a 136 percent increase in the number of cases with charges filed (Soler, 1987).

Prosecutorial Control Over Criminal Charges

In stranger cases, prosecutors usually sign the complaints. In abuse cases, however, prosecutors have tended to require victims to sign as a way of testing their resolve to go forward with prosecution. This discouraged prosecution and was often dangerous to the victim, leaving her vulnerable to further attack or intimidation to force her to drop the charges. If prosecutors take responsibility for the prosecution and treat the victims as key witnesses, offenders get the message that their violence is a crime against the state and not a personal or private matter. This absolves victims of the onerous responsibility of "throwing the book" at their partners and encourages them to cooperate with prosecutors.

In accordance with the policy that prosecution is the obligation of the prosecutor and not of the victim, some offices have adopted procedures that give prosecutors control over whether charges are filed and pursued. These policies may deter batterers from successfully pressuring victims to drop charges and, more fundamentally, these policies indicate the strong condemnation by society of the batterer's conduct (Waits, 1985). These procedures also result in prosecutors taking abuse cases more seriously (Goolkasian, 1986).

Critics of these policies argue that battered women have the right to decide whether they want criminal justice intervention and that prosecutors should not take that choice away (Goolkasian, 1986). Some prosecutors have even jailed victims for not cooperating (Waits, 1985). Nonetheless, policies that encourage prosecutorial action demonstrate that the criminal justice system can protect victims and act on batterers to try to deter them from engaging in further violence (Lerman, 1981).

Prosecutors have implemented a number of policies to encourage battered women to cooperate with them. Perhaps the most important policy in both practical and symbolic terms is for prosecutors to affirm their official responsibilities by signing criminal complaints themselves rather than requiring victims to do so (Goolkasian, 1986; Pence, 1984). A prosecutor signing a complaint indicates that it is government, not victims, that is answerable for charging the abusers (Attorney General's Task Force, 1984).

Other policies adopted by prosecutors prevent victims from dismissing charges ("no-drop" policies). A victim who wants to drop charges in Alexandria, Virginia must appear on the day of the trial to discuss the case with the prosecuting attorney. Victims are advised that if they do not appear, a judge may assess court costs against them. Since this approach can be criticized as being punitive rather than supportive of victims, many prosecutors offer counseling, protection, and encouragement at this point. This is the approach of prosecutors in Brooklyn, New York who will eventually let victims drop charges but only after the victims see a counselor (Holtzman, 1988a). However, the prosecutor's office in South Bend retains control over the decision to dismiss or to drop charges (Hile, 1988). And Dane County, Wisconsin has a prosecution policy under which it will not reduce or dismiss charges, regardless of a victim's requests, unless there are "extraordinary circumstances" (Held, 1986). It has also decided to pursue most aggressively those cases in which any number of the following factors are present:

(1) The perpetrator has caused serious bodily harm to the victim, requiring medical treatment or hospitalization;

(2) The perpetrator has used a weapon or a weapon-like instrument to cause bodily harm to the victim;

(3) The perpetrator has previously been convicted of any assaultive crime;

(4) The perpetrator has demonstrated a repeated pattern of assaultive behavior as evidenced by prior police reports, arrests, or convictions; and

(5) The perpetrator has repeatedly harassed or threatened the victim before or after the assault (Held, 1986).

Another policy showing that it is the prosecutor, rather than the victim, who controls a case is to subpoena victims/witnesses when they must be present in court. This may protect victims from being intimidated into not appearing in court because they can show abusers that they have been ordered to attend. The Portland, Oregon District Attorney's office has set up a subpoena process under which witnesses in felony abuse cases are subpoenaed to appear before the grand jury and at trial (Abraham, 1987).

Finally, prosecutors have been able to obtain convictions even without victim or witness cooperation. The Seattle City Attorney and Philadelphia District Attorney have prosecuted abusers without victim testimony by using other eyewitnesses or photographs of injuries (Lerman, 1981). The St. Joseph, Indiana prosecutor's office videotapes all domestic violence complaints so that it has a record in case a victim forgets or is unwilling to testify at a trial (Hile, 1988). This office has an internal memorandum that regulates how and when videotapes can be used at trial.

Victim Advocates

Battered women need to understand the criminal justice process. Many victims who become witnesses in criminal cases against their abusers are subject to threats, retaliation, and intimidation to coerce their noncooperation with prosecutors. Others have ambivalent relationships with their abusers and go through periods of reconciliation; often they believe that the role of witness is inconsistent with that of partner.

It is well-established that the use of victim advocates as contact points for abused women increases the rate of cooperation and increases the victims' satisfaction with the justice system. The functions performed by advocates include: in-depth interviewing of victims to assess their immediate safety needs and to gain an understanding of the facts of each case; explaining the criminal process and its likely outcome; providing victim information to prosecutors; counseling victims about intimidation, ambivalence or other problems while charges are pending; preparing testimony; and accompanying victims to court (Goolkasian, 1986).

There are several models for victim/witness programs. Perhaps the most successful are programs based outside of a prosecutor's office but which work very closely with its prosecutor, as in the Duluth Domestic Abuse Intervention Project and the Domestic Abuse Project in Minneapolis, Minnesota. Although the prosecutor's office and other law enforcement agencies participate, the projects receive funding from outside sources (Brygger, 1989; Pence, 1983). The Minneapolis project has 13 staff members and approximately 50 volunteers. After the police make an arrest, the projects follow up with victims and meet with prosecutors before arraignment to ensure that they have information about victims and do not drop charges. Both projects track every case through the criminal justice system, help ensure that prosecutors have all available evidence, and prepare victims for court proceedings. There is a follow-up contact with victims after six months and one year. Aurora, Colorado has adopted a variation of this model. Volunteer victim advocates (coordinated by the battered women's shelter working with the city's criminal justice system) contact victims for their court appearances and transmit information about violent incidents from the victims to prosecutors (Mickish & Schoen, 1988).

A second model involves the victim/witness advocacy programs based in prosecutors' offices, as in Seattle, Washington or Baltimore, Maryland. In Seattle, a staff member of the Victim Advocates Unit contacts each victim and conducts a phone interview with her within a few hours after an arrest is made (Baird, 1988). Advocates may hold plea negotiations and recommend an appropriate disposition of each case too (Goolkasian, 1986). The Unit has also developed a cooperative volunteer program for misdemeanor abuse cases. During a seven-month period ending on March 31, 1988, when there were approximately 230 cases, the Unit contacted 90 percent of identified victims at least once and communicated with victims an average of five times about their court cases (Baird, 1988).

The Brooklyn, New York District Attorney's office has its own counseling facility staffed by social workers (Holtzman, 1988a). The office also provides victim advocates to help battered women obtain civil protection orders. Additionally, in conjunction with other agencies, the district attorney has published a booklet which lists services for victims of crimes, including spouse, child, and elder abuse (Holtzman, 1988b). San Francisco has developed a variation of this model. The prosecutor's office there funds a domestic violence project offering advocacy services but the project is physically separate from the prosecutor's office.

Victim/witness advocates have been very effective in encouraging witnesses to pursue criminal prosecution. The San Francisco Family Violence Project found that, in the first year after it established a Domestic Violence Victim Services Unit, 70 percent of the victims assisted by the unit said they would not have pursued their cases without the help they received (Soler, 1987). In its first six years, the Project worked with more than 5,000 battered women.

Case Assignments

How an abuse case is handled in a prosecutor's office is crucial. A victim who must repeat her story to three or four different attorneys may feel traumatized and angry at the criminal justice system for forcing her to overcome many hurdles before she receives action. In response to this problem, prosecutors have developed case assignment methods that provide continuity and support to victims. Some offices which handle a large number of abuse cases have established special abuse units, designated certain attorneys to handle all abuse cases, or provided for "vertical prosecution" in which one attorney works with each victim from initial intake through trial. In addition to benefiting the victim, these special case assignment methods allow prosecutors to develop expertise in handling abuse cases.

The San Francisco Family Violence Project has implemented a vertical prosecution policy for felony cases (Soler, 1987). Its staff has estimated that a prosecutor needs at least six months to become familiar with the special issues in abuse cases (Goolkasian, 1986). In Brooklyn, abuse cases are handled by special units staffed by prosecutors with special training to make them more sensitive to victim concerns (Holtzman, 1988b). The Domestic Violence Unit of the Portland, Oregon prosecutor's office is responsible for almost all the county's abuse cases. It is staffed by an attorney and a victim advocate (Abraham, 1987).

Post-Charge and Sentencing Options

Once charges are filed, an abuser may be eligible for a pretrial diversion program under which prosecution is suspended while he completes a counseling or other intervention program; or the case may proceed to trial, at which a prosecutor may recommend a variety of sentencing options.

Prosecution may be deferred at any point until the final verdict with diversion. In many cases, the terms of diversion are similar to what would be the conditions of probation after conviction (Lerman, 1981). The disposition reached through diversion may take only a few days, as opposed to waiting months for a trial to be scheduled. If diversion is successful, then the victim need not testify. Parenthetically, some diversion programs use mediation or couples counseling. These strategies are misguided because they undermine the message of abuser responsibility for violence that should be communicated by prosecution.

Battered women's advocates differ about whether diversion is prudent. Some believe diversion may be more responsive than traditional prosecution to the concerns of victims whose goals may be stopping the violence rather than punishing their abusers (Lerman, 1984). On the other hand, most advocates now see that diversion does not convey the strong societal disapproval of abuse that traditional prosecution does (Brygger, 1989). Rarely are diversion cases brought back into the criminal justice system unless there is a second assault, which is itself a basis for a new criminal charge (Brygger, 1989). Thus, the effectiveness of a diversion program depends on a prosecutor's office developing detailed guidelines to ensure a careful screening of participants, intensive supervision of abusers (by prosecutors or court personnel), regular and frequent counseling, and the ability to reinstate criminal charges if abusers fail to comply at any time while charges are deferred. In addition, before diversion programs can be implemented, there must be counseling programs that accept court referrals and that provide alcohol and drug treatment as well as group therapy for batterers (Lerman & Cahn, forthcoming).

The San Francisco Felony Protocol states that felony charges are too serious to be reduced to charges for which an abuser may be eligible for diversion. According to the Misdemeanor Protocol, diversion is only possible when, among other conditions, the charge is a misdemeanor (although not one involving a child), the defendant has no convictions for any violent offenses within the past seven years, and the defendant has not been diverted for abuse during the previous five years. A victim's response to the disposition is another factor in determining the appropriateness of diversion.

In Bellevue, Washington, eligibility for diversion is decided on the basis of the individual abuser's prior record and attitude, and the victim's wishes. If diversion is appropriate, prosecutors draft a Stipulated Order of Continuance which sets out the conditions for diversion. At the same time, prosecutors decide whether a No Contact Order is also appropriate. Both documents are then presented to the judge for signature and copies are given to the victim, defendant, probation officer, and prosecutor (Bellevue Police Department, 1984). Any violation of the conditions of diversion is discussed by prosecutors and probation officers to determine if diversion should be revoked and the case should go forward. In Dane County, Wisconsin the use of deferred prosecution has almost eliminated dismissal of charges at the victim's request (Held, 1986).

Some offices have developed post-trial sentencing options instead of using diversion programs. These sentencing options may be implemented after a trial, upon a finding of guilty, or through plea bargaining when an abuser pleads guilty in front of the judge but has his sentence suspended pending completion of these alternative sentencing provisions. These programs have a greater ability to coerce abuser participation than diversion because of the immediate threat of jail upon violation. However, they often require more victim cooperation than diversion programs because sentencing generally occurs later in the prosecutorial process than diversion.

In Brooklyn, New York, the district attorney and the victim services agency have developed a program called "Alternatives to Violence." It is a treatment for batterers to learn how to avoid future violence (Holtzman, 1988b). In Denver, a defendant in diversion must plead guilty but judgment and sentencing are deferred while he completes a court-mandated program (Denver Domestic Violence Manual, 1986). Once the defendant is accepted into the program, he is referred to a treatment agency that has an agreement with the Domestic Violence unit of the city attorney's office. It verifies the defendant's compliance with the program while a victim advocate from the diversion program attempts to contact the victim on a monthly basis to determine whether the abuse has ended.

In Duluth, judges order presentence investigations on all abuse cases and choose from sentencing options developed by the Domestic Abuse Intervention Project (Pence, 1983). There is a presumptive sentence of 30-60 days in jail, with the sentence stayed for one year based on conditions which protect the victim and are designed to rehabilitate the abuser, such as his participation in a counseling and education program and his agreement to stay away from the victim (Goolkasian, 1986). A probation officer must set up a reporting schedule to monitor the abuser's participation in counseling.

Johnson County, Iowa has developed guidelines for determining jail sentences and probation periods. The criteria include the severity of a victim's injury, the abuser's prior criminal history and past incidents of abuse, whether the defendant contests the charges, and whether the parties want to maintain their relationship (Johnson County Attorney, 1987).

Other Programs

Overcoming Evidentiary Problems

Juries often find it difficult to believe testimony that a woman has actually been battered if she returns to an abusive situation after having been battered. At least one prosecutor has used expert testimony on the "battered woman syndrome" in prosecuting an abuser in a rape case to explain why the victim continually returned to him despite the abuse she suffered. The expert testified about the behavioral characteristics of battered women and the diagnosis of post-traumatic stress disorder. The Supreme Court of Washington upheld the trial court's use of this testimony (*Washington v. Ciskie*).

Other Innovations

In several cities in Washington state, prosecutors work closely with domestic violence networks (Washington State Shelter Network, Evergreen Legal

Services & Washington Women Lawyers, 1984) to monitor existing policies and implement new ones. Other prosecutors have worked with battered women's advocates to develop community education and better training programs.

Prosecutors in these programs are generally pleased with them. While there are relatively little before and after data, prosecutors report that these programs facilitate treating woman abuse as a crime. The Orleans County, Vermont prosecutor's office attributes its 92 percent conviction rate in abuse cases from July, 1982 through June, 1985 to the adoption of an interagency domestic violence protocol. In San Francisco, "positive disposition" (cases which resulted in a disposition that required a court to exercise jurisdiction over a defendant) increased 136 percent in the two years following implementation of the felony protocol (Soler, 1987). After adoption of the misdemeanor protocol, the Project found that the conviction rate increased "dramatically" to 90 percent (Soler, 1987). In Bellevue, Washington the percentage of cases not prosecuted because the victim failed to appear in court for misdemeanor cases dropped from 25 percent to 12 percent (Bellevue Police Department, 1984).

THE DIFFICULTY OF IMPLEMENTATION

In light of the range of different and successful innovations, why haven't more prosecutors adopted them? The implementation of these programs is not easy and there are many obstacles to reform. First, there is an evidentiary problem in battering cases because there is generally just one witness (other than the abuser). Many prosecutors do not want to waste their time wrestling with a problem that could deny them a conviction. Second, coordinated projects can be expensive. For example, California passed legislation authorizing funding for special domestic violence programs; but in the first two years after the legislation was enacted, there was no money appropriated for these projects. Third, battering cases may require a substantial time commitment from prosecutors. The caseloads of most prosecutors are overwhelming and do not leave time to spend encouraging victims to cooperate. Fourth, successful programs require coordination between prosecutors, police, and the battered women's community. And finally and most important, many prosecutors still do not believe abuse is a crime and do not want to intervene in "private, family matters."

Many of these problems can be overcome. Where prosecutors persist in refusing to take abuse seriously, battered women's advocates must apply pressure to get them to change. Advocates should consider joining the staffs of prosecutors' offices to ensure that their concerns are handled effectively. Another strategy is for advocates to lobby legislatures to enact statutes setting out policies for the criminal handling of abuse as occurred in Washington and California.

Model legislation on the prosecution of abuse includes provisions on special training for police officers, prosecutors, and judges, the establishment of victim advocacy programs, and the streamlining of prosecutorial procedures, such as required notification of victims within a set time of whether prosecutors will institute criminal proceedings (California Penal Code, 1989; Lerman, 1984; Washington Code, 1989).

While no one set of innovations will work in every community, there are some steps that all communities can take regardless of legislative direction. In fact, prosecutors should take these steps not only to prevent abuse but also to protect themselves from legal liability for failing to do so. Prosecutors have been sued for their unwillingness to initiate prosecutions in abuse cases (Woods, 1981). As the result of one lawsuit, prosecutors in Cleveland, Ohio agreed to change their procedures by considering each abuse case on its own merits and advising police officers that abusers would be prosecuted (Woods, 1981).

The first step in developing a successful program is to make abuse a prosecutorial priority by recognizing that it is a crime and that the criminal justice system can contribute to decreasing its incidence (Washington State Shelter Network et al., 1984). The primary goal of intervention should be ending the violence, not saving a relationship. Prosecutors might adopt a policy statement like the following:

> All cases of domestic violence will be treated as alleged criminal conduct. A person who commits domestic violence has committed a crime against the state (city, county). Perpetrators should receive consistent, direct, clear messages of the criminal nature of domestic violence, and that they are responsible for their behavior, regardless of alleged "provocation."
>
> All perpetrators should receive appropriate criminal sanctions as well as monitored treatment for domestic violence. All victims should receive appropriate supportive services (Mickish & Schoen, 1988).

Once a prosecutor's office is committed to more effective handling of abuse it can develop appropriate standard policies and guidelines. The exact form of these guidelines depends on available resources, such as the existence of a well-organized battered women's coalition or victim services agency and cooperative personnel in other criminal justice agencies. The guidelines may require that:

* all police officers, prosecutors, and judges be trained on issues related to abuse;
* special forms be used by all persons involved in the criminal justice response to abuse;

* police refer all victims to a particular person in the prosecutor's office who is responsible for all abuse cases and for contacting victims within 48 hours of incidents;
* prosecutors file charges based on the sufficiency of evidence, regardless of the relationship of the parties, and prosecutors sign the charges;
* the decision to prosecute be made within five days of an incident and the case proceed with as few continuances as possible;
* prosecutors implement a no-drop policy;
* prosecutors work with community mental health agencies to develop programs to help abusers so sentencing recommendations can request that abusers enter these programs; and
* prosecutors use diversion programs only if abusers have no criminal record and diversion is in accord with victim wishes and be prepared to continue prosecution if the abusers violate the conditions of diversion (Lerman, 1981).

To develop these guidelines, all members of local criminal justice systems must cooperate and work with the battered women's community. This will help to ensure that new projects address actual victim needs.

Finally, any successful program needs a mechanism to monitor compliance. Given the great discretion of criminal justice officials, periodic effort must be made to ensure that practice conforms to policy. Even communities with policies calling for arrest and prosecution may experience widespread noncompliance (Pence, 1983).

Prosecution of woman abuse cases can make a difference by protecting victims and by forcing abusers to recognize that their conduct is criminal. But prosecutors must work with the police, social service agencies, and the courts to be effective. Once police see that abusers are prosecuted, they may be more likely to arrest; and once criminal court judges see increasing numbers of abuse cases with carefully gathered and presented evidence, they may take these cases more seriously. Successful prosecution is only possible when all elements of the criminal justice system work together.

NOTES

1 Prosecutors are variously referred to as district attorneys, city attorneys, or county attorneys depending on the structure of the local government.

2 We use this term to refer to adult domestic violence, most often committed by men against women.

REFERENCES

Abraham, L. (1987). *Domestic Violence Unit Procedure Manual.* Portland, OR: District Attorney's Office.

Attorney General's Task Force on Family Violence (1984). *Final Report.* Washington, DC: U.S. Department of Justice.

Baird, R. (1988). King County Prosecuting Attorney's Victim Assistance Unit Status Report.

Baker, K., N. Cahn & S. Sands (1989). *Report on District of Columbia Police Response to Domestic Violence.* Washington, DC.

Bellevue Police Department. (1984). *A Community Approach to Domestic Violence.* Bellevue, Washington.

Brygger, M.P. (1989). Interview with N. Cahn. Director, National Woman Abuse Prevention Project.

California Penal Code, ch. 2, 273 (Deering Supp. 1989).

City of Alexandria, Virginia Domestic Violence Intervention Project (1988). *Policies and Procedures.*

Denver Domestic Violence Manual Task Force (1986). *The Denver Domestic Violence Manual.* Denver, CO.

Elliott, D. (1989). "Criminal Justice Procedures in Family Violence Crimes." In L. Ohlin & M. Tonry (eds.) *Family Violence*, pp. 427-480. Chicago: University of Chicago Press.

Ellis, J. (1984). "Prosecutorial Discretion to Charge in Cases of Spousal Assault: A Dialogue." *Journal of Criminal Law and Criminology*, 75:56-102.

Fromson, T. (1977). "The Case for Legal Remedies for Abused Women." New York: *University Review of Law and Social Change*, 6:135-174.

Goolkasian, G. (1986). *Confronting Domestic Violence: A Guide for Criminal Justice Agencies.* Washington, DC: National Institute for Justice.

Held, Catherine. (1986). "Law Enforcement and Prosecution Responses to Domestic Violence; Non-involvement to the Application of Criminal Justice Sanctions." *Wisc. Women's L.J.*, 2:95-124.

Hile, J. (1988). *Letter to L. Lerman.* South Bend, IN: Office of Prosecuting Attorney.

Holtzman, E. (1988a). *Counseling Services for Victims of Crime.* Brooklyn, NY: Office of District Attorney.

_____ (1988b). *Testimony on the Legal Needs of Battered Women Before the New York City Council Committee on Women.*

Johnson County Attorney. (1987). *Johnson County Domestic Assault Mandatory Arrest Guidelines.* Iowa City, IA: Johnson County Attorney.

Langan, P.A. & C.A. Innes (1986). *Preventing Domestic Violence Against Women.* Washington, DC: Bureau of Justice Statistics.

Lerman, L. (1981). *Prosecution of Spouse Abuse: Innovations in Criminal Justice Response.* Washington, DC: Center for Women Policy Studies.

_____ (1984). "A Model State Act: Remedies for Domestic Abuse." *Harvard Journal on Legislation,* 21:61-143.

Lerman, L. & N. Cahn (forthcoming). "Stopping Adult Domestic Violence; The Role of Mental Health Professionals in the Legal System." In R.T. Ammerman & M. Hersen (eds.) *Case Studies in Domestic Violence.* New York: Plenum Press.

Meier, J. (1987). *Battered Justice.* The Washington Monthly, 37-45.

Mickish, J. & K. Schoen (1988). "Domestic Violence: Developing and Maintaining an Effective Policy." *The Prosecutor,* 15-20.

National Woman Abuse Prevention Project. (1988). *Domestic Violence Fact Sheets.* Washington, DC: NWAPP.

Orleans County, Vermont. (1983). *Interagency Protocol for Response to Domestic Complaints and Enforcement of Relief from Abuse Orders.*

Pensworth, L. (1989). Interview with N. Cahn. Former Assistant District Attorney.

Pence, E. (1983). "The Duluth Domestic Abuse Intervention Project." *Hamline Law Review,* 6:247-275.

_____ (1984). *Criminal Justice Response to Domestic Assault Cases: A Guide for Police Development.* Duluth, MN: Region 3 Council for Battered Women.

San Francisco District Attorney's Office (1982). *Felony Protocol.*

_____ (1985). *Misdemeanor Protocol.*

Schmidt, J. & E. Steury (1989). "Prosecutorial Discretion in Filing Charges in Domestic Violence Cases." *Criminology*, 27:487-510.

Sherman, L. (1985). *Domestic Violence*. Washington, DC: National Institute of Justice.

Soler, E. (1987). *The San Francisco Family Violence Project: An Overview*. San Francisco: District Attorney's Office.

Spohn, C., J. Gruhl & S. Welch (1987). "The Impact of the Ethnicity and Gender of Defendants on the Decision to Reject or Dismiss Felony Charges." *Criminology*, 25:175-191.

Waits, K. (1985). "The Criminal Justice System's Response to Battering: Understanding the Problem, Forging the Solutions." *Washington Law Review*, 60:267-329.

Washington v. Ciskie, 110 Wash. 2d 263, 751 P.2d 1165 (1988).

Washington Code Annotated, ch. 10.99 (West 1980 & Supp. 1989).

Washington State Shelter Network, Evergreen Legal Services & Washington Women Lawyers (1984). *The Domestic Violence Act Evaluation Project*. Olympia, WA: Washington State Shelter Network.

White, P. (1985). *Fifth Annual Report of the Orleans County (Vermont) State's Attorney's Office for the Period July 1, 1984 through June 30, 1985.*

Woods, L. (1981). "Litigation on Behalf of Battered Women." *Women's Rights Law Reporter*, 7:39-45.

6

Counseling and Shelter Services for Battered Women

Mary Ann Dutton-Douglas
Nova University

Dorothy Dionne
Nova University

INTRODUCTION

While the problem of woman battering has been recognized for some time now, the development and evaluation of comprehensive and effective intervention strategies for addressing it continues to be a need. Battered women's shelters provided the first recognized efforts to address the immediate needs of victims and their children. Since the development of the first shelter in 1972 in England (Pizzey, 1974), more than 700 shelters have been established in the United States (Berk, Newton & Berk, 1986). More recently, mainstream mental health, social service, and legal service delivery systems have also begun working to help victims and reduce battering rates.

The purposes of this chapter are (1) to identify the problems for which battered women need counseling and shelter services; (2) to discuss the types of interventions currently available from these services and review empirical data concerning their effectiveness; and (3) to discuss the interactions of these services with criminal justice agencies. Methodological and philosophical issues related to defining effectiveness and ethical issues are also addressed as are the implications for treatment of the diversity that exists among victims as far as race, social class, and sexual preference.

INTERVENTIONS FOR BATTERED WOMEN

Both victim needs and the interventions designed to address them are related to three areas of concern: (1) crisis issues such as physical danger, suicide, and homicide; (2) transition issues involving choice-making about relationships, living arrangements, and divorce; and (3) recovery from the traumatic psychological effects of abuse (Douglas, 1987). Efforts to treat these needs involve applying interventions for each simultaneously and in a coordinated manner.

Needs and Problems Facing Battered Women

The most immediate need facing the battered woman still involved in a battering relationship, regardless of whether she is living with an offender, is safety for herself and her children. The fear resulting from actual violence or the threat of violence often explains why battered women seek help.

A second set of needs facing battered women relates to transition issues and involves making some serious choices. Examples of such choices include whether to leave or stay in the relationship with an abusive partner, to press criminal charges against him, to stop living with the offender independent of a decision to terminate her relationship with him, and to get a job to be financially independent of the offender.

A third set of needs among victims concerns the psychological effects produced by the trauma of battering. The woman who is psychologically, physically, and/or sexually abused experiences predictable reactions which have been collectively described and termed the Battered Woman Syndrome (Walker, 1984). More recently, the Battered Woman Syndrome has been typed as a special case of Post-Traumatic Stress Disorder (PTSD; Douglas, 1987; Ochberg, 1988), a diagnostic category within the Diagnostic and Statistical Manual (DSM-III-R; APA, 1987). Victims also experience the effects of psychological, physical, and sexual abuse beyond the specific criteria of PTSD.

Specific emotional, cognitive, and behavioral responses that are characteristic products of battering include anger, fear and anxiety, depression, low self-esteem, suicide or a high risk of it, confusion, feelings of being overwhelmed, memory loss, poor concentration, physical problems, suspiciousness and paranoia, and recurrent experiencing of the trauma of abuse and an avoidance of the emotions associated with it, including dissociation (cf. Douglas, 1984; Hilberman & Munson, 1978; Stark & Flitcraft, 1981; Walker, 1984). A number of responses often function as coping mechanisms for battered women. These include denial and minimization of the severity of abuse, of the likelihood of its reoccurrence, of the risk of lethality, and of the difficulty of safe retreat. Self-blame and responsibility for either the cause of the violence or for providing a solution to it are other coping mechanisms.

Intervention Strategies

There are a variety of methods that shelter and counseling services utilize to help battered women. Some, like emotional support and validation, can be used at any point of intervention. Others, like exploring past abuse and victimization, are best left to the later stages of healing. The following paragraphs discuss intervention strategies commonly used within the crisis, transition, and recovery phases.

Crisis Stage. During the crisis stage, interventions help victims escape abuse, safeguard them and their children, and assess their potential for suicide and/or homicide. While this is typically the shortest of the three phases, it is likely to recur and is a time when there is a great potential for positive change. Making shelters or safehouses available to victims is one of the most important intervention strategies. They provide a higher degree of certainty that battered women and their children will be safe from danger than most other alternatives.

Because many battered women do not seek shelter protection (Bowker, 1983), other interventions are needed to satisfy safety needs. One involves escape plans. Developing a plan encourages the battered woman to think of ways to avoid further abuse. These include identifying important cues to danger, creating and accessing resources necessary to make an escape (e.g., telling neighbors of plans, making arrangements with others for a place to go, accumulating money, making spare keys, keeping an extra distributor wire in the trunk), and establishing a specific behavioral plan of action. Older children may be informed of the plan ahead of time and/or may be involved in its development. It is important to remember that using an escape plan does not guarantee a victim's safety. And, under certain circumstances, it may be impossible to use.

Transition Stage. The *transition stage* is often a time of decision-making for a woman. She may need assistance exploring alternatives to her current living situation and identifying sources of financial support before she will realistically be able to consider leaving the abusive relationship as a viable option. A counselor can take a woman through the steps of problem-solving including brainstorming possible options and plans, assessing their feasibility and consequences, choice-making among alternatives, and formulating ways to assess their effectiveness. This should be done with an emphasis on exploring options while helping the woman reclaim her power in making decisions for herself. Aiding decision-making requires a basic acceptance of the woman and her right to make a decision on her own, regardless of the therapist's personal views about what she should do. This in no way implies, however, that the counselor should give victims assessments of the feasibility of options based on experience in working with other battered women. Empowerment at this point of intervention means providing the battered woman with all the information and resources available to make a particular choice and then respecting the woman's right to act while maintaining active support and acceptance of her.

Helping a woman see her battering as a larger social problem is also an important tool, one consistent with principles of feminist therapy (Rosewater & Walker, 1985). Many women suffer abuse and the isolation of believing that it is their unique, personal problem. The analysis of battering as a larger social problem helps the battered woman recognize that she is not alone and that the cause of the abuse is deeply rooted in the social structure. This understanding, which is central to feminist analysis and to feminist therapy, can facilitate a far more powerful and effective response to the problem of battering than one which is based on addressing individual psychopathology. Understanding oppressive attitudes toward women and other minority status groups that permeate society makes it clear that a woman's victimization, in part, is a function of her gender alone, not due to what she does or who she is as an individual. Seeing herself as part of a larger community of women can give her strength and support to continue her personal fight against oppression. She may find strength in numbers which she does not feel alone.

Social and emotional support are critical components at any point in the intervention process. Messages from others telling her she is a good person and does not deserve abuse help to counteract messages from her abuser that she is worthless and deserving of punishment. Support from others can also provide a critical link to safety if a woman should need to flee. Knowing that someone else understands and is available to help can make the difference between life and death for a battered woman.

Teaching victims about battering generally goes a long way toward building self-esteem. Learning about the cycle of violence (Walker, 1984) with its tension-building, acute battering, and contrite loving phases may allow a woman to see that the abuse she suffers is not a result of her inability to stop her partner's battering. She may also learn that battering is a behavior pattern that she can escape or avoid, but not directly change. Applying the cycle of violence theory to her own life may help the battered woman predict her batterer's behavior better and thus avoid or escape future violence. Additionally, it may help her to see her situation in a broader perspective and devise more options for herself.

Education about the effects of abuse helps a battered woman redefine her pain. Instead of seeing her depression, anxiety, and self-hatred as proof that her abuser is right and she is "crazy," she can define those responses as common reactions to trauma and as efforts to cope with a "crazy" situation. In some ways, this redefinition can lessen the pain by allowing a woman to trust her feelings and perceptions rather than fear that her own connection with reality is distorted.

Skill development is another component of the educational process. Simply because a battered woman does not use certain behaviors with her batterer, e.g., assertiveness, does not mean that she lacks skills to do so. Many behaviors that most people take for granted, like making requests or expressing feelings, can result in abuse from a batterer and therefore are avoided as a means of staying safe. Some battered women have few vocational or social skills. They may have had these skills at one time but, because they lost control over their lives to their abuser, they cannot use them effectively in employment or other interpersonal situations. Other women never had the opportunity to develop these skills. Acquiring them and learning when they may be helpful can increase the battered woman's confidence and her ability to get more of what she needs in the world. Providing information about opportunities to develop new skills or how to use existing skills effectively, i.e., vocational training, is an important intervention. Teaching a woman how to access social agencies is another means of empowering her and allows her the option of moving toward greater independence. Advocacy for battered women as an intervention can take many forms. It can be expressed through political action such as working to change laws that compromise the safety of battered women or limit their rights or drafting new legislation to improve the availability of services. Efforts to educate the public about the effects of battering and how they parallel the kinds of victimization many women experience in a sexist and violent society is advocacy too. Defining battering as a use of power and control in the dominance of one over another makes battering resemble other forms of oppressive behavior such as rape and sexual harassment in the workplace. Education about battering as a problem of power and control, not just a specific set of physically abusive behaviors, is especially important in the criminal justice system. It can help defense attorneys, prosecutors, and judges learn about the dynamics of family violence and about how they can help stop it, help the battered woman protect herself, and facilitate her healing and recovery. Education is equally important in the medical profession. Medical treatment facilities and professionals must help identify battering victims and provide necessary support and referral.

Advocacy can also involve working to satisfy an individual woman's needs and to protect her rights. Visiting her in prison, accompanying her to the hospital for medical care, standing by as she testifies about her abuse in court, and asserting her right to know about the status and location of her batterer as he moves through the criminal justice system to ensure her safety are all examples of advocacy that validate the battered woman and her right to be safe.

Recovery Phase. The previous areas of intervention lead up to and render the *recovery phase* of intervention possible. During it, a battered woman has the opportunity to rebuild her self-esteem by seeing herself as a survivor rather than a victim. She comes to see her emotional and physical scars not only as symbols of pain, but as representative of her strength and will to endure and overcome. She can assign responsibility for her victimization to her abuser and responsibility for survival to herself. She can accept what her experiences have to teach her about herself while resolving never to accept abuse again. She can learn to reach out to others and see her own ability to nurture others as a strength, not a weakness. The first step in this process occurs when the battered woman revisits past instances of abuse and experiences the full range of emotions they provoke.

After an abusive incident a woman is likely to experience anger, emotional hurt, and physical injury. But if she expresses her feelings openly, she may face a high probability of even more abuse from her partner. As a result, the battered woman may redirect, suppress, or deny the anger or redefine it not as rage at her abuser, but at herself. During the recovery process, a woman is given an opportunity to revisit her anger and pain, acknowledge it as justified, and direct it not at herself and others, but at the partner who abused her and toward the system that maintained that abuse and failed to protect her from it. The expression of anger is essential to recovery and often provides the emotional energy necessary to become independent of an abusive relationship.

It is paradoxical that the very step that can open the door to life after abuse, the appropriate expression of justified anger, is the very one most likely to be resisted by others. Our society sees an angry woman as out of control, demanding, and unacceptable. Those who encounter an abused woman when she is angry often back away until she can "act more appropriately" or, alternatively, may become angry in response to her. She may be expected to play the role of a passive victim, accepting the ministrations of others gratefully rather than standing up and demanding that justice be served, restitution made, and her suffering acknowledged. That is one reason why the criminal justice system is in such an important position to empower a victim by recognizing and validating her feelings and her attempts to respond to abuse. Not to do so is to revictimize her (Douglas, 1988).

SERVICE DELIVERY SYSTEMS FOR BATTERED WOMEN

It is important to identify battered women and to make them aware of the services available to assist them. As with other victims of crime and abuse, battered women can be identified during contacts with community agencies and professionals as well as through their contact with programs specifically designed to serve them. Many battered women seek medical attention from emergency rooms, family doctors, or paramedics. Some have contact with police officers who have responded to a battering incident. A smaller number of battered women have consulted attorneys or mental health counselors in their search for relief. Agencies that oversee welfare programs for women and children encounter significant numbers of battered women who often are not identified as such. Many probation officers see probationers or their partners who are victims of abuse. These contacts are critical opportunities to recognize the battered woman as a victim and to make her aware of services that can protect her.

Emergency Hotlines

Emergency hotlines are often operated by a shelter and can act as triage centers to establish contact between the battered woman and a helping network. They provide information and referrals on alternative housing, financial help, legal aide, medical services, vocational resources, and many other services a woman might need to protect herself and her children from abuse. In addition, hotlines are often a woman's first attempt at seeking help and the understanding and acceptance she receives can mean the difference between continued isolation or a first step toward healing and growth.

Shelters

Hotlines often help battered women get into shelters which provide a safe place to sleep and food to eat in a secure environment. Many shelters also go beyond providing these essentials and offer supportive counseling, child care, advocacy services, and a community of other women to help alleviate a woman's feelings of isolation.

Counseling given to women during their stay at a shelter is usually supportive and goal directed. Its emphasis is on establishing plans for safety and, if the woman chooses, an independent life for herself. Analysis of her personal dynamics and growth are deemphasized in favor of the more immediate and pragmatic issues discussed earlier regarding crisis interventions. A common goal is that the battered woman leave the shelter with a clearer understanding of her situation, her options, and the fact that she is only responsible for her safety, not for her abuse.

Advocacy is another important component of most shelter services. Victim advocates help the woman gather information necessary to apply for economic assistance or vocational training. In addition, advocates facilitate her involvement with the court system in obtaining restraining orders, pressing charges, contacting attorneys to represent her, and tracking the status of her abuser if he is involved in the criminal justice system.

Support Groups and Special Programs

Support groups often provide a unique network of women who have experienced abuse. These groups ease the feelings of isolation and shame many women experience as a consequence of their abuse. They also act to raise women's consciousness of battering as a widespread, societal problem rather than a feature of their own troubled marriages.

Specialized community treatment programs for battered women are less common. These programs are designed to provide counseling and advocacy interventions not offered by a shelter. Thus, women who do not contact a shelter can use these programs. Some specialized programs work closely with shelters and provide more long-term involvement than may be available through a shelter. While these programs can provide assistance at any point in a woman's struggle, they are particularly suited for responding to issues in the transition and recovery phases of intervention. However, it is important that they make crisis services available too, directly or through networking with other services, since safety issues often reemerge at all phases of intervention.

Special programs often target particular groups of battered women who may need specific or intensive types of help, for example, incarcerated women. Many women in jails and prisons are victims of battering which in some instances contributed to the crimes for which they were charged, i.e., killing an abusive partner in self-defense or committing criminal acts under duress from an abuser. These women are often further abused and neglected by the criminal justice system with its lack of awareness and understanding of battering. Support groups run for women in correctional institutions help women understand the effects of abuse in their own lives and aid in their recovery. They can also help women advocate for themselves in areas such as visitation with their children, clemency, and establishing support systems following release.

Other Services

In addition to specialized programs, women can also receive services from other providers, including inpatient crisis stabilization units, outpatient community mental health centers, private counseling agencies, or clergy. While many women have received help and support from these sources, a caveat is necessary. Practitioners and helping professionals not experienced with battering can indulge in well-meaning victim-blaming under the guise of assessing pathology, helping the victim recognize her responsibility for her abuse, reminding her of her duty to home and family, and her need to forgive those who have injured her. These are not legitimate goals for victims of abuse if they further damage victims' fragile self-esteem and make them feel more guilty and hopeless. Therefore, women who are victims of abuse should be referred to helpers with experience in mitigating and healing the effects of abuse.

EFFECTIVENESS OF SHELTERS AND COUNSELING SERVICES

The literature addressing the effectiveness of shelters and counseling services to battered women is in its infancy. This literature uses three criteria to evaluate interventions with battered women: (1) the decision to leave or the actual leaving of the abusive relationship, (2) the recurrence of more violence, and (3) self-reported ratings of effectiveness.

Decision to Leave the Relationship

The first criterion, the decision to leave the abusive relationship, implies that leaving the relationship is the desired outcome. While a battered woman's leaving the abusive relationship is often important in her efforts to increase her own safety, there is no guarantee that she will be safe simply because she no longer resides with her abuser or is divorced from him. In fact, the woman's leaving may be directly related to an escalation of violence even to the point of lethality (Berk, Newton & Berk, 1986; Browne, 1987). In a study of spouse murder in Florida (Barnard, Vera, Vera & Newman, 1982), 57 percent of the men who had killed their wives were living apart from them at the time of the incident. So, although leaving the relationship may be desirable as an overall outcome, it is dangerous to consider it as a goal unrelated to considerations of a woman's immediate safety.

Many empirical studies of the effectiveness of shelter or counseling interventions have measured the outcome criterion of "leaving the relationship" in terms of actual living arrangements (cf. Synder & Scheer, 1981). Others have also measured it as a decision or intent to return to the batterer (cf. Schutte, Bouleige & Malouff, 1986) and as a decision to seek a divorce (cf. Stone, 1984). In a review of the empirical literature, Strube (1988) grouped research into two categories: (1) indirect studies examining the decision to leave an abusive relationship, and (2) studies which directly address relationship termination.

Although most studies have looked at the decision to return to live with batterers after women have been in shelters, two studies have examined battered women's living arrangements after some form of counseling. Among the latter, by the end of treatment, 53 percent of women referred for psychiatric evaluation and treatment (Hilberman & Munson, 1978) and 68 percent of women receiving counseling (Rounsaville, 1978) were living with their abusers. Studies of women's return following shelter by definition examine women who had left their relationship to enter a shelter. Comparatively, those studies addressing return following counseling included both women who had actually left the relationship, either at the time of counseling or previously, as well as those who had never left. As a result comparing rates based on the decision to leave versus the actual behavior of leaving is somewhat confounded.

One problem with studies of the battered woman's return to the abuser following shelter is the lack of uniformity in the time frame within which information is gathered. Difficulty contacting women following discharge from shelter or counseling also presents an obstacle to adequate assessment (Gondolf, 1988). Finally, most studies do not take into account whether the battered woman lived with the batterer prior to seeking help, an important variable that is probably related to her returning to him following shelter or counseling.

Labell (1979) found that immediately following discharge from a shelter, only 26.6 percent of women moved into independent living arrangements. This suggests that their reported 28 percent of women returning to the batterer may represent an underestimate since many battered women eventually return following a brief separation. Based on a follow-up sample of 40 percent of an original sample, Snyder and Fruchtman (1981) reported an overall return rate of 60 percent within 6-10 weeks following shelter, although the rate varied from 39 to 89 percent across empirically constructed clusters of battered women. Giles-Sims (1983) reported a return rate of 42 percent at six months and Stone (1984) a 41.9 percent rate at 1 and 3 months.

Studies which have examined the intent to return to the batterer after shelter also differ according to when the question is asked. Snyder & Fruchtman (1981) reported that 34 percent of their sample intended to return at time of discharge (although 60 percent of those contacted actually had done so at follow-up). Snyder and Scheer (1981) reported a 13 percent rate of intent to return among women being admitted to a shelter and a 33 percent rate of intent to return at discharge. Gondolf (1988) reported that 24 percent of his sample of shelter women planned to return to their abusers following shelter. Of the remaining women, only 26 percent planned to live independently suggesting that the actual return rate might actually be greater within a relatively short period.

To summarize these findings, many battered women state their intent to return to their abusers following shelter, although fewer appear to do so at admission than discharge. And even more women actually live with abusers again at some point following separation. Future studies should examine the cycles many battered women go through of leaving and returning repeatedly (Gondolf, 1988) before permanently leaving abusers to measure outcome effectiveness adequately. Simply measuring return to the batterer seems insufficient to capture a true measure of effect for shelter or counseling interventions. For example, even after a battered woman's return to her batterer following contact with a shelter, her eventual propensity to leave as a measure of escape may be altered as a function of her stay, certainly a positive outcome of her shelter experience.

A few studies have examined factors to predict a battered woman's decision to return to her partner. Snyder and Scheer (1981), using a discriminate analysis, found that three variables (length of relationship, previous separations, and religious affiliation) predicted relationship status following a brief stay in a shelter. Strube and Barbour (1983) in studying data collected from battered women during intake interviews at a counseling program found that economic dependence (employment status, subjective reports of economic hardship, having nowhere else to go) and psychological commitment (length of relationship and subjective report of love) predicted relationship status at follow-up 1-18 months later.

At best, "return to batterer" is only an indirect measure of intervention effectiveness. The most relevant measure is whether a woman continues to be abused.

Recurrence of Violence

Few studies have actually examined the recurrence of violence following the provision of shelter or counseling services in part because of the difficulty of maintaining contact with victims through follow-up (Gondolf, 1988). Follow-up periods that exceed a batterer's usual cycle of violent episodes are necessary in order to determine how a woman's success in avoiding further victimization is related to her partner's attempts at violence.

Giles-Sims (1983) found that among women who could be contacted 6 months after shelter stay, 44 percent of those who never returned to their partner and 57 percent of those who did return reported at least one recurrence of violence. Snyder and Scheer (1981) noted that of the 55 percent of women in their original sample who returned to their partners, 12 percent had experienced more physical abuse and an additional 15 percent received more psychological abuse within a 6-10 week follow-up period. Berk et al. (1986), in a study of women whose abuse was recognized by either a shelter or a prosecutor's office, reported that 76 percent of the sample was living with their abusers at the beginning of the study. Six weeks later 19 percent of the women had experienced another incident of violence.

Taken together, these studies suggest that following shelter intervention, a significant number of battered women continue to be at risk. Berk et al. (1986) suggest that shelter residence can even trigger new incidents of violence as the batterer retaliates against the woman's efforts to protect herself and/or to live independent of his control.

There is little evidence identifying the components of shelter and/or counseling interventions that are related to ameliorative outcomes. However, Berk et al.'s (1986) data indicate that for victims who use a shelter, each additional effort to obtain help (e.g., calling police, obtaining a restraining order, seeking prosecution, previous shelter stay, seeking help from an attorney or legal aid) reduces the number of subsequent violent episodes.

Assessing outcomes in terms of a cessation of violence suggests that interventions can stop further victimization. That is, when a battered woman can escape attempted violence she can free herself from repeated victimization. More realistically, however, a battered woman is not responsible for and often cannot stop her abuser's violence (Ganley, 1987). Even when she has made numerous attempts to escape the violence against her, she alone cannot control the outcome of her efforts. For example, she may call the police, seek prosecution, divorce her batterer, obtain a new residence and job and still be subject to repeated violence, even death, if her partner persists in tracking her down. Other women, having made many failed attempts to escape further violence, find that they have to fight back in self-defense. As a result, some of them face homicide charges and are sentenced to prison (Bauschard & Kimbrough, 1986). However, others are acquitted by juries or given reduced sentences by judges who understand the mitigating circumstances leading to their actions.

Self-Reports of Effectiveness

Few studies have asked battered women directly about the effectiveness of the shelter or counseling services they have received. Bowker and Maurer (1986) compared effectiveness ratings of three sources of counseling services for battered women: the clergy, social services/counseling agencies, and women's groups. Based on written responses to a *Woman's Day* questionnaire from 1,000 women, they found that although women were more likely to receive help from counseling agencies (50%) or the clergy (33%) than women's groups (21%), their ratings of effectiveness were greater for women's groups. Sixty percent rated women's groups as very or somewhat effective compared to 47 percent for counseling agencies and 34 percent for the clergy. Women's groups were also rated least often as not effective or causing increased violence (23%) compared to counseling agencies (37%) and the clergy (46%).

Although self-reports allow each woman to define effectiveness according to her own needs, their utility is limited by the inherent reporting bias associated with subjective measures (Evans, 1986). However, their use in combination with other measures seems essential in order to understand fully whether particular services are effective for battered women.

THE INTERACTION OF VICTIM SERVICES AND CRIMINAL JUSTICE AGENCIES

Criminal justice agencies are becoming increasingly involved in treating the problem of battering and in influencing the lives of battered women. The Attorney General's Task Force on Family Violence (U.S. Department of Justice, 1984) offers recommendations about how to handle battering for law enforcement officers, prosecutors, and judges. In considering what these officials should do, it is important to stress the necessity of building networks so that they can work with victim advocacy and service agencies. It is only through such coordination that criminal justice agencies can protect battered women from further violence and give them an opportunity to heal from its devastating effects.

Diversity Issues

Coordinated interventions are needed to offset the effects of oppression based on race, ethnicity, sexual preference, language, age, and ablebodiedness. The dynamics of power and control that define battering are compounded by the oppression of battered women flowing from sexism, racism, or homophobia by personnel in criminal justice, mental health, and social service agencies. Guidelines for criminal justice agencies (National Institute of Justice, 1986) state the importance of addressing the special needs of non-English speaking women and women of color by recognizing and working to remove the additional barriers to justice that face these women. This is especially important given the disproportionate numbers of minority group members involved in reported cases of battering. Recognizing and overcoming these barriers is equally important for mental health professionals (Schechter, 1987).

ETHICAL ISSUES

Ethical issues involved in providing services to battered women are sensitive, vitally important, and susceptible to mitigation or resolution by coordination. The most essential ethical issue is confidentiality. Without the assurance of it and its protection by law, battered women easily fall victim to their abusers' use of the legal system to hurt and harass them further. Confidentiality must be honored by shelter workers and counselors to protect the safety of battered women and to build trust in their healing relationship with them. It is essential when developing plans (e.g., escape plans) to protect abused women that the women make full and honest disclosures of their situations so that they can be aided in developing realistic plans. If a woman fears that her communications with counselors may be revealed to her abuser, she may withhold information in an attempt to stay safe. A helping system must provide battered women with confidentiality so that they do not think they have to protect themselves by keeping information from the very people who want to help them.

Abusers often monitor the movements of their victims in order to control them. As a result, women who seek help or a means of escape risk being discovered and punished for their efforts. It is important that any communication with helping persons be protected so that battered women will not suffer more for trying to protect themselves.

Frequently, men trying to defend themselves against battering charges or who are involved in divorce or custody proceedings try to impune or discredit victims. Through the use of subpoenas or court orders a batterer may seek access to a woman's records from her stay at a shelter or her participation in counseling. Even if the records contain no information pertinent to his defense, he can threaten his victim with the exposure of all her "craziness" and "incompetence" in open court and subject her to public humiliation. This is no idle threat as victims who are called to testify frequently have their mental stability, morality, past conduct, and/or their judgment questioned by the defense. Encouraging women to press charges and testify against their abusers requires that their own communications with helpers not be used against them.

Currently, attorneys can issue subpoenas for confidential information without judicial review. If an opposing motion to quash a subpoena is not filed, the propriety of using a subpoena is not likely to be considered by a judge. Many women and the agencies that serve them do not know how to challenge a subpoena or lack the resources to hire an attorney to file the necessary motions. Therefore, they release information that might otherwise have been protected.

Ideally, a judicial hearing to determine relevance should be held to prevent the unnecessary release of confidential information about a battered woman. Release of confidential information directly to a judge who could issue a ruling concerning its relevance prior to its release would also help protect confidential information about a battered woman from misuse by an abuser or his attorney.

A related issue is the extent to which a helping agency should have contact with a batterer and how it should be managed to ensure a woman's safety. Helpers who treat battering can become enmeshed in abusive relationships (Bograd, 1986) and actually contribute to further abuse. For instance, it is common for both men and women seeking services to request counseling as a couple. Many women note that their partners will not seek help for their battering unless they participate with them. Men frequently report physical violence by their partners and insist on counseling for women's abusive tendencies too. Not analyzing such charges carefully impedes meaningful interventions for both batterers and victims.

It is nearly impossible and often not safe for a battered woman to detail her abuse in the presence of her abuser. She knows the controlling, intimidating, and abusive behavior that will follow her speaking of the truth during and/or after the session. Furthermore, therapists who assign equal responsibility to each partner for changing a relationship assume that each has equal power over the other. The idea that a woman can control her abuser and his violent and controlling behavior is a form of abuse perpetrated by the helping profession. The batterer in this situation is sure to dispute his victim's recollection of events and try to justify his actions. This puts the helper in a nearly impossible situation. If the helper does not validate the victim's experience as truth, she undermines and revictimizes the woman. If she finds fault with the batterer because of his actions, the helper is seen by him as siding with the victim before the helper can develop a therapeutic alliance with him. This may end the therapeutic relationship with the batterer who often insists that the woman do the same. Because of the danger joint counseling presents for battered women and its ineffectiveness as a treatment for batterers, separate programs must be maintained for batterers, especially early in the intervention process.

More agencies are offering services to both the battered woman and the batterer. This presents the possibility that both are receiving services in the same location, perhaps with appointments close in time. Programs need to be aware of the potential danger this creates. The actual location of a program can become a site for further control and intimidation of a victim by her abuser, often in a parking lot, hallway, or waiting room. Safety precautions for victims and staff members and adequate crisis plans demand the attention of program staff and criminal justice agencies. Referral of a batterer to an alternative program elsewhere may be required, although this may merely make it more inconvenient for him to continue his abuse rather than stop it.

Finally, using volunteers or staff with minimal or informal training can present an ethical dilemma. Shelter and battered women's programs are often grassroots movements comprised mainly of women who have suffered abuse themselves. It is the policy of many shelters to have the majority of their staffs comprised of such women because they can offer invaluable empathy to victims and serve as powerful role models of survival. At the same time, shelter staffs are called upon to treat a woman's complex reality and help her change it in a manner she chooses. In doing so, they may encounter a wide variety of problems, including alcohol and drug abuse, severe depressive reactions with suicidal intent, psychotic or extreme dissociative reactions, and intense anxiety reactions with panic attacks. It is often unreasonable to expect untrained persons, regardless of their level of empathy, to assess and respond to these situations effectively. Thus, it is important for shelters and battered women's programs to utilize the services of trained professionals who understand abuse and victimization issues. These professionals can in no way replace or exceed the support offered by volunteer shelter staff, but can serve as an important adjunct to providing safety and healing to battered women. And to the extent that coordinated networks have been established, the use of trained professionals can make the delivery of criminal justice interventions more sensitive to victim needs and more effective.

REFERENCES

American Psychiatric Association (1987). *Diagnostic and Statistical Manual of Mental Disorders.* (DSM-III-R). Washington, DC: Author.

Barnard, G.W., H. Vera, M. Vera & G. Newman (1982). "Till Death Do Us Part." *Bulletin of the American Academy of Psychiatry and the Law*, 10(4):271-280.

Bauschard, L. & M. Kimbrough (1986). *Voices Set Free.* St. Louis, MO: Women's Self Help Center.

Berk, R.A., P.J. Newton & S.F. Berk (1986). "What a Difference a Day Makes: An Empirical Study of the Impact of Shelters for Battered Women." *Journal of Marriage and the Family*, 48:481-490.

Bograd, M. (1986). "Holding the Line: Confronting the Abusive Partner." *The Family Therapy Networker*, 10(4):44-47.

Bowker, L.H. (1983). *Beating Wife Beating.* Lexington, MA: Lexington Books.

Bowker, L.H. & L. Maurer (1986). "The Effectiveness of Counseling Services Utilized by Battered Women." *Women & Therapy*, 5(4):65-82.

Browne, A. (1987). *When Battered Women Kill.* New York: The Free Press.

Douglas, M.A. (1984). "Mental Health Risks: A Study of Battered Women and Abusive Men." Paper presented at the Second National Conference for Family Violence Researchers, Durham, New Hampshire.

_____ (1987). "The Battered Woman Syndrome." In D. Sonkin (ed.) *Domestic Violence on Trial.* New York: Springer Publishing.

_____ (1988). "Victimization or Empowerment: The Judicial Process." In F.W. Kaslow (Chair), *Alternative Treatment Methods for Reducing Marital Violence.* Symposium conducted at the Annual Conference of the American Psychological Association, Atlanta, Georgia, August.

Evans, I.M. (1986). "Response Structure and the Triple-Response-Mode Concept." In R.O. Nelson & S.C. Hayes (eds.) *Conceptual Foundations of Behavioral Assessment.* New York: Guilford Press.

Ganley, A.L. (1987). "Perpetrators of Domestic Violence: An Overview of Counseling the Court-Mandated Client." In D.J. Sonkin (ed.) *Domestic Violence on Trial.* New York: Springer Publishing.

Giles-Sims, J. (1983). *Wife-Battering: A Systems Theory Approach.* New York: Guilford Press.

Gondolf, E.W. (1988). *Battered Women as Survivors: An Alternative to Treating Learned Helplessness.* Lexington, MA: Lexington Books.

Hilberman, E. & L. Munson (1978). "Sixty Battered Women." *Victimology: An International Journal,* 2(3-4):1336-1347.

Labell, L.S. (1979). "Wife Abuse: A Sociological Study of Battered Women and Their Mates." *Victimology: An International Journal,* 4:258-267.

National Institute of Justice. (1986). *Confronting Domestic Violence: A Guide for Criminal Justice Agencies.* Washington, DC: U.S. Government Printing Office.

Ochberg, F.M. (1988). *Post-Traumatic Therapy and Victims of Violence.* New York: Brunner/Mazel.

Pizzey, E. (1974). *Scream Quietly or the Neighbors Will Hear.* London: Penguin Books.

Rosewater, L. & L.E. Walker (1985). *Handbook of Feminist Therapy.* New York: Springer Publishing.

Rounsaville, B.J. (1978). "Battered Wives: Barriers to Identification and Treatment." *American Journal of Orthopsychiatry,* 48(3):487-494.

Schechter, S. (1987). *Guidelines for Mental Health Practitioners in Domestic Violence Cases.* Washington, DC: National Coalition Against Domestic Violence.

Schutte, N.S., L. Bouleige & J.M. Malouff (1986). "Returning to Partner After Leaving a Crisis Shelter: A Decision Faced by Battered Women." *Journal of Social Behavior and Personality,* 1(2):295-298.

Snyder, D.K. & L.A. Fruchtman (1981). "Differential Patterns of Wife Abuse: A Data-Based Topology." *Journal of Consulting and Clinical Psychology*, 49(6):878-885.

Snyder, D.K. & N.S. Scheer (1981). "Predicting Disposition Following Brief Residence at a Shelter for Battered Women." *American Journal of Community Psychology*, 9(5):559-566.

Stark, E. & A. Flitcraft (1983). "Social Knowledge, Social Policy and the Abuse of Women: The Case Against Patriarchal Benevolence." In D. Finkelhor, R.J. Gelles, G. Hotaling & M. Straus (eds.) *The Dark Side of Families*, pp. 330-348. Beverly Hills, CA: Sage Publications.

Stone, L.H. (1984). "Shelters for Battered Women: A Temporary Escape from Danger or the First Step Toward Divorce?" *Victimology: An International Journal*, 9(2):284-289.

Strube, M.J. (1988). "The Decision to Leave an Abusive Relationship: Empirical Evidence and Theoretical Issues." *Psychological Bulletin*, 104(2):236-250.

Strube, M.J. & L.S. Barbour (1983). "The Decision to Leave an Abusive Relationship: Economic Dependence and Psychological Commitment." *Journal of Marriage and the Family*, 45:785-793.

U.S. Department of Justice. (1984). *Attorney General's Task Force on Family Violence (Final Report)*. Washington, DC: U.S. Government Printing Office.

Walker, L. (1984). *The Battered Woman Syndrome*. New York: Springer Publishing.

7

The Symbiosis of Arrest and Treatment for Wife Assault: The Case for Combined Intervention

Donald G. Dutton
University of British Columbia

Barbara M.S. McGregor
University of British Columbia

INTRODUCTION

As recently as the late 1970s, the criminal justice system's response to wife assault was weak and ineffective; its agencies tended to view family violence as neither serious nor state business (Dutton, 1987).[1] Women who were assaulted by male partners were routinely discouraged from proceeding with charges (Dutton, 1981b).

Although some attempts were made to improve the handling of spousal violence cases, they tended to be unsuccessful. For example, in 1975 one urban police force endeavored to improve its response to "domestic" calls through policy changes and extensive police training (Dutton, 1981b, 1988). The program failed to generate higher arrest rates. Police officers were not motivated to lay charges because they continued to believe that they would not be aggressively prosecuted, as was indeed the case. Prosecutors believed that judges would dismiss all but the most egregious violations with a simple admonishment, and that was also true. Judges were frustrated by what they considered to be a lack of acceptable sentencing options; not wanting to separate wage earners from their families, or believing that violence in a domestic setting was not truly "criminal" behavior, they only infrequently punished guilty offenders with fines or jail time. The ripple effect of lenient sentencing was felt throughout the criminal justice system and generated a ceiling on arrest rates and encouraged the police tendency to define wife assault as inappropriate for arrest (Dutton, 1988). Consequently, only 21 percent of assaults (for which there was prima facie evidence) actually led to arrest, and less than 1 in 200 wife assaults resulted in fines or jail (Dutton, 1987).

Treatment groups for wife assaulters originated from public pressure on the criminal justice system to respond more effectively to this problem (U.S. Commission on Civil Rights, 1978; Dutton, 1981a; Standing Committee on Health, Welfare and Social Affairs, Canada, 1982). It was hoped that such groups would provide a viable sentencing option to judges (Dutton, 1981a), in addition to improving protection for women who opt to remain in a relationship with a partner who will not seek treatment voluntarily.

In an early attempt at system change, Dutton (1981a, 1981b) speculated that when judges are offered what they believe to be an effective sentencing alternative, they would be more inclined to define wife assault cases as appropriate for their court. And when judges are more willing to convict and sentence, prosecutors become more willing to proceed with cases, and police more willing to charge the perpetrator. Although we are unaware of any cross-jurisdictional study correlating arrest and prosecution rates for spousal violence with the existence of court-mandated treatment groups, we suspect the correlation would be high. Indeed, court-mandated treatment groups may prove to be a partial antidote to the reluctance of the criminal justice system to take action against wife assaulters.

PURPOSE OF TREATMENT

Bandura (1979) describes in detail the psychological mechanisms that allow "reprehensible conduct" such as wife assault to recur. These include cognitive distortions that minimize or deny the reprehensible behavior and/or locate its cause outside the self (usually in the victim or alcohol). To the extent that a wife assaulter believes that: (1) his wife's injuries were minimal, or (2) she was to blame for the conflict, or (3) his use of violence was justified, his subsequent arrest and conviction are more likely to be viewed as unjust.

While both arrest and treatment challenge the assaulter's denial of the seriousness of his behavior and its consequences, treatment can also confront inappropriate causal attributions and justifications. Thus, an objective of treatment is to undermine the cognitive, habit-sustaining mechanisms that cannot be changed by punishment alone (Ganley, 1981; Dutton, 1988, Ch. 6).

A second objective of treatment is to enable wife assaulters to improve their ability to detect the warning signs of their own violence (e.g., increased arousal, anger, etc.) and to develop a more elaborate set of behaviors to manage previously violence-evoking situations. Many men come to treatment for assaultive behavior with the belief that their violence is "hard wired" or immutable. When a therapist confronts their interpretations of their wives' motives, their denials of emotions other than anger, and their refusals to use other behaviors to express anger, the men gradually develop a perception that alternatives to violence are possible. This presents the possibility of learning new behaviors that have less destructive consequences.

Another objective of treatment is to help assaultive men recognize the long-term costs of the short-term gains achieved by violence. Men who repeatedly assault their wives gain personal feelings of power (Novaco, 1976) and control over a conflict that felt unmanageable prior to the violence (Sonkin, Martin & Walker, 1985). However, for most men, these "gains" are expensive; they are obtained through the use of conduct that is not normatively acceptable (Stark & McEvoy, 1970) and that erodes the quality of the marital relationship.

In sum, the purpose of treatment is to provide a means through which "hard core," or repeat, wife assaulters can learn alternative skills for conflict management, improve their ability to detect and express anger, and have the negative consequences of their violence made salient to them.

TREATMENT PHILOSOPHY

Since we are describing a therapeutic form that is to be used by the criminal justice system as a condition of probation for men convicted of wife assault, it must have a philosophical base that is compatible with criminal justice ideology. As criminal justice philosophy usually emphasizes individual responsibility for an action, a treatment philosophy with a similar orientation is recommended.

In some areas of human conduct, a division exists between legal philosophy, stressing individual responsibility, and social science explanation, emphasizing situational determinism (see Fincham & Jaspars, 1980; Dutton, 1986). Social learning theory, the basis of many treatment groups for assaultive husbands, acknowledges the formative role of situational events in shaping habits. It suggests that learning influences the event-reaction process at four levels: (1) the appraisal of the event as maliciously intended or threatening, (2) the affective (emotional) reaction to the consequent arousal, (3) the mode of behavioral expression of anger, and (4) the choice of a "target" for abuse. However, social learning theory also stresses choice and responsibility for individual action. In fact, it could be argued that this approach is not only consistent with the criminal justice emphasis on individual responsibility, but has a more stringent view of personal accountability. Contrary to the criminal justice system, social learning philosophy does not allow clients to attribute their behavior to any external causes. For example, the courts routinely accept a defense of "diminished responsibility" when alcohol has been consumed. The social learning view is that, while alcohol may "disinhibit" behaviors that are normally suppressed, those behaviors are themselves learned on the basis of each individual's unique reinforcement history, and can ultimately be "unlearned" and/or replaced by new, non-destructive behaviors. Hence, each individual has the ability and responsibility to learn appropriate behaviors.

The resultant therapeutic imperative for a counselor is that he/she must repeatedly challenge a client's statements that his violence was caused by an external force, a short-term situation, and/or an uncontrollable predisposition (e.g., his wife did not force him to hit her, other men get drunk and do not become violent, and/or he does not attack fellow workers because of his "bad temper"). Thus, while acknowledging that situational and/or dispositional predilections for violence may exist, the therapist helps the client appreciate that all his actions have an element of choice and that he has a greater ability to control his behavior than formerly realized.

THERAPEUTIC TECHNIQUES

Clinical descriptions of men who are court-directed for treatment for wife assault underscore the need for highly structured, confrontational techniques (Ganley, 1981; Sonkin et al., 1985). These men are described as cognitively (perceptually) rigid and unassertive, with strong tendencies to externalize blame for their behavior. They have rarely had experience in psychological treatment groups (unless involved in alcohol treatment programs) and, typically, have had little interest in self-change. Hence, highly directive treatment and the provision of "motivation builders" are required.

Descriptions of therapy with assaultive males (e.g., Ganley, 1981; Gondolf, 1985; Sonkin et al., 1985) outline a variety of techniques that are used in treatment groups to generate the learning of new perceptions and behaviors. These include having the men keep diaries in which they log the instigators of their anger, group analysis of angry and/or violent events, a discussion of affective reactions to specific behaviors of others (empathy building), and relaxation exercises while imagining anger-provoking situations. While the emphasis and form of these practices may vary from group to group, the objective remains constant: to demonstrate to the clients how their use of violence is a learned behavior sustained by their own perceptions.

Since many court-directed treatment programs are short-term in nature (i.e., 3-6 months), therapeutic priorities must be selected carefully. It is unlikely, for example, that a man socialized into a "macho" working environment is going to embrace a feminist view of male socialization during weekly treatment sessions, especially when he returns to a work milieu that is philosophically contradictory to a feminist perspective (cf. Ptacek, 1984). Men in these groups frequently feel powerless, or disenfranchised, and are not sympathetic to a perspective that views society as patriarchal and them as the ruling class. However, demonstrating to them that their sex-role expectations may differ from those of their wives, and teaching them skills to negotiate those differences, are not necessarily incompatible with their social milieus. Accordingly, we favor specific anger management techniques that can be adapted to a variety of social situations, rather than attempts to generate ideological change that may be incompatible with the client's background and needs.

Cognitive-Behavioral Therapy

Cognitive-behavioral therapy, the treatment application of the social learning approach, is based on three fundamental assumptions: (1) that cognition (perception) affects behavior, (2) that cognition may be monitored and altered, and (3) that behavior change can be generated through changing cognitions (Dobson & Block, 1987). Stemming from a growing body of literature in the 1970s emphasizing the role of cognition in anxiety (Lazarus & Averill, 1972) and depression (Beck, 1976), and from a dissatisfaction with the results of long-term psychodynamically oriented psychotherapy, which views assaultive behavior as a symptom of a personality disorder (Eysenck, 1969; Rachman & Wilson, 1980), cognitive-behavioral treatment began to be applied to a wide variety of affective (emotional) and behavioral disorders (Dobson & Block, 1987). These included problems with "self-control" (Mahoney & Thoreson, 1979), anxiety (Meichenbaum, 1977), depression (Beck, 1976), and anger (Novaco, 1975).

The cognitive-behavioral approach to anger has been used in individual, men's, and couple's groups formats (e.g., Edleson, Syers & Brygger, 1987; Sonkin et al., 1985; Neidig & Friedman, 1984; Saunders, 1984; Ganley, 1981). Typically, this approach uses a treatment "package" consisting of thought-stopping (Bass, 1973), assertiveness training (Foy, Eisler & Pinkston, 1975; Bower & Bower, 1976), behavioral contracting and communication training (Saunders, 1977), a combination of relaxation training and cognitive restructuring (Novaco, 1975; Edleson et al., 1987), and building awareness of the personal and social roots of aggression.

Novaco's (1975) application of cognitive-behavioral therapy to anger management focuses on the interrelationship of physiological and cognitive determinants. He emphasizes the positive functions of anger arousal: it is energized behavior, it is expressive (advertising potency and determination), and it is defensive (overrides feelings of anxiety, vulnerability and ego threat).

If anger serves this variety of functions, therapy must include alternative means for clients to satisfy each one. This is not easily accomplished in short-term therapy. For example, if anxiety and vulnerability increase as a result of a client's learning to reinterpret his anger, limited therapeutic time may not permit the development of adequate strategies to deal with these alternative, and male sex-role dissonant, feelings. For this reason , a less ambitious therapeutic objective may be the development of the client's awareness that other feelings can provide a base for anger.

Novaco's (1975) "anger management" treatment was designed to alter clients' anger-enhancing cognitions. To this end, Novaco focused on: (1) changing clients' perceptions of an "aversive stimulus" (e.g., a personal affront, a task that requires a solution), (2) teaching clients to use their own arousal as a cue for non-aggressive coping strategies, (3) increasing clients' perceptions that they are in control of themselves in provoking circumstances, (4) teaching clients to analyze "provocation sequences" in stages, with self-instructions for managing each stage, and (5) teaching relation techniques to enable clients to reduce anger-arousal. In other words, Novaco's techniques would apply to all four learned aspects of the stimulus-response chain. In social learning terms, anger management attempts to modify both the perception of the instigators of aggression and its cognitive regulators.

Gondolf and Russell (1986) raised concerns about the "anger control" focus in the cognitive-behavioral approach. They suggest that because not all aggression is anger-based, this approach may be a dangerous "quick fix" that prolongs denial and does not address the social system reinforcers of male violence. Tolman and Saunders (1988) responded by noting that some of this criticism can be applied to all treatment approaches, and that cognitive-behavioral approaches are empirically-grounded methods that are likely to end the violence quickly, thus allowing other methods to be used. They state that "anger regulation" is a more accurate term for the methods used and agree that victims must be warned about false hopes for treatment success. They suggest that anger regulation training should be only one part of a multi-systems approach (cf. Edleson et al., 1987).

Therapeutic Techniques: Ganley Method

The development of treatment groups specifically for wife assaulters was pioneered by Anne Ganley (Ganley & Harris, 1978; Ganley, 1981). Ganley views battering as a learned tension-reducing response. It occurs in the family setting because that is the safest place to aggress without punishment, because batterers have stereotyped views of men as absolute rulers of their homes, and because of conflict resolution techniques learned in their families of origin.

Ganley bases her treatment program on the social learning premise that wife assaulters did not have the opportunity to develop good conflict resolution skills while growing up. In their families of origin, violence was often the only means of dealing with conflict-generated anger: listening skills were poor, verbal problem-solving skills were inadequate, and emotional self-disclosure was equated with loss of control. As a step toward rectifying these deficits, Ganley includes assertiveness training in her treatment model.

As batterers tend to express emotions such as hurt, anxiety, excitement, sadness, guilt, humiliation, and helplessness as anger, they are often unaware of their true feelings before and after a violent act. Ganley's treatment program develops a batterer's motivation to change by helping him to identify correctly his emotions and the negative feelings his violence generates. Ganley describes, as has been discussed above, the tendency of batterers to deny or minimize their violence, and to externalize it by holding others responsible and culpable for their own moods and outbursts. She recommends confrontation as a therapeutic strategy for dealing with these forms of "neutralization of self-punishment." Her highly structured treatment format stresses personal accountability for each participant. Exercises, such as maintaining an anger diary, emphasize the need for individual responsibility in monitoring anger and develop an understanding of that anger. In addition, anger diaries help each man identify instigators of his anger and his physical and cognitive responses to anger. The man lists the "triggers" (instigators) of his anger (e.g., what another person did or said to him), how angry he became (on a 10-point scale), how he knew he was angry (e.g., physiological responses), "talk up" (what he said to himself to increase his anger), and "talk down" (what he said to himself to calm down). The man lists the "triggers" as an objective recording of events. He is taught to be specific, to record only what was seen or heard, and not to make assumptions about the other's motives.

Comparisons of the "trigger" and "talk up" columns emphasize the interpretative or subjective quality of his anger responses. The "talk up" column generally contains blaming statements that serve to increase the man's self-generated anger; this exercise forces him to analyze how frequently he imputes negative motives to others and the extent to which those assumptions generate anger. "Talk down," or anger-decreasing statements, have to be taught to most batterers. These statements are formulated to redirect the client's focus from the external, rage-inducing event, to the internal process of anger. This procedure teaches the client to redirect his focus onto self-statements that will help him control the internal process, rather than on attempting to control the external stimulus.

The statements in the anger diaries acknowledge the individual's feelings of anger and help him to improve his ability to detect anger cues. They also generate self-control as he changes his statements of external blame to acknowledgment of internal feelings. For a complete description and examples of anger diaries, see Sonkin and Durphy (1982) or Sonkin, Martin, and Walker (1985). When men show progress in treatment groups and consistently complete anger diaries, the diaries are used as a step to assertiveness training.

Therapeutic Techniques: Assertiveness Training

Bower and Bower (1976) develop assertiveness by having clients verbalize a "DESC script." DESC is an acronym for "describe, express, specify, and consequences." Clients are asked to *describe* what behaviors the other person has that bother them, to *express* how those behaviors make them feel, to *specify* what new behavior they want, and to express the (positive) *consequences* for the other person if she performs those behaviors. This assertiveness exercise becomes a first step in teaching clients to negotiate interpersonal differences.

The bridge from the anger diary to the DESC script is built as follows: the "triggers" from the anger diary (specific acts or statements) provide the *describe* portion of the DESC script. The specificity learned in keeping an anger diary helps the man to focus his verbal statements on his behavior, rather than on the other person's disposition. The "talk down" column (statement of feeling) then becomes the *express* part of the DESC script. Hence, the anger diary provides the first half of an assertive statement, often improving communication before addressing the *specify* and *consequences* portions. These latter steps teach the man to assert what changes he wants and what changes he is willing to make as a consequence. They develop a problem-oriented, or negotiation, approach to the communication of anger.

After rehearsal and practice in the treatment group, men are encouraged to continue with couples communication therapy. It should be emphasized that we recommend such treatment *only* when the use of violence by the man is under control. The communication aspect of treatment, which is designed to improve the conflict climate of the primary relationship, can only be effective if the man's partner no longer is at risk of further violence. Typically, this is determined by the client's successful demonstration of anger control techniques and the absence of abuse for a period of time that indicates a major change in his methods of dealing with conflict and anger (the actual length of time will vary depending on the individual's history). Wives' reports are used to confirm or deny the apparent changes in behavior.

Therapeutic Techniques: Sex-Role Socialization, Power, and Group Processes

While anger recognition and improved communication skills provide the essence of therapy for assaultive males, other issues also constitute an important adjunct to this treatment.

Since treatment is for male-female violence, the contribution of sex-role socialization to setting the stage for violence is important. Male socialization both narrows the range of "acceptable" emotions (Fasteau, 1974; Pleck, 1981) and creates occasionally unrealistic expectations about family roles. This can be a source of chronic conflict in a relationship (Coleman & Straus, 1985). Treatment must address these issues and attempt to develop empathy for the victim.

One way to develop empathy is to have assaultive males describe their own experiences as victims of abuse by their parents. Exploring the feelings connected to these experiences as victims, can serve to strengthen empathy. This process makes salient the negative consequences of violence for the victim. Treatment should also include an attempt to have males think about power in a different way. A man typically enters treatment thinking about power vis-à-vis his wife in an adversarial fashion: his gain is his wife's loss and vice versa. The therapist encourages each man to view power in interdependent terms: that by diminishing his wife he loses a vital partner and by accepting her empowerment he actually gains. This is done by making salient the personal losses he sustains as a result of violence toward his wife (e.g., her emotional and sexual withdrawal, mistrust, and chronic anger toward him). By repeatedly "yoking" the couple's gains and losses, the concept of power interdependence becomes clearer. In this way an objective of feminist therapy is addressed by a means consonant with a dominant, male-oriented social milieu.

Feminist therapy works toward a recognition that violence is used to maintain the power imbalance in a patriarchal society, and that such an imbalance is unhealthy and unproductive for all concerned. However, to attempt to change assaultive males' attitudes about patriarchy in a limited therapeutic time period would be ineffective; it would, for most individuals, simply offer an opportunity to cast responsibility for their behavior onto the social system, rather than onto themselves. What therapy can do is clarify the negative consequences of each individual's attempts to achieve greater power in his relationship and the positive consequences of sharing that power. Thus, the assaultive male moves closer to a feminist perspective, but on an individual rather than a systems level.

Finally, since treatment for assaultive males usually occurs in a group setting, group process issues (Yalom, 1975) are also important. Most clinical texts describe assaultive males as being isolated (Ganley, 1981; Sonkin et al., 1985). They frequently feel anxious about describing personal problems and feelings in front of other men. Therapists do considerable "bridge building" by explicitly connecting the experiences of men in the groups in order to establish some camaraderie and a sense of safety in self-disclosure.

On the other hand, the therapist cannot allow group cohesiveness to generate mutual protection in the service of denial and minimizing. Since men in these groups may have a shared sense of outrage at the "injustice" of an arrest for what they consider to be a minimal act, they may try to feed each other's tendency to blame the victim, women in general, or the criminal justice system. The therapeutic objective is to allow resentments to be expressed in the group, while still confronting the men's perceptions of blame. Having a reformed client or clients participate in group sessions can be extremely useful in diffusing the individually confrontative role the therapist would otherwise have to assume.

Regardless of whether the therapist operates alone or with reformed clients when confronting individuals in the group, if some or all of the clients perceive the challenges as attacks, group polarization can occur as a form of defense. The therapist must make it clear that confrontation is used to help each individual accept responsibility for his actions and learn new ways to manage conflict; they are not used to attack or judge.

TREATMENT—CRIMINAL JUSTICE SYSTEM INTERFACE

Descriptions of wife assaulters who attend court-mandated groups indicate that most are men with little or no previous experience with group therapy (the typical exceptions are those men who have attended substance abuse treatment groups). Given the average man's unfamiliarity with the treatment context in which intimate feelings are shared, it is understandable that many men would find the new experience of group therapy highly stressful. That stress is exacerbated by the confrontational techniques used to challenge the men's strong denial and/or minimization of their violence.

One way for a client to deal with the anxiety created by group therapy is to drop out. An advantage of nesting treatment within a criminal justice system context is that court authority can be used to ensure attendance. Typically, men attend court-mandated groups as a condition of probation; failure to attend constitutes a technical breach of that probation. In some jurisdictions, probation orders can be worded so that the man must attend and participate to the satisfaction of the therapist (i.e., the men can literally be passed or failed for their performance in the group). Many groups favor a practice wherein men accept and sign a participation agreement that stipulates what is expected of them. Non-compliance is dealt with by a warning. Subsequent non-compliance results in a breach of probation that is reported to the probation officer.

The consequences of breaching probation vary considerably from one court to another. As a result, anxiety about the consequences may vary as a function of each client's prior experience with the criminal justice system. However, the majority of men who come into court-mandated groups do indicate anxiety about further criminal justice system involvement (Dutton & Hart, 1988), and completion rates suggest that the leverage generated by the possibility of breaching probation does operate effectively for most clients. For example, in a court-mandated treatment program in which the first author is a director (the Assaultive Husbands Project in Vancouver, British Columbia), the completion rate for 16-week groups has been 88 percent (71/81) during the last two years.

While the leverage created by the fear of a probation breach can be used to generate simple compliance (e.g., attending the meetings, keeping anger diaries, etc.), more complex issues, such as developing real change in a client's perceptions of the causes and controls of his violence, are not as easily addressed. These issues require considerable therapeutic skill. Court-mandated groups do, however, create the opportunity for that skill to be practiced with otherwise recalcitrant clients.

Can the existence of court-mandated groups increase voluntary (i.e., self- and/or wife-mandated) referrals? Although we are not aware of any empirical studies of this question, some treatment programs have a mechanism in place to promote such an increase and could be studied. These programs have a second phase: after the expiry of the court-mandated treatment sessions, men can choose to attend additional, voluntary sessions. In this phase, the men continue to explore psychological issues and have the option of "sponsoring" previously untreated, self-referred men to the group. This model, similar to that of Alcoholics Anonymous, results in an increase in the community outreach of the program. An example of this format is the Family Violence Project in Victoria, British Columbia.

ARE TREATMENT GROUPS EFFECTIVE?

The main issue surrounding court-mandated treatment groups is, of course, their effectiveness. Victim advocacy groups have criticized such treatment for being only a "Band-Aid" solution to the problem of wife assault and for promising more than it can deliver. The first charge is true and evident; any program depending on criminal justice system selection cannot deal widely with a systemic problem. Only 1 out of 7 wife assaults is reported to the police, and less than 1 man in 100 (for whom prima facie evidence of wife assault exists) is convicted in court (Dutton, 1987). Obviously, court-mandated treatment deals with a highly selected sub-group of wife assaulters.

The second charge is somewhat unfair and raises the question of what should constitute the criterion of success for these groups. From a victim advocate's point of view, the glass may appear half empty: some victims may return to an abusive relationship because of a misapprehension that the group will definitely "cure" their partner. Clearly, therapists must warn victims that therapy does not guarantee a "cure" in any particular case. However, from the therapist's point of view, the glass is half full: any successes (in terms of cessation of violence) are notable, given the plethora of problems many clients bring to the group (e.g., major psychological dysfunction, family situations characterized by high levels of ambient conflict).

The last decade has seen a proliferation of court-mandated treatment groups for men convicted of wife assault. Browning (1984) and Eddy and Meyers (1984) provide descriptive profiles on 24 Canadian and 54 U.S. treatment programs for assaultive males. Both reviews outline referral processes, treatment procedures and funding issues for such programs, and agree on the need for an evaluation of treatment effectiveness. Unfortunately, attempts at assessing treatment programs have not been as systematic or thorough as one might expect. This is surprising given the importance of these programs from a policy perspective.

Developing Effectiveness Studies

The "effect side" of treatment (Rosenthal, 1983) for wife assaulters can be established by estimating what percentage of men would not repeat assault without treatment. Surveys by Schulman (1979) and Straus, Gelles and Steinmetz (1980) found that single events of severe violence occurred for about 33 percent of couples reporting physical assaults and repeated events of assault for the remaining 66 percent. As far as determining the effectiveness of treatment, the following implications may be drawn from these surveys: (1) if a post-treatment evaluation period is one year or less, 33 percent of "treated" men would be expected not to repeat assault even without treatment; (2) since frequency rates vary greatly, some pre-post individual comparisons should be made to relate post-treatment behavior to each man's pre-treatment individual frequency rate; and (3) for post-treatment evaluation periods of more than one year, additional mean of generating baseline incidence will be required.

The Straus et al. and Schulman samples consisted of men who may or may not have had criminal justice contact, whereas most treatment for wife assault follows arrest and conviction. Sherman and Berk (1984) studied the specific deterrence effect of arrest and short term incarceration for misdemeanor wife assault. Their six-month follow-up of 161 "domestics," where police contact occurred, indicated an overall recidivism rate of 28.9 percent, and a 13 percent rate for men who were actually arrested and briefly jailed.[2] Despite interpretative problems, the Sherman and Berk study allows us to estimate expected recidivism with surveillance (e.g., probation) after criminal justice intervention. Specifically, if a "treated" population has been arrested prior to treatment, we might expect a 13 percent recidivism rate in the first six months.

A major problem in assessing treatment effects has been the lack of baseline measure of recidivism for a matched group of untreated offenders. In the absence of randomized designs, the next best comparison group is a group of males demographically similar to the treated group with similar arrest patterns prior to the latest arrest and, if available, similar patterns of frequency of wife assault. The Sherman and Berk study, and that of Jaffe, Wolfe, Telford and Austin (1986) who also examined pre- and post-arrest violence, can provide comparison groups against which we can judge the effectiveness of a treated group through a matching of demographics and arrest records.

Without control groups and reliable data, it is difficult to draw conclusions from effectiveness studies. For example, Pirog-Good and Stets (1986) evaluated treatment success by surveying leaders of therapy groups for batterers in the United States and reporting recidivism rates for 72 such programs. Pirog-Good and Stets found from their survey that, of every 100 men who enroll in treatment programs for batterers, 60 complete the program. Of those 60, 42-53 do not return to battering the year following treatment. Thus the "success" rate in absolute terms is 79 percent. However, this study has two major problems. One is that the recidivism measure was not systematic; it was "based on the educated estimates of (program) administrators." These "personal estimates," as the authors admit, can be unreliable. The second problem is that no controls were used, thus we do not know what percentage of non-recidivists would have stopped battering without treatment.

Another example of the difficulties of conducting effectiveness studies is demonstrated by Saunders and Hanusa (1984). They used self-reports to evaluate 25 men who completed 20 sessions of a cognitive-behavioral treatment that was comprised of assertiveness training, relaxation training, and cognitive restructuring. Saunders and Hanusa reported decreases in "threat from female competence" and depression, but no significant drop in anger scale scores. Actually, there was a decrease reported in pre-post anger scores (on a modified version of the Novaco anger scale), but when social desirability scores (attempts by the subject to look good in their responses, measured by the Marlowe-Crowne Social Desirability Scale (Crowne & Marlowe, 1960)) were used to adjust anger scores, the significant differences disappeared, emphasizing once again the problem of relying exclusively on self-report measures of treatment effectiveness. Thus, the methodology used in effectiveness studies must be carefully considered before drawing strong conclusions about their findings.

Effectiveness Studies: Arrest Reports

Douglas and Perrin (1987) noted changes over the course of a six-session cognitive-behavioral program for 20 men diverted from prosecution. The program focused on the causes and effects of abuse, anger recognition and regulation, emphatic listening, and handling jealousy. Following treatment, the men revealed significantly higher scores on assertiveness and lower scores on alcohol use. They did not show changes on measures of depression or sexist attitudes toward women. Three of the men (15%) were re-arrested for a violent crime (not necessarily wife assault) between 2 and 23 months after treatment (mean=6.1). By comparison, five men (29%) in a matched group of non-completers were arrested. The completers differed minimally from the recidivism rate of a group of untreated, arrested men in another city (Sherman & Berk, 1984).

Effectiveness Studies: Self-Reports

Kelso and Personette (1985) assessed the outcome of a skills-training approach to treatment. The overall goals were to lessen the guilt and isolation of the men, to confront the violent attitudes, to provide support, and to teach interpersonal skills. The skills taught were "time-outs" (brief separations when angry), cognitive restructuring, assertiveness, and the use of physical exercise and relaxation for anger reduction. Most of the men received group treatment, but about one-third received individual and/or group counseling. The treatment was to be weekly for six months, but the average length of treatment was 4.5 months and only 28 percent of the men completed the therapy.

Although assessment was called "follow-up," it was made over the six months when treatment was in progress. Contacts with the men were attempted monthly; only 48 percent agreed to participate or had complete data. The frequency, severity, and number of different acts of violence were measured separately and in combination. Comparisons were made with a post-hoc baseline six months before treatment. As in studies by the Domestic Abuse Project (to be discussed), mental abuse was most likely to occur (35% to 61% monthly rate), and was almost always present with physical or sexual violence. All of the violence ratings declined over the course of treatment.

This study also related client characteristics and use of acquired skills with outcome. Court-ordered men reported less violence after treatment, but this difference did not exist after controlling for age and length of the relationship. There was no relationship between social support and violence. Violence did reportedly decrease as alcohol use diminished. Unexpectedly, more frequent use of acquired skills and more frequent contact with public agencies was associated with more reported violence. Those who completed treatment, however, reported less violence, and the completers used the skills less often. Therefore, the authors speculate that the skills may have been used more often, but unsuccessfully, by those reporting more violence. In a multiple regression analysis, the strongest predictor of violence was the level of pre-treatment violence, which was especially high among young, court-ordered men. This study's use of a composite index of violence and attempts to predict characteristics of successful clients are noteworthy and bear further study.

DeMaris and Jackson (1987) also relied on abusers' self-reports of recidivism. Voluntarily referred men attended an open-ended therapy group which emphasized communication of feelings, coping with stress, and examination of one's expectations of women. Court-ordered men attended a program much more structured and didactic in nature. It covered the topics in the voluntary group in addition to, for example, jealousy, substance abuse, and "time-out" procedures. Seventeen percent (n=53) of the men returned mailed questionnaires. Those who responded were less likely to have alcohol problems, witnessed parental violence, and "beaten up" their partners. Thus, there was a major bias in the evaluation.

The total group of respondents reported a recidivism rate of 35 percent, but that figure rose to 40 to 42 percent for couples living together or currently involved. Significantly higher recidivism rates were reported by those with alcohol problems, with parental violence, and who did not call a counselor when violence seemed imminent. Abuse as a child, court-ordered participation, and number of sessions attended, did not seem to be related to recidivism, although the dichotomization of all variables may have reduced the chance of finding significance. Violence reduction was greatest for men who were voluntary participants, paid attention to physiological signs of anger, used "time-outs," and whose partner had also been violent. The authors are aware of the tentative nature of their results because the men were likely to have given socially approved answers; the results are more useful if one assumes that response bias does not differ within the sample.

Effectiveness Studies: Self-Reports and Wives' Reports

Hamberger and Hastings (1986) used a cognitive-behavioral approach in their group therapy. They compared partners' reports of 32 men who completed treatment and 36 men who did not complete treatment. The partners reported that 72 percent of the completers and 53 percent of the non-completers were not violent during a one-year follow-up. For those who completed treatment, there were significant decreases in scores on the Conflict Tactics Scale (Straus, 1979) from before treatment to after, with a maintenance in the change at one-year follow-up. (The Conflict Tactics Scale determines the degree and quantity of verbal and physical abuse in the relationship in the past year.) There were significant decreases in self-reported depression and anger over the course of treatment.

Maiuro and his associates (Maiuro, Cahn, Vitaliano & Zegree, 1986) assessed 65 men before and after they completed an anger management program and compared them with 25 men on a waiting list. Treatment consisted of a structured group using mostly cognitive-behavioral methods. Sex-role resocialization focused on expanding affective repertoires and cognitive distortions regarding women. Group process methods included modeling from a male-female therapy team and mutual support and confrontation among group members. The wait-list control group received minimal treatment, consisting of an intake evaluation, contacts with program personnel, and probationary monitoring of court-referred cases (60%). They were reassessed after a mean of 19 (18-20) weeks.

The treated men showed significant decreases in anger and aggression, by their reports and those of their partners. The treatment group also reported decreases in depression and maladaptive coping (wishful thinking, avoidance) and increases in problem-focused coping and seeking social support. In contrast, the wait-list group showed positive change on only one of twelve pre-post measures.

Saunders and Hanusa (1986) evaluated 92 assaultive husbands before and after treatment. Treatment consisted of 12 sessions (30 hours) of cognitive-behavioral group treatment and eight sessions (16 hours) of a guided self-help group. There were significant decreases in the men's self-reported levels of depression, anger toward their partners, anger toward work or friend situations, and jealousy, and more liberal scores on the Attitudes Toward Women Scale, a measure of views on women's roles. These changes were maintained even after statistically controlling for the tendency to give socially approved responses. The anger measures were shown to be related significantly with the women's reports of changes in aggressiveness from before treatment through the follow-up period.

Shepard (1987) compared the reports of the partners of men in group therapy at different phases of treatment: before (n=30), middle (n=18), and end (n=16). There were also follow-up reports received from the women 14 months after treatment. She used a behavior checklist that assessed both psychological and physical abuse and contained some items in common with the Conflict Tactics Scales. The men were matched on a number of demographic factors. The first three months of treatment consisted of cognitive-behavioral approaches with confrontational techniques for increasing client accountability. The next three months were spent in an educational group that focused on attitudes about control of the victim.

Sixty-one percent of the victims reported no violence during the first three month session and 69 percent reported no violence during the second session and at the 14 month follow-up. Psychological abuse did not change over the course of treatment but did diminish over the follow-up period. It should be noted that about 60 percent of the couples were living together at the time of each phase of the study. This is not a true comparison between methods because no random assignment was conducted.

Lund, Larsen and Schultz (1982) report on the effects of a comprehensive treatment approach at the Domestic Abuse Project of Minneapolis. The project has programs for men, women and children. The men's service reported in the study consisted of 16 sessions of cognitive-behavioral treatment followed by a self-help group. Of the sample of 86 men, 57 of their partners could be contacted at follow-up (an average of six months after program completion). Sixty-seven percent of the partners of men completing the program (n=27) reported that the violence had not recurred. This figure compares with a reported success rate of 54 percent by the partners of men who dropped out of treatment (n=30). However, this form of comparison does not control for factors associated with program completion and higher motivation levels that might be responsible for the positive change.

For example, those who completed the program were more likely to be better educated and might have learned to change on their own without treatment. Moreover, when threats were added to the list of abuse items, there was no significant difference between groups. Other limitations of the study were a lack of knowledge about the frequency of violence before treatment and using a non-standard follow-up period that may not have been long enough. Although the men reported that they became less traditional in their views of women's roles and that they improved their levels of affective communication, they did not change in their self-reports of a "need for control."

Two other studies at the Domestic Abuse Project are described by Edleson and Gruszski (1988). In one study, an assessment was made of the effectiveness of 16 sessions of cognitive-behavioral group treatment, followed by 16 sessions of traditional group psychotherapy. Forty-two women and 17 men were contacted at a point averaging 9.5 months after treatments. Based solely on the women's reports, 68 percent of the men were non-violent during the follow-up period. Forty-one percent reported that they were free of both violence and threats.

In a third study from the project, Edleson and Gruszski evaluated the same two treatments as described above. This time completers and non-completers were compared. There were no significant differences between these two groups on demographic variables, childhood violence, prior help-seeking, or source of referral. Of the 159 subjects selected for participation, 112 completers and 42 randomly selected non-completers were successfully interviewed. Based on the women's reports approximately six months after treatment, 59 percent of the completers and 52 percent of the non-completers were non-violent. This difference was not statistically significant. The difference was greatest for the category of severe violence, where the partners of 15 percent of the completers and 22 percent of the non-completers reported such activity. None of the men, in either condition, admitted to severe violence.

Edleson and Grusznski (1988) speculate that the results of the third study were not as impressive as the other two because the men were more difficult to treat: substantially more were unemployed and had prior mental health and chemical dependency counseling. They also note that because of the liberal definition of a non-completer, many individuals in that category attended all 16 sessions of the cognitive-behavioral therapy group and some of the group sessions. It is possible that some of the men who dropped out learned the skills quickly and no longer needed treatment. Further, the success rate may have been inflated because of a design problem: the follow-up interviews included couples who were living apart. Violence may not decrease with separation, but will decrease with separation and no contact (Kelso & Personnette, 1985).

From a methodological standpoint, these studies underscore the need to rely on reports from the victims of abuse and to include measures of verbal abuse. The authors speculate that "many men who end their violence may resort to the use of threats as legal, but hardly less terrorizing, forms of control." The methods of these studies also could not disentangle the deterrent effects of criminal justice sanctions for the many men who were court-ordered. Dutton and Hart (1988) have shown that untreated men are on their "best behavior" for short periods of time during probation, most likely due to criminal justice sanctions. About 40 percent of these men eventually re-offend without treatment.

Effectiveness Studies: Arrest, Wives' and Self-Reports

Dutton (1986) attempted to disentangle these issues in a quasi-experimental design that assessed recidivism reports by police, wife assaulters, and their victims. He compared recidivism in 50 treated and 50 untreated men who had been convicted of wife assault. The untreated individuals were deemed unsuitable for treatment by the therapist (n=8) or were not treated for practical reasons (n=42). Treatment consisted of four months of court-mandated group therapy that included cognitive-behavior modification, anger management, and assertiveness training. Comparison was also made with a study of men who had been arrested but not treated (Jaffe, Wolfe, Telford & Austin, 1986). The sample was matched for prior violence and criminal justice contact. In that study, Jaffe et al.

assessed recidivism by utilizing both police records and wives' reports for a one-year period after arrest.

The treated men and their partners competed Conflict Tactics Scales (Straus, 1979) before treatment and six months to three years after treatment (n=37). On these scales, both husbands' and wives' reports of verbal abuse, all violence, and "severe" violence (slapping, kicking, biting, hitting, threatening, or using a weapon) showed significant pre-post decreases. Eighty-four percent of the wives reported no severe violence during the follow-up period. Twenty-one percent of the wives, however, reported an increase in verbal aggression. Comparing the wives' reports of severe violence with those of wives whose partners were arrested but not treated in both his and the Jaffe et al. study, Dutton found significantly greater reductions in severe violence in the arrested and treated group compared with those who were only arrested. The re-arrest rate for the untreated group was 40 percent within 2.5 years after arrest, whereas it was only 4 percent for the treated group. (The "treated" group was defined as men who had completed treatment. A more comprehensive study should assign men at random to treatment/non-treatment conditions and measure recidivism in both drop-outs and completers in the treatment group.)

SUMMARY AND EPILOGUE

In this chapter we have developed a treatment philosophy for wife assaulters that holds men responsible for their use of violence and helps them to analyze and control their anger. We have traced the development of treatment programs based on a cognitive-behavioral approach, and reviewed evidence for their success.

Given the limited success of other forms of offender treatment (Shore & Massimo, 1979; Gendreau & Ross, 1980), some criminal justice officials are skeptical about the success of therapy groups for wife assaulters. They tend to view a false dichotomy between treatment and "law and order" approaches to violence. But in actuality, both have the same objective: to prevent repeat violence. Anger management-assertiveness treatment uses a philosophy of personal responsibility that is compatible with criminal justice philosophy; preliminary evidence suggests that the two approaches complement each other.

Incarceration for first-time wife assaulters is rare unless the assault was extremely violent and caused serious injury. Although 33 to 60 percent of these men will probably not re-offend (Schulman, 1979; Straus, 1977; Sherman & Berk, 1984), proponents of treatment groups argue that the 40 percent to 67 percent who probably will re-offend require therapeutic intervention to alter habitual methods of dealing with conflict through the use of violence (Ganley, 1981).

The results of the above outcome evaluations, although preliminary, tend to support this view.

In the arrest-treatment model, "law and order" and treatment approaches operate symbiotically to reduce further violence. Arrest serves both a didactic and deterrent function, showing the man that wife assault is unacceptable and will be punished by the state. Treatment then provides the opportunity for the man to learn new responses to the interchanges with his wife that formerly generated violent behavior.

The model presented in this chapter is a conservative approach that seeks to change individuals to fit the social system; it does not try to change the system itself. It acknowledges that social change is a complex, ongoing process and that a time-constrained therapy program has limitations in what it can do. Thus, it is a pragmatic "Band-Aid" for dealing with spousal violence in a manner that is compatible with criminal justice philosophy and the values of the culture in which it is nested. It would be an error to view such treatment groups as a comprehensive solution to the social problem of wife assault. To effectively end this form of violence in our society, we must buttress this approach with other therapeutic forms, community consciousness raising, and by constant agitation for social change.

NOTES

1 The term "wife assault" is used to refer to violence against women committed by intimate male partners, regardless of legal marriage.

2 Some problems exist with Sherman and Berk's (1984) explanation that the lower recidivism rate for their arrested group was due to deterrence. Dutton and Hart (1988) demonstrated that wife assaulters can be affected by a number of informal events as a consequence of arrest. These include an equalization of the perceived power distribution in the man's relationship with his wife and the number of persons to whom the man's violence is disclosed. These factors could also play a role in recidivism reduction, apart from deterrence per se. For a fuller discussion of these issues see Dutton and Hart (1988).

REFERENCES

Bandura, A. (1979). "The Social Learning Perspective: Mechanisms of Aggression." In H. Toch (ed.) *Psychology of Crime and Criminal Justice.* New York: Holt, Rinehart & Winston.

Bass, B. (1973). "An Unusual Behavioral Technique for Treating Obsessive Ruminations." *Psychotherapy: Theory, Research, and Practice,* 10:191-192.

Beck, A.T. (1976). *Cognitive Theory and the Emotional Disorders.* New York: International Universities Press.

Bower, S.A. & G.H. Bower (1976). *Asserting Yourself: A Practical Guide for Positive Change.* Reading, MA: Addison-Wesley.

Browning, J.J. (1984). *Stopping the Violence: Canadian Programmes for Assaultive Men.* Ottawa: Health and Welfare Canada.

Coleman, D.H. & M.A. Straus (1985). "Marital Power, Conflict, and Violence." Paper presented at the meeting of the American Society of Criminology, San Diego, California.

Crowne, D.P. & D.A. Marlowe (1960). "A New Scale of Social Desirability Independent of Psychopathology." *Journal of Consulting Psychology,* 24:349-354.

DeMaris, A. & J. Jackson (1987). "Batterers' Reports of Recidivism After Counseling." *Social Casework,* 68:458-465.

Dobson, K.S. & L. Block (1987). "Historical and Philosophical Bases of the Cognitive-Behavioral Therapies." In K.S. Dobson (ed.) *Handbook of Cognitive-Behavioral Therapies.* New York: Guilford Press.

Douglas, M.A. & S. Perrin (1987). "Recidivism and Accuracy of Self-Reported Violence and Arrest in Court Ordered to Treatment Batterers." Paper presented at the Third National Family Violence Research Conference, Durham, New Hampshire.

Dutton, D.G. (1981a). *The Criminal Justice System Response to Wife Assault.* Ottawa: Solicitor General of Canada, Research Division.

_____ (1981b). "Training Police Officers to Intervene in Domestic Violence." In R.B. Stuart (ed.) *Violent Behavior.* New York: Brunner/Mazel.

_____ (1986). "The Outcome of Court-Mandated Treatment for Wife Assault: A Quasi-Experimental Evaluation." *Violence and Victims,* I(3):163-175.

_____ (1987). "The Criminal Justice Response to Wife Assault." *Law and Human Behavior,* II(3):189-206.

_____ (1988). *The Domestic Assault of Women: Psychological and Criminal Justice Perspectives.* Allyn and Bacon: Boston.

Dutton, D.G. & S.G. Hart (1988). "The Prediction of Recidivist Wife Assault: Subjective Perceptions of Consequences for Future Assault in a Population of Convicted Wife Assaulters." Paper presented at the American Psychology and Law Society, Miami, Florida.

Eddy, M.J. & T. Meyers (1984). *Helping Men Who Batter: A Profile of Programs in the United States.* Texas Council on Family Violence, Arlington, Texas.

Edleson, J.L. & R.J. Grusznski (1988). "Treating Men Who Batter: Four Years of Outcome Data From the Domestic Abuse Project." *Journal of Social Service Research,* 12:3-22.

Edleson, J.L., M. Syers & M.P. Brygger (1987). "Comparative Effectiveness of Group Treatment for Men Who Batter." Paper presented at the Third National Family Violence Conference, Durham, New Hampshire.

Eysenck, H. (1969). *The Effects of Psychotherapy.* New York: Science House.

Fasteau, M.F. (1974). *The Male Machine.* New York: McGraw Hill.

Fincham, F. & J. Jaspars (1980). "Attribution of Responsibility from Man the Scientist to Man as Lawyer." *Advances in Experimental Social Psychology,* 13:81-138.

Foy, D.W., R.M. Eisler & S. Pinkston (1975). "Modeled Assertion in a Case of Explosive Rage." *Journal of Behavior Therapy and Experimental Psychiatry,* 6:135-137.

Ganley, A. (1981). *Participant's Manual: Court Mandated Therapy for Men Who Batter: A Three-Day Workshop for Professionals.* Washington, DC: Center for Women Policy Studies.

Ganley, A. & L. Harris (1978). "Domestic Violence: Issues in Designing and Implementing Programs for Male Batterers." Paper presented at the 86th annual convention of the American Psychological Association, Toronto.

Gondolf, E.W. (1985). *Men Who Batter: An Integrated Approach for Stopping Wife Abuse.* Holmes Beach, CA: Learning Publications.

Gondolf, E.W. & D. Russell (1986). "The Case Against Anger Control Treatment for Batterers." *Response,* 9(3):2-5.

Hamberger, L.K. & J.E. Hastings (1986). "Characteristics of Male Spouse Abusers: Is Psychopathology Part of the Picture?" Paper presented at American Society of Criminology, Atlanta, Georgia.

Jaffe, P., D.A. Wolfe, A. Telford & G. Austin (1986). "The Impact of Police Charges in Incidents of Wife Abuse." *Journal of Family Violence,* I(1):37-49.

Kelso, D. & L. Personnette (1985). *Domestic Violence and Treatment Services for Victims and Abusers.* Anchorage, AK: Altam Assoc.

Lazarus, R.A. & J.R. Averill (1972). "Emotion and Cognition: With Special Reference to Anxiety." In C.D. Spielberger (ed.) *Anxiety: Current Trends in Theory and Research (Vol. II).* New York: Academic.

Lund, S.H., N.E. Larsen & S.K. Schultz (1982). *Exploratory Evaluation of the Domestic Abuse Project.* Unpublished manuscript, Program Evaluation Resource Center, Minneapolis.

Mahoney, M.J. & C.E. Thoreson (1979). *Self-Control: Power to the Person.* Monterey, CA: Brooks/Cole.

Maiuro, R.D., T.S. Cahn, P.P. Vitaliano & J.B. Zegree (1986). "Anger Control Treatment for Men Who Engage in Domestic Violence: A Controlled Outcome Study." Paper presented at the annual convention of the Western Psychological Association, Seattle, Washington.

Meichenbaum, D. (1977). *Cognitive Behavior Modification.* New York: Plenum Press.

Neidig, P.H. & D.H. Friedman (1984). *Spouse Abuse: A Treatment Program for Couples.* Champaign, IL: Research Press.

Novaco, R. (1975). *Anger Control: The Development and Evaluation of an Experimental Treatment.* Lexington, MA: Lexington Books.

_____ (1976). "The Functions and Regulations of the Arousal of Anger." *American Journal of Psychiatry*, 133(1):1124-1128, October.

Pirog-Good, M.A. & J. Stets (1986). "Recidivism in Programs for Abusers." *Victimology: An International Journal*, 11(forthcoming).

Pleck, J.H. (1981). *The Myth of Masculinity.* Cambridge, MA: M.I.T. Press.

Ptacek, J. (1984). "The Clinical Literature on Men Who Batter: A Review and Critique." Paper presented at the Second National Conference on Family Violence Research, University of New Hampshire, Durham, New Hampshire.

Rachman, S.J. & G.T. Wilson (1980). *The Effects of Psychological Therapy* (2nd ed.). Oxford: Pergamon Press.

Saunders, D.G. (1977). "Marital Violence: Dimensions of the Problem and Modes of Intervention." *Journal of Marriage and Family Counselling*, 3:43-52.

_____ (1984). "Helping Husbands Who Batter." *Social Casework*, 65:347-356.

Saunders, D.G. & D.R. Hanusa (1984). "Cognitive-Behavioral Treatment for Abusive Husbands: The Short-Term Effects of Group Therapy." Paper presented at the Second National Conference on Family Violence Research, Durham, New Hampshire.

_____ (1986). "Cognitive-Behavioral Treatment for Men Who Batter: The Short-Term Effects of Group Therapy." *Journal of Family Violence*, 1(4):357-372.

Schulman, M. (1979). *A Survey of Spousal Violence Against Women in Kentucky.* Washington, DC: U.S. Department of Justice, Law Enforcement.

Shepard, M. (1987). "Interventions with Men Who Batter: An Evaluation of a Domestic Abuse Program." Paper presented at the Third National Conference on Family Violence Research Conference, Durham, New Hampshire.

Sherman, L.W. & R.A. Berk (1984). "The Specific Deterrent Effects of Arrest for Domestic Assault." *American Sociological Review*, 49:261-272.

Sonkin, D.J. & M. Durphy (1982). *Learning to Live Without Violence: A Handbook for Men.* San Francisco: Volcano Press.

Sonkin, D.J., D. Martin & L. Walker (1985). *The Male Batterer: A Treatment Approach.* New York: Springer Publishing.

Standing Committee on Health, Welfare, and Social Affairs. (1982). *Report on Violence in the Family: Wife Battering*. House of Commons, Ottawa.

Stark, R. & J. McEvoy (1970). "Middle Class Violence." *Psychology Today*, 4(6):107-112.

Straus, M.A. (1979). "Measuring Family Conflict and Violence: The Conflict Tactics Scale." *Journal of Marriage and the Family*, 41:75-88.

Straus, M.A., R.J. Gelles & S. Steinmetz (1980). *Behind Closed Doors: Violence in the American Family*. Doubleday, NY: Anchor Press.

Tolman, R.M. & D.G. Saunders (1988). "The Case for the Cautious Use of Anger Control with Men Who Batter." *Response*, 11(2):15-20.

U.S. Commission on Civil Rights (1978). *Battered Women: Issues of Public Policy.* Washington, DC: U.S. Government Printing House.

Yalom, T.D. (1975). *The Theory and Practice of Group Psychotherapy.* New York: Basic Books.

8

Civil Protection Orders: A Flawed Opportunity for Intervention*

Peter Finn
Abt Associates

INTRODUCTION

Communities across the country are making increased use of civil protection orders as a means of reducing the appalling level of abuse documented in other chapters of this book. Yet, there are widespread doubts within and outside the justice system about whether civil protection orders are—or ever can be—truly effective. Protection orders have been criticized for failing to prevent further violence, for reinforcing a "soft" approach to a serious criminal problem, for being susceptible to fraud, and for being difficult to enforce. After a brief review of the principal features of protection orders, this chapter marshals evidence that suggests that while protection orders to date may indeed have fallen far short of their intended goal, properly issued and enforced they provide a

* This chapter is based largely on a study conducted by the author for the National Institute of Justice, U.S. Department of Justice, under contract OJP-86-C-002. All opinions are those of the author and do not necessarily reflect the positions or policies of the U.S. Department of Justice.
I wish to thank the many individuals who provided assistance during the study, including Cynthia Carlson, Jane R. Chapman, Sarah Colson, Gail Goolkasian, Gladys Kessler, Lisa G. Lerman, Taylor McNeil, Ellen Pence, Carol Petrie, Marianne Takas, Deborah Welch, and Barbara T. Yanick.

unique opportunity to help reduce violence between partners in intimate relationships.

Information for the chapter comes from four sources: a review of pertinent state statutes and case law; telephone interviews with twelve judges and twelve victim advocates; examination of program documentation in two sites (Duluth, Minnesota and Seattle, Washington); and site visits to Portland, Maine and Portland, Oregon; Springfield and Chicago, Illinois; and Nashville, Philadelphia, and Colorado Springs. These sites were chosen to represent a range of reportedly effective approaches. Site visits involved interviews with judges, prosecutors, law enforcement officers, women's advocates, and battered women; courtroom observation; and (in two sites) ride-alongs with police officers.

Civil protection orders grant immediate relief to battered women by enjoining abusers from further violence against their partners. These orders may provide further protection by authorizing judges to evict a batterer from a shared residence, arrange for temporary custody of children, limit child visitation rights, require payment of child support, and order a batterer to attend counseling. Temporary orders can be obtained in an ex parte proceeding to provide for a victim's immediate safety when there is insufficient time to give notice to a batterer. After the respondent receives notice, the court holds a hearing at which both parties have an opportunity to be heard. At this time, a temporary order may become "permanent," usually for up to a year.

Civil protection order hearings differ from criminal prosecutions in two important respects. First, they involve civil rules of procedure. This means that the standard of proof for granting an order is a preponderance of the evidence, not proof beyond a reasonable doubt. And second, hearings are designed to separate the parties and prevent future unlawful conduct rather than to vindicate the state's interest in punishing past offenses.

Petitioning for an order does not preclude a victim from bringing criminal charges against a batterer at the same time (except in New York State). Indeed, many observers recommend that battered women pursue their cases both civilly and criminally. They argue that batterers should always be arrested and prosecuted.

In most jurisdictions a protection order can also be issued as a condition of bail or pretrial release in a criminal case. However, this route is foreclosed when the abuse is not an "arrestable" offense or presents insufficient evidence to bring criminal charges.

The District of Columbia and every state except Arkansas and Delaware have statutes authorizing civil orders of protection for abuse. The following section lists the features of all 49 statutes and briefly discusses several of the more common provisions. Detailed examinations of the types of relief authorized by statute, temporary ex parte orders, and the petitioning process follow. The principal advantages and limitations of protection orders are treated next.

The chapter concludes with a brief discussion of the need for a coordinated community-wide effort if the unique potential of protection orders is to be fully realized.

THE LEGAL BASIS FOR CIVIL PROTECTION ORDERS

In the past, problems with the use of civil protection orders often stemmed from lack of clarity and limitations of scope concerning eligible victims, offenses that permit an order of protection, kinds of relief authorized, and provisions for enforcement. As a result, many state statutes have been revised to include clearer and more comprehensive procedures for courts and law enforcement agencies to follow in issuing and enforcing protection orders.

Figure 8.1 presents significant provisions of the civil protection order statute of every state and the District of Columbia as of March, 1988. Examination of the matrix suggests that current problems in using and enforcing civil protection orders do not usually reflect deficiencies in the enabling legislation. Indeed, most statutes provide very broad authority for issuing and enforcing orders. But the statutes are often interpreted more narrowly than intended. Often, this is because judges and law enforcement officers are concerned about affording victims more protection than is constitutionally permissible. However, courts and police are probably on safe ground interpreting the statutes broadly and enforcing them vigorously given statutory language and case law that has consistently rejected challenges to the constitutionality of the relief authorized.

Several features of the statutes are reviewed below to illustrate the ample opportunity they offer judges to protect women from further violence. Because types of relief, temporary ex parte eviction of an offender, and the petitioning process are crucial yet often troubling features of protection orders, they are treated separately and in greater detail in the following sections.

Eligible Petitioners

Statutes in 48 states and the District of Columbia make spouses eligible for protection orders. Former spouses are eligible in 46 jurisdictions, persons living as spouses qualify in 39, and any family member is eligible in 42. Twenty-three statutes explicitly extend relief to household members who are unrelated. For example, several states qualify "persons cohabiting" or "persons jointly residing." Missouri and New Jersey include non-family members but limit eligibility to cohabitants "of the opposite sex." Judges in several other states have granted orders to homosexual couples living together on the grounds that state statutes do not explicitly deny eligibility to them.

Figure 8.1*

STATUTORY FEATURE	Total No. of States	AL	AK	AZ	CA	CO	CT	FL	GA	HI	ID	IL	IN	IA	KS	KY	LA	ME	MD	MA
I. ELIGIBILITY																				
A. Who may be covered																				
Spouse	49	✓	✓	✓	✓	✓	✓	✓	✓	✓	✓	✓	✓	✓	✓	✓	✓	✓	✓	✓
Former spouse	46		✓	✓	✓	✓	✓	✓	✓	✓	✓	✓	✓	✓	✓	✓	✓	✓		✓
Person living as spouse	39	✓	✓	✓	✓		✓		✓	✓	✓	✓	✓	✓	✓			✓		
Person formerly living as spouse	36		✓	✓	✓		✓		✓	✓	✓	✓	✓		✓			✓		
Family member	42	✓		✓	✓	✓	✓	✓	✓	✓	✓	✓	✓	✓	✓	✓	✓	✓	✓	✓
Household member related by blood or marriage	43	✓	✓		✓	✓	✓	✓	✓	✓	✓	✓	✓	✓	✓		✓	✓	✓	✓
Unrelated household member	24		✓		✓	✓	✓			✓	✓	✓	✓		✓					✓
Former household member	24				✓		✓			✓	✓	✓	✓		✓			✓		✓
Persons with a child in common	30		✓		✓		✓		✓	✓	✓	✓	✓			✓		✓	✓	✓
Minor child of one or both parties	30	✓	✓	✓	✓		✓		✓	✓		✓			✓	✓	✓	✓	✓	✓
Eligible if victim leaves residence	36	✓	✓		✓	✓	✓	✓	✓	✓	✓	✓	✓		✓	✓	✓	✓	✓	
Self-defense permitted	6										✓	✓						✓	✓	
B. Who may petition																				
Victim	48	✓	✓	✓	✓	✓	✓	✓	✓	✓	✓	✓	✓	✓	✓	✓	✓	✓	✓	✓
Adult household member for minor	26	✓	✓				✓			✓		✓			✓	✓	✓	✓	✓	
C. Abuse which qualifies																				
Physical abuse																				
(a) of an adult	49	✓	✓	✓	✓	✓	✓	✓	✓	✓	✓	✓	✓	✓	✓	✓	✓	✓	✓	✓
(b) of a child	33	✓	✓	✓	✓		✓		✓	✓	✓	✓			✓	✓	✓	✓	✓	✓
Threat of physical abuse	43	✓	✓	✓		✓	✓	✓		✓	✓	✓	✓	✓	✓	✓	✓	✓	✓	✓
Attempt at physical abuse	40	✓	✓	✓			✓	✓	✓		✓	✓	✓		✓		✓	✓	✓	✓
Sexual abuse																				
(a) of an adult	28		✓				✓	✓	✓		✓	✓					✓	✓	✓	✓
(b) of a child	22		✓	✓			✓				✓	✓			✓		✓	✓		✓

Figure 8.1*

STATUTORY FEATURE	Total No. of States	AL	AK	AZ	CA	CO	CT	FL	GA	HI	ID	IL	IN	IA	KS	KY	LA	ME	MD	MA
II. DURATION PROVISIONS																				
A. Full orders																				
Maximum duration (days)		365	90	183	3yrs		90	365	183	180	30	730	5	365	365	365	90	365	30	365
Extendable	22		✓	✓	✓		✓	✓				✓			✓		✓	✓		✓
B. Ex Parte Relief																				
Available	49	✓	✓	✓	✓	✓	✓	✓	✓	✓	✓	✓	✓	✓	✓	✓	✓	✓	✓	✓
Maximum duration (days)		1	20		25		14	30	10	30	14	14	10	10	20	14	30	21	5	5
Extendable	26	✓	✓				✓	✓			✓	✓		✓			✓	✓	✓	✓
Lasts until full hearing held	29					✓	✓	✓	✓		✓				✓		✓	✓	✓	
C. Evening/Weekend Relief																				
Available	23	✓	✓		✓	✓						✓		✓	✓		✓	✓		✓
Maximum duration (days)		10	20		4	3						14		3	3		30			
Immediate court certification	14	✓			✓	✓						✓		✓	✓			✓		✓
III. FILING PROVISIONS																				
Filing fee	23		✓	✓			✓	✓	✓			✓	✓	✓						
Filing fee waived for indigents	26		✓	✓			✓	✓	✓			✓	✓	✓			✓		✓	
Special forms	35		✓	✓	✓		✓	✓	✓	✓	✓	✓			✓	✓	✓	✓		✓
Assistance available for forms	28		✓	✓	✓			✓	✓	✓		✓					✓	✓		✓
Victim may file pro se	10		✓	✓			✓	✓	✓		✓	✓					✓	✓		✓

MI	MN	MS	MO	MT	NE	NV	NH	NJ	NM	NY	NC	ND	OH	OK	OR	PA	RI	SC	SD	TN	TX	UT	VT	VA	WA	WV	WI	WY	DC
✓	✓	✓	✓	✓	✓	✓	✓	✓	✓	✓	✓	✓	✓	✓	✓	✓	✓	✓	✓	✓	✓	✓	✓	✓	✓	✓	✓	✓	✓
✓	✓	✓	✓	✓	✓	✓	✓	✓	✓	✓	✓	✓	✓	✓	✓	✓	✓	✓	✓	✓	✓	✓	✓		✓	✓	✓	✓	✓
✓	✓	✓	✓	✓	✓	✓	✓	✓			✓	✓	✓	✓	✓	✓	✓	✓		✓	✓	✓	✓		✓	✓	✓	✓	✓
✓	✓	✓	✓	✓	✓	✓	✓	✓			✓	✓	✓	✓	✓	✓	✓		✓	✓		✓	✓		✓	✓	✓	✓	✓
✓		✓	✓		✓	✓	✓	✓		✓		✓	✓	✓	✓	✓	✓	✓	✓	✓	✓	✓	✓		✓	✓	✓		✓
✓	✓	✓	✓	✓	✓	✓	✓		✓			✓	✓	✓	✓	✓	✓	✓	✓	✓	✓	✓	✓		✓	✓	✓	✓	✓
✓	✓		✓			✓						✓		✓		✓	✓			✓	✓	✓			✓		✓	✓	
✓	✓		✓	✓	✓							✓	✓	✓		✓				✓	✓	✓			✓	✓	✓		
	✓	✓			✓	✓		✓	✓	✓		✓	✓		✓	✓	✓	✓	✓		✓				✓	✓			✓
✓	✓	✓			✓	✓				✓			✓	✓		✓		✓	✓		✓		✓		✓	✓			✓
	✓	✓	✓	✓	✓	✓	✓	✓		✓				✓	✓	✓	✓	✓	✓		✓	✓			✓	✓	✓		
																		✓		✓									
✓	✓	✓	✓	✓	✓	✓	✓	✓	✓	✓	✓	✓	✓	✓	✓	✓	✓	✓	✓	✓	✓	✓	✓	✓	✓	✓	✓	✓	✓
	✓	✓				✓				✓			✓	✓		✓	✓	✓		✓	✓		✓		✓	✓	✓	✓	
✓	✓	✓	✓	✓	✓	✓	✓	✓	✓	✓	✓	✓	✓	✓	✓	✓	✓	✓	✓	✓	✓	✓	✓	✓	✓	✓	✓	✓	✓
	✓	✓			✓	✓							✓	✓		✓	✓	✓	✓	✓	✓		✓		✓	✓	✓	✓	✓
✓	✓		✓	✓	✓	✓	✓	✓			✓	✓	✓	✓	✓	✓	✓	✓	✓		✓	✓	✓	✓	✓	✓	✓	✓	✓
✓		✓	✓	✓	✓	✓	✓	✓	✓	✓		✓	✓	✓	✓	✓	✓		✓	✓	✓	✓	✓	✓		✓	✓	✓	✓
			✓			✓	✓	✓	✓	✓			✓	✓	✓	✓	✓	✓				✓			✓	✓	✓	✓	✓
	✓	✓											✓	✓		✓	✓	✓					✓		✓	✓	✓	✓	✓

MI	MN	MS	MO	MT	NE	NV	NH	NJ	NM	NY	NC	ND	OH	OK	OR	PA	RI	SC	SD	TN	TX	UT	VT	VA	WA	WV	WI	WY	DC
	365	365	180	365			365		90	365	365		365		365	365	365	183	365	365	365	60	365	365	365	365	730	180	365
	✓		✓				✓		✓						✓		✓	✓		✓			✓			✓		✓	✓
✓	✓	✓	✓	✓	✓	✓	✓	✓	✓	✓	✓	✓	✓	✓	✓	✓	✓	✓	✓	✓	✓	✓	✓	✓	✓	✓	✓	✓	✓
	14	10		20		30		10	✓		10	30	10		365	365	20		21		20	10	10	15	14	5	7	3	14
	✓	✓				✓			✓	✓		✓	✓		✓		✓			✓	✓				✓	✓	✓	✓	
		✓	✓		✓	✓	✓	✓	✓	✓	✓	✓	✓	✓		✓		✓				✓	✓	✓		✓	✓	✓	
		✓	✓	✓				✓		✓		✓				✓	✓	✓					✓	✓		✓			
		10						10						3												5			14
			✓					✓				✓				✓	✓						✓						
✓	✓		✓	✓					✓			✓				✓		✓		✓	✓	✓			✓	✓	✓	✓	
✓	✓		✓	✓	✓				✓			✓				✓		✓		✓	✓	✓			✓	✓	✓	✓	
	✓		✓	✓		✓	✓	✓	✓	✓				✓	✓	✓	✓	✓		✓		✓	✓		✓	✓	✓	✓	✓
	✓		✓	✓		✓		✓	✓					✓	✓	✓	✓			✓		✓	✓		✓	✓	✓	✓	✓
	✓		✓			✓	✓	✓	✓	✓			✓		✓	✓	✓	✓		✓	✓	✓	✓		✓		✓	✓	✓

Figure 8.1*

STATUTORY FEATURE	Total No. of States	AL	AK	AZ	CA	CO	CT	FL	GA	HI	ID	IL	IN	IA	KS	KY	LA	ME	MD	MA
IV. WHAT RELIEF, EXPLICITLY MENTIONED IN STATUTE, MAY BE GRANTED IN FULL ORDER																				
No further abuse	46	✓	✓	✓	✓		✓	✓	✓	✓	✓	✓	✓	✓	✓	✓	✓	✓	✓	✓
No contact	26		✓	✓	✓		✓	✓	✓	✓	✓	✓					✓	✓		
Stay away from residence, etc.	39		✓	✓	✓	✓	✓	✓	✓	✓	✓	✓		✓	✓		✓	✓	✓	
Eviction from residence	48	✓	✓	✓	✓	✓	✓	✓	✓	✓	✓	✓	✓	✓	✓	✓	✓	✓	✓	✓
Abuser pays for alternate housing for victim	18		✓		✓				✓			✓			✓					
Temporary custody/visitation	41	✓	✓		✓		✓	✓	✓	✓	✓	✓	✓	✓	✓	✓	✓	✓	✓	✓
Temporary child support	27	✓	✓		✓			✓	✓			✓	✓	✓	✓		✓	✓		✓
Temporary support of spouse	29	✓	✓					✓	✓			✓	✓	✓	✓	✓	✓	✓		✓
Use of certain property	18		✓		✓				✓			✓			✓		✓	✓		
Monetary compensation	14				✓						✓	✓						✓		✓
No disposition of property	17											✓	✓		✓	✓	✓	✓		
Counseling	28		✓		✓			✓	✓	✓	✓	✓	✓	✓	✓	✓	✓	✓	✓	
Costs and attorneys fees	24	✓	✓		✓				✓		✓	✓			✓			✓		
Court may order other relief	38	✓	✓	✓	✓		✓	✓		✓	✓	✓	✓	✓		✓	✓	✓	✓	✓
V. ENFORCEMENT																				
Order given to victim by court	28	✓	✓		✓		✓	✓				✓		✓	✓		✓	✓	✓	
Order issued to abuser by court	32	✓	✓		✓	✓	✓	✓		✓	✓	✓	✓	✓	✓		✓	✓	✓	
Order issued to police/sheriff	46	✓	✓	✓	✓	✓	✓	✓	✓	✓	✓	✓		✓	✓	✓	✓	✓	✓	✓
Order enforceable statewide	24		✓		✓	✓	✓				✓	✓			✓	✓		✓	✓	
VI. PENALTIES FOR VIOLATION																				
A. Charge																				
Civil Contempt	31	✓	✓	✓	✓	✓	✓	✓	✓			✓		✓	✓	✓	✓	✓	✓	✓
Criminal Contempt	21		✓			✓		✓				✓			✓		✓	✓		✓
Misdemeanor	30			✓	✓		✓	✓	✓	✓		✓			✓		✓	✓		✓
B. Sanction																				
Maximum jail sentance (days)	26				180	180	365										180	3yrs	60	913
Maximum fine ($) (K=$1000)	27				1K	5K	1K	1K									500	1K	500	5K

Figure 8.1*

STATUTORY FEATURE	Total No. of States	AL	AK	AZ	CA	CO	CT	FL	GA	HI	ID	IL	IN	IA	KS	KY	LA	ME	MD	MA
VII. POLICE INTERVENTION																				
A. Discretionary Arrest—Warrantless																				
(a) If probable cause of abuse	24		✓	✓				✓	✓		✓	✓	✓	✓	✓	✓	✓			✓
(b) If probable cause of order violation	25		✓	✓		✓	✓	✓			✓	✓			✓		✓	✓		✓
B. Mandatory arrest—Warrantless																				
(a) If probable cause of abuse	10						✓							✓			✓			
(b) If probable cause of order violation	13													✓				✓		
C. Other police responsibilities																				
Train officers	15		✓		✓		✓	✓	✓		✓					✓		✓		
Establish procedure for verifying orders in effect to field officers	28		✓	✓	✓		✓	✓		✓		✓				✓		✓		✓
Use all means to prevent abuse	12											✓		✓		✓	✓	✓		✓
Enforce orders	28		✓		✓	✓	✓	✓	✓					✓		✓	✓	✓		✓
Provide victim assistance	24		✓		✓		✓	✓			✓	✓		✓	✓	✓	✓	✓		✓
Inform victim of legal rights	30		✓	✓	✓		✓	✓			✓	✓		✓		✓	✓	✓		✓
Supervise eviction of abuser	16		✓		✓				✓	✓		✓				✓	✓			
Report and keep records	22		✓		✓		✓	✓		✓	✓	✓		✓		✓	✓	✓		

MI	MN	MS	MO	MT	NE	NV	NH	NJ	NM	NY	NC	ND	OH	OK	OR	PA	RI	SC	SD	TN	TX	UT	VT	VA	WA	WV	WI	WY	DC
✓	✓	✓	✓	✓		✓	✓	✓	✓	✓	✓	✓	✓	✓	✓	✓	✓	✓	✓	✓	✓	✓	✓	✓	✓	✓		✓	✓
			✓			✓		✓	✓	✓			✓	✓		✓	✓	✓		✓				✓			✓	✓	✓
✓	✓		✓		✓	✓	✓	✓	✓	✓		✓	✓	✓	✓	✓	✓	✓		✓	✓	✓		✓	✓		✓	✓	✓
	✓	✓	✓	✓	✓	✓	✓	✓	✓	✓	✓	✓	✓	✓	✓	✓	✓	✓	✓	✓	✓	✓	✓	✓	✓	✓	✓	✓	✓
		✓	✓			✓	✓	✓			✓	✓	✓			✓				✓				✓		✓		✓	
	✓	✓	✓			✓	✓	✓	✓	✓	✓	✓	✓		✓	✓	✓	✓		✓	✓		✓	✓	✓	✓	✓	✓	✓
	✓		✓				✓	✓	✓		✓	✓	✓			✓		✓		✓	✓			✓		✓		✓	
	✓	✓	✓				✓	✓	✓		✓	✓	✓			✓		✓	✓	✓	✓			✓		✓		✓	
	✓		✓				✓		✓				✓					✓			✓			✓		✓	✓		✓
		✓	✓			✓	✓	✓			✓		✓			✓		✓											
		✓	✓	✓					✓				✓	✓				✓			✓					✓		✓	✓
	✓	✓	✓			✓		✓		✓		✓	✓						✓		✓			✓	✓			✓	✓
		✓	✓				✓			✓	✓	✓	✓	✓		✓		✓		✓		✓		✓	✓		✓		✓
✓	✓		✓	✓			✓	✓	✓	✓		✓	✓	✓		✓	✓	✓	✓		✓	✓		✓	✓	✓	✓	✓	
			✓				✓		✓	✓			✓		✓	✓	✓	✓	✓	✓	✓		✓	✓	✓	✓			✓
			✓		✓			✓	✓	✓			✓		✓	✓	✓	✓	✓	✓	✓		✓			✓		✓	✓
✓	✓		✓	✓	✓	✓	✓	✓		✓	✓	✓	✓	✓	✓	✓	✓	✓	✓	✓	✓	✓	✓	✓	✓	✓	✓	✓	✓
✓	✓			✓					✓	✓		✓	✓	✓	✓		✓						✓	✓	✓			✓	
	✓				✓		✓	✓		✓	✓		✓		✓	✓	✓			✓	✓	✓		✓	✓				
✓		✓	✓					✓	✓			✓				✓		✓			✓		✓			✓		✓	✓
	✓		✓	✓		✓		✓			✓	✓	✓	✓	✓		✓	✓	✓		✓	✓	✓		✓		✓	✓	
90	90	180	365		7			180		180		365	5yrs	365	180	180	365	365		10	365	180	180			30	270		180
500	700	1K	1K		500			1K		250			2.5K	1K	300		1K	1.5K			2K	1K	1K			1K	1K		300

MI	MN	MS	MO	MT	NE	NV	NH	NJ	NM	NY	NC	ND	OH	OK	OR	PA	RI	SC	SD	TN	TX	UT	VT	VA	WA	WV	WI	WY	DC
			✓				✓		✓			✓	✓	✓		✓		✓		✓	✓	✓						✓	
✓			✓				✓			✓		✓	✓			✓		✓		✓	✓	✓	✓			✓		✓	
						✓		✓							✓		✓							✓	✓		✓		
	✓					✓		✓	✓		✓				✓		✓			✓	✓				✓		✓		
			✓		✓			✓					✓			✓	✓											✓	
	✓		✓	✓			✓	✓				✓	✓		✓	✓			✓	✓	✓	✓	✓		✓	✓	✓	✓	
							✓				✓				✓		✓	✓										✓	
	✓					✓		✓	✓				✓		✓	✓	✓	✓		✓		✓	✓		✓		✓	✓	✓
✓							✓			✓	✓	✓					✓	✓		✓		✓	✓	✓				✓	
✓	✓		✓				✓	✓		✓	✓		✓	✓	✓	✓	✓	✓		✓	✓	✓		✓				✓	
	✓						✓	✓				✓	✓				✓	✓					✓	✓				✓	
	✓		✓					✓				✓	✓	✓			✓			✓	✓			✓				✓	

*The matrix that was used for this chart is adapted from Lerman and Livingston, "State Legislation on Domestic Violence," *Response to Violence in the Family and Sexual Assault*, Vol. 6, No. 5 (Center for Women Policy Studies [CWPS] Sept./Oct. 1983). The CWPS matrix was more detailed and covered more types of provisions. The content of this chart is not taken from the CWPS chart but is based on independent analysis of the statutes. This analysis was verified by an attorney in each state except Minnesota and North Carolina in 1988.

Most states allow at least some individuals to petition for an order even if they are not currently living with the respondent. Forty-five states and the District of Columbia provide for relief to former spouses and 35 states and the District of Columbia authorize orders for never-married individuals who once lived together as spouses. Being able to grant protection orders to victims who no longer live with their abusers is important. A study of emergency room records found that 72 percent of the abuse victims in the sample were not living with abusers at the time of the assault.[1] Anecdotal evidence suggests that many abusive former husbands and boyfriends make repeated attempts to harass or injure their former partners.

Most states do not preclude a victim from obtaining an order because she is involved in a divorce or separation from the batterer. Some statutes authorize this explicitly. Several states simply require that petitioners disclose to the court any other pending family court actions. However, statutes in Arizona, Texas, and West Virginia explicitly state that no order may be issued if an action for legal separation or dissolution of marriage is pending between the parties.

Qualifying Behavior

Victims of physical abuse are eligible for protection orders in all 49 jurisdictions. In addition, victims may petition on the basis of attempted physical abuse in 39 states and the District of Columbia and on the basis of threatened physical abuse in 42 states and the District of Columbia.

Some judges are concerned that issuing an order when threats are alleged but no actual battery has occurred may exceed their authority. One judge, for example, grants orders only if there have been several threats and the abuser has the ability to carry out his menaces. However, 42 states and the District of Columbia expressly permit an order on the basis of assault without battery. Often the statutory language is couched in terms of intimidating the victim, as in Maine, which includes "attempting to place or placing another in fear of imminent bodily injury" within its definition of abuse.

Once a batterer has exhibited behavior that qualifies for relief, statutes in 36 states provide that the victim remains eligible even if she has left the residence to escape further abuse. Most state statutes are silent, however, regarding how recent the latest incident must be to qualify the victim for an order. While of questionable legality, many judges establish their own guidelines in this matter. For example, one judge will not issue an order unless the most recent incident occurred within the past 48 hours. However, many judges have found that victims often need several days or even weeks after an incident to learn about the availability of protection orders, to seek encouragement from family, friends, or victim advocates to initiate legal action, and to make the invariably difficult decision to petition for an order. As a result, a number of judges will grant orders as long as an incident did not take place more than a month before the petition was filed. Courts in Oregon are permitted by statute to consider women eligible who have been abused any time in the preceding 180 days.

Standard of Proof

Most statutes are silent regarding the proper standard of proof in protection order hearings. Although a civil hearing should require a standard less stringent than the criminal standard of "beyond a reasonable doubt," some judges are uncertain about which civil standard to use in determining whether abuse has occurred. Some—perhaps most—judges base their decisions to grant an order on a preponderance of the evidence. This is in keeping with the fact that 11 of the 13 states that have prescribed the standard by statute have specified "a preponderance of evidence." (Maryland requires "clear and convincing" evidence of abuse and Wisconsin requires "reasonable grounds.") Given the absence of specific guidelines in most civil protection order statutes, judges should examine other civil code provisions to determine the proper rules of evidence that apply.

Remedies for Violations

Figure 8.1 shows the charges that may be brought in each state for violating a protection order. As shown, violation of a protection order is a misdemeanor offense in 30 states. In some states, the offense is more seriously classified with subsequent violations. Ohio, for example, has made a first violation a misdemeanor of the fourth degree, a second violation a misdemeanor of the first degree, and a third and subsequent violation a felony of the fourth degree. By making a violation a crime in itself, these statutes give law enforcement officers clear authority under their arrest powers to detain anyone who commits a violation they have witnessed—in particular, the mere presence of the offender in the victim's (or family's) residence, when such is prohibited by the order. However, enabling police to make a misdemeanor arrest of any offender who violates an order gives victims little protection because most repeat offenders have fled the scene before officers arrive—and officers must usually obtain a warrant before arresting anyone for a misdemeanor they have not witnessed. To address this dilemma, 25 states permit or require officers to make an arrest without a warrant when they have probable cause to believe the respondent has violated an order.

In several states, the failure of police to arrest violators of protection orders has led to considerable public concern, particularly when serious injury or death later resulted. In response to these concerns, 13 states mandate, rather than permit, warrantless arrest for violation of an order. For example, the Minnesota statute prescribes that:

> A peace officer shall arrest without a warrant and take into custody a person whom the peace officer has probable cause to believe has violated an order granted pursuant to this section restraining the person or excluding the person from the residence, if the existence of the order can be verified by the officer.

This law and one in New Hampshire require arrest even if the offender is found in the home and the victim has not reported his presence to the police. Oregon's statute mandates arrest even if the victim objects to the perpetrator's being taken into custody. This removes the onus of "you had me arrested" from the victim.

Nine states classify violation of a protection order exclusively as criminal contempt rather than as a misdemeanor offense. This approach offers less protection for victims than classifying a violation as a misdemeanor. This is because many—perhaps most—police officers are unaware that they may arrest any offender they witness violating orders even if the charge is only criminal contempt, and that they may make arrests based on probable cause without having seen the violation if state statute permits warrantless arrest for a violation. According to constitutional law scholars, criminal contempt is treated the same as a misdemeanor for purposes of arrest powers unless otherwise provided for by state statute, state constitution, or state appellate court ruling.

Violation constitutes exclusively civil contempt in 19 states. Statutes that make a violation merely civil contempt fail to provide immediate protection to a victim when there is a violation which does not otherwise qualify as an arrestable offense. Unless otherwise specified in legislation, police have no arrest powers for civil contempt because a defendant must be given an opportunity by a judge to "undo" his behavior, since the purpose of a civil contempt finding is not to punish but to secure compliance with the directives of the court.

Finally, many protection order statutes refer only to "contempt" without indicating whether a violation constitutes civil contempt or criminal contempt; other statutes provide for both civil and criminal contempt. In these jurisdictions, other statutes or case law must be consulted to determine which type of contempt may be charged.

Figure 8.2 summarizes the arrest powers of law enforcement officers depending on whether (1) a violation is a misdemeanor, criminal contempt, or civil contempt, and (2) there is statutory authorization to make a warrantless probable cause arrest for a violation.

Figure 8.2 **Law Enforcement Officers' Arrest Powers Under Six Combinations of Statutory Provisions**

Statutory Provisions	Arrest Powers[a]
I. a. Violation is a misdemeanor b. Warrantless probable cause arrest for violation	— Peace officers may make warrantless arrest for violation of any provision of protection order[b]
II. a. Violation is a misdemeanor b. No warrantless probable cause arrest for violation	— Peace officers may arrest for violation of any provision of protection order that they witness — Peace officers may arrest a violator who is found in the victim's home if the order includes an eviction provision
III. a. Violation is criminal contempt b. No warrantless probable cause arrest for violation	— Peace officers may make warrantless arrest for violation of any provision of protection order[b] — Peace officers may arrest a violator who is found in the defendant's home if the order includes an eviction provision
IV. a. Violation is criminal contempt b. No warrantless probable cause arrest for violation	— Peace officers may arrest for violation of any provision of protection order that they witness — Peace officers may arrest a violator who is found in the defendant's home if the order includes an eviction provision
V. a. Violation is civil contempt b. Warrantless probable cause arrest for violation	— Peace officer may not arrest for violation (because defendant must be given opportunity by judge to "undo" his behavior—court's role is not to punish but to achieve compliance)
VI. a. Violation is civil contempt b. No warrantless probable cause arrest for violation	— Peace officers may not arrest for violation (because defendant must be given opportunity by judge to "undo" his behavior—court's role is not to punish but to achieve compliance)

[a] In addition to any powers granted by statute to arrest on the grounds of a violation of a protection order, police officers may in all cases arrest for any *witnessed* act that by statute is *misdemeanor* offense in their jurisdiction (e.g., simple assault, threats, trespass, breaking and entering), and they may arrest on probable cause for *any act* that is a *felony* (e.g., threatening with a firearm, aggravated assault).

[b] Federal appeals courts have placed two limitations on warrantless searches regardless of purpose. In *Payton v. New York*, 445 U.S. 573 (1980), the court ruled that, absent consent or exigent circumstances, entry into a home to conduct a search or to make an arrest is unreasonable under the Fourth Amendment unless done pursuant to a warrant. In addition, in *Steagald v. United States*, 451 U.S. 204 (1981), the court ruled that, absent exigent circumstances or consent, police must obtain a search warrant to enter the residence of a third party where the offender is located in order to arrest him. The search warrant must be based on probable cause that the offender is at the location to be searched.

Common Statutory Weaknesses

Deficiencies in many statutes reduce the ability of the courts or law enforcement to protect victims as completely as possible. The most serious weaknesses relate to filing fees, training for clerks, emergency orders, service, monitoring, and enforcement. Each of these deficiencies is addressed elsewhere in this chapter. However, despite these weaknesses, current legislation in most states provides judges and law enforcement ample opportunity to use protection orders to help protect many women from further abuse.

TYPES OF RELIEF

As Figure 8.1 shows, most state statutes authorize a broad range of relief. However, the maximum relief is authorized in the 38 states that explicitly grant judges the latitude to grant any constitutionally defensible relief that is warranted. Such a provision means, for example, that a court does not need specific statutory authority to impound a victim's address if this measure is considered necessary to protect her safety.

In some states all the relief authorized for inclusion in a permanent order may also be provided in an emergency ex parte order. More commonly, however, statutes exclude some types of relief from emergency orders. For example, some states exclude spouse support, mandatory counseling, or child support. At a minimum, however, every statute permits eviction of the batterer in a temporary ex parte order and most authorize awarding the victim temporary custody of the children. A few states also authorize courts to grant such additional relief as they deem proper in an emergency proceeding.

To be effective, temporary and permanent civil protection orders should include *all* the statutorily authorized protection against further abuse that the victim needs given *her* particular circumstances. In intimate relationships, the victim needs a high level of protection because, unlike most stranger-to-stranger crimes, the batterer typically has ready access to her.

Each type of relief provided should also be fully explained in the order. For example, if a batterer might abuse a petitioner at school or her place of work, the order should explicitly enjoin him from appearing there. Providing precise conditions of relief makes the batterer aware of the specific behavior he must avoid. A high degree of specificity also makes it easier for police and other judges to know later whether the respondent has violated the order. Five types of relief (in addition to evicting the batterer) require special discussion.

No Contact

Many judges specify in an order the types of contact a respondent may and may not have with a victim—even when the order enjoins any contact at all. For example, the need to identify the victim's workplace may be important. One batterer terrified his wife by repeatedly parking across the street from where she worked so she could see him from her desk. Her supervisor became angry as her work began to deteriorate. However, the police reported there was nothing they could do because this behavior was not specifically prohibited in the order. Thus, unless the victim's work address is unknown to the abuser and the victim feels safer keeping it confidential, it should be specified. Similarly, in some cases in-laws can threaten a victim unless the order explicitly enjoins them, too, from contact with her.

Visitation

Nowhere is the potential for renewed violence greater than during visitation. Many batterers take advantage of the exchange of children to threaten or assault victims if the children are not ready quite on time or are sick and cannot join them. Some fathers keep the children longer than permitted as a way of tormenting the mother. Furthermore, men who batter women may also abuse children; as a result, judges need to consider the vulnerability of the children as well as that of the petitioner in deciding whether to award visitation and, if so, what limitations to place on it.

Recognizing these dangers, some judges are careful to include explicit conditions for visitation in their orders, specifying neutral pick-up and drop-off locations, times and days of the week, and the involvement of neutral third parties. In some jurisdictions, courts have helped locate safe places for visitation, such as churches and synagogues. Duluth has a visitation center where offenders can schedule visitation without having to telephone victims, victims can deliver their children to offenders and pick them up in the presence of center staff, or supervised visitation can take place to prevent child abuse. One judge sometimes suggests that the victim have the father come to the police station to pick up and drop off the children. Some judges also stipulate that the respondent may not drink or take drugs before or during the visit and that the woman may refuse visitation if the offender appears to have violated this condition. Permitting the order to indicate that visitation "will be arranged later" is particularly risky.

Child Custody

Many judges feel they do not have enough information to make custody decisions as part of a protection order. Other judges feel that some women with an impending divorce action use civil protection orders inappropriately to gain quick custody of the children. However, it is important to award custody to mothers who obtain an order because, as noted, men who batter their partners may abuse their children too. Even if there is no evidence that either parent has harmed the children, if one party has been violent towards the other that should be sufficient basis to grant custody to the victimized partner. Moreover, batterers who retain custody of the children sometimes use them to abuse or "get at" the mother emotionally by, for example, taking them out of state.

Statutes in 40 states and the District of Columbia specifically authorize judges to award temporary custody of any children to victims. In 1982, the Missouri Supreme Court upheld against due process challenge a statutory provision authorizing the ex parte award of temporary custody of minor children to the plaintiff.[2] The court ruled that, although the liberty interest in custody of one's children was a significant private interest, the governmental interest in preventing abuse outweighed the private interest because of the high incidence and severity of abuse. The court also based its decision on the statute's 15-day limitation on the effectiveness of an ex parte order, after which a hearing must take place where a batterer may contest the custody provision of the temporary order.

Mandatory Counseling

Statutes in 28 states and the District of Columbia authorize judges to order counseling for respondents. Even without specific authorization, judges can often require counseling based on statutory authorization for the court to provide for "such additional relief as the judge deems proper."

Mandatory counseling that is specifically designed to treat abuse appears to teach some batterers non-abusive ways of relating to women intimates. However, even if counseling cannot accomplish this goal it can serve a purpose by reinforcing court sanctions. The counseling sessions become a constant reminder to the batterer that the court and community will not tolerate his violent behavior.

Many judges and victims want batterers who are substance abusers to enter outpatient or voluntary inpatient treatment programs because these men become violent only when they are drunk or drugged. However, these programs do not address the issues of violence or control and are not effective substitutes for batterer counseling. In some cases, addiction counseling may be needed first (to get the offender sober enough to address his violence problem) with batterer counseling afterwards.

In jurisdictions that do not monitor attendance, batterers may attend a couple of sessions and think they are "cured." Unmonitored counseling can also lead to a false sense of security among victims. These problems have led some jurisdictions to establish monitoring arrangements. Duluth has one of the most carefully monitored counseling systems. Judges there normally order respondents who will have ongoing contact with victims to be evaluated by the Domestic Abuse Intervention Program, a local counseling program for men who batter. Protection orders require the men to follow the program's recommendations. Typically, the program will contract with the batterer for a 26-week counseling and education program. The batterer may also be required to participate in individual therapy, seek psychiatric help, or participate in an outpatient drug dependency program. The Domestic Abuse Intervention Program is then appointed by the court as an interested third party in the case, permitting the program to request a review hearing or ask the court to initiate a contempt of court action in the event of attendance problems.

Most state statutes that provide for mandatory batterer counseling also authorize mandatory counseling for victims. However, it is inappropriate to require counseling of a victim who has committed no offense. Furthermore, requiring a victim to enter counseling puts her in more jeopardy because it may suggest to her batterer that he is not responsible for his violence and give him an excuse to continue his violence. Couples' counseling has the same effect and it creates a setting in which the woman is at an inherent disadvantage given her fear of the batterer. Some judges and many victim advocates do suggest to victims that they seek counseling for help in dealing with the emotional trauma they are experiencing, not because they are in any way responsible for their abuse. For example, victims in Duluth are encouraged by the court and victim advocates to attend educational groups held by a local woman's coalition.

Courts have occasionally found unmistakable evidence that both partners have a problem with violent behavior. Usually, this involves a woman who has retaliated against a man's violence by reacting violently herself. For example, of 34 female assailants evaluated by the Duluth Domestic Abuse Intervention Program, all but 3 had been repeatedly assaulted by their partners. There are also rare instances in which a woman will ineffectually strike her husband or boyfriend first, only to have the man respond with overwhelming force and hurt her. When there is clear-cut evidence that she is also violent, it may be appropriate to order individual counseling for the petitioner as well as for the respondent. For example, the Duluth program mandated the 34 women assailants into counseling, making clear to them that they may act violently in self-defense but not in retaliation for their partners' abuse. However, a protection order still must be issued to protect these women from the disproportionate violence of the stronger partner.

Mutual Orders

When both parties appear to have engaged in violent behavior, judges sometimes issue mutual orders enjoining both from engaging in violence. This is often because of the difficulty or inconvenience of evaluating the evidence and determining the true perpetrator. There are compelling reasons to use this remedy sparingly. The Minnesota Court of Appeals ruled that the issuance of a mutual restraining order in a domestic abuse action after a hearing where only the wife requested an order was erroneous when no evidence existed that the wife abused the husband.[3] In appealing the mutual order, the wife claimed she was prejudiced by the order because it suggested that she was found to have committed acts of abuse and because it gave the abuser the message that he was not going to be held accountable for his violent behavior. The petitioner also asserted that mutual restraining orders are less enforceable than orders against just the batterer because the police may be misled about which party actually has a history of battering. Indeed, a number of police officers report that when a victimized woman calls them to the scene of a violation they are uncertain how to proceed when there is a mutual order; they typically end up doing nothing or arresting both parties. As a result, when batterers request mutual orders, judges should tell them that they must file for protection orders of their own—and then evaluate carefully the credibility of their allegations before granting an order.

TEMPORARY EX PARTE ORDERS

Perhaps nothing is more controversial than the emergency ex parte procedure authorized in every state statute for issuing a temporary order typically valid for up to 10 or 14 days. Its most controversial feature is the inclusion of a provision evicting the batterer from the residence he shares with a petitioner for a brief period before he has had a chance to state his side of the case. Some judges believe—and some defense attorneys have contended—that an ex parte hearing that results in the exclusion of the batterer from the home might violate the respondent's due process rights to proper notice and a hearing. Many people have expressed concern that a man might be forced to undergo the hardship of leaving home on the basis of a fraudulent claim by a petitioner. Finally, society as a whole has been conditioned to treat a man's home as "his castle," making it seem unfair to force him to leave for any reason.

However, ex parte eviction is almost always the single most effective protection the court can provide battered women because it provides for victims' immediate safety when there is insufficient time to provide batterers with immediate hearings. There is a long history in American civil law of issuing temporary restraining orders as a means of preventing immediate and irreparable harm by enjoining a given party from specific, imminent behavior that may occur in the interval between the time the court learns of the danger and the time a hearing can be held to adjudicate the matter in the presence of both parties. As a result, many courts include this relief when victims ask for it.

Of course, a man who is determined to do violence to his partner will not be deterred by a court order alone. But many batterers will think twice about committing renewed violence when a police officer arrives, gives the abuser 10 minutes to pack up and leave, and warns that if he returns he will be arrested and possibly jailed.

Furthermore, while many courts and law enforcement agencies have their "horror story" about a woman who made life difficult for her husband or boyfriend through fraudulent claims of abuse, documented instances of women abusing the process are rare. Judges and victim advocates report that abuses of the protection order process that do occur are usually by men requesting mutual orders out of spite or to gain a tactical advantage, or by men who file for orders to gain quick custody of their children. In addition, the fact that it is unusual for a batterer to request an emergency hearing to oppose his eviction suggests that the burden on these men is neither unjust nor onerous. For example, during a six-month period in Chicago only three out of several hundred men evicted from the residence appealed the ex parte order. In Springfield, Illinois, even with a court summons only one-third of all respondents show up at scheduled hearings for permanent orders. Furthermore, when they do come, they generally admit to having assaulted their wives or girlfriends (but claim that the beatings were not "serious"). The reason they appear at all is usually to contest custody or visitation provisions, not eviction.

Perhaps the most important reason for using temporary ex parte relief and eviction provisions is that they are well-founded in both state statutes and case law.

Statutory Safeguards

Nearly every state permits judges to evict batterers temporarily as part of an ex parte proceeding. However, every statute specifies certain conditions for granting an ex parte order that are intended to safeguard the respondent from either an unconstitutional deprivation of his due process rights or unfair hardship. Most statutes require evidence indicating a greater degree of danger to issue an ex parte order than to issue a permanent one. Specifically, a situation must be an emergency in which any delay might seriously endanger the petitioner's safety. Most states also specify that evicting a batterer from his residence does not change his interest in real property. Finally, and most importantly, statutes generally make provision for respondents who have been evicted in an ex parte proceeding to receive a hearing within a few days to contest the eviction.

Many observers feel that the opportunity afforded a respondent to obtain an emergency hearing on short notice to contest an eviction is the strongest ethical and legal justification for granting this relief. One judge reported, "I used to worry about signing temporary restraining orders and excluding the man from the home, but because he can contest the order within 48 hours I don't feel so bad anymore." Of course, even if this safeguard is not adequately addressed in legislation, any judge can grant an immediate hearing to permit a respondent to contest an order.

Many judges will not evict a man when he is the sole owner of the home or exclusive holder of the lease. Often, this reflects what is permitted by statute. Most states require the petitioner to have an interest in the property for a judge to evict the batterer. However, a few states authorize granting exclusive possession to the petitioner when the respondent has sole interest in the residence but owes the petitioner support. The Wisconsin statute provides for the court to "order the respondent to avoid the premises for a reasonable time until the petitioner relocates..." regardless of who has title to the property. California, New Jersey, and Oregon explicitly authorize the court to evict the batterer even when he is the sole owner or renter of the residence.

It is important that statutes provide judges with this discretion. Ordinarily, both parties have contributed to the family either financially or in homemaking services, but the property may be titled in the husband's name for legal reasons, tax purposes, or to retain greater control over battered women.

Case Law

There are no United States Supreme Court cases that deal directly with ex parte civil protection orders. However, three Supreme Court cases establish the constitutionality of temporary ex parte orders in other circumstances and appear to be controlling. In 1970, the court balanced three factors in determining whether ex parte termination of disability benefits violated due process: the private interests affected versus the asserted governmental interest; the fairness and reliability of existing procedures; and the probable value, if any, of additional procedural safeguards.[4] In 1972, the court held that a court may forego notice in certain prejudgment replevin cases if the pending action is necessary to protect an important governmental or public interest or if a situation requires prompt action.[5] Finally, the court ruled in 1973 that providing relief prior to notice and deferring a hearing on deprivation of property may be permissible if (1) the petition includes statements of specific facts that justify the requested relief, (2) notice and opportunity for a full hearing are given as soon as possible, preferably within a few days after the order is issued, and (3) the temporary injunction is issued by a judge.[6]

Two state supreme courts have upheld the constitutionality of ex parte evictions in abuse cases. In response to an offender's argument that a Pennsylvania statute permitted a taking of property without due process of law by not providing him with timely notice and an opportunity to be heard before the eviction, the Pennsylvania Supreme Court noted that providing notice before the presentation of the petition would defeat the act's purpose of providing the victim with immediate protection.[7] Although a notice requirement would better meet the goals of the Fourteenth Amendment, it would increase the risk of violence. The court held further that subordinating the respondent's due process rights to the victim's right to immediate protection was consistent with U.S. case law holding that a court may forego notice in certain prejudgment replevin cases if a situation requires prompt action.

In 1982, the Missouri Supreme Court upheld the constitutionality of a state statute against a due process challenge.[8] A wife had sought a writ of mandamus to compel a trial court to issue a protection order to restrain her husband from entering their home. The trial court denied relief because it held the act was unenforceable on the grounds that it violated the United States and Missouri Constitutions by excluding the respondent from the home without notice or hearing. In reversing the trial court, the Missouri court held that the ex parte order provisions satisfied due process requirements because the provisions were a reasonable means to achieve the state's legitimate goal of preventing abuse and because the provisions afforded adequate procedural safeguards before and after any deprivation of rights.

THE PETITIONING PROCESS

There are a number of potentially significant bottlenecks in the process of petitioning for a protection order. However, some legislators, judges, and victim advocates have found remedies for them that simultaneously provide victims with maximum protection and streamline the process for the court.

Filing Fees

Many observers have expressed concern that 23 states require a filing fee to petition for a protection order. While every state but Hawaii permits an indigent woman to have the fee waived, completing the necessary affidavit of indigency can be a discouraging bureaucratic burden. More important, nearly all of these states include the man's income in determining a petitioner's eligibility for a fee waiver. A battered woman whose husband controls the family finances is usually afraid to ask him for the money—if she did, she would probably suffer additional violence.

Because of these problems, statutes in at least 5 states prohibit a filing fee. An alternative remedy is to exclude the man's income in the fee waiver determination. Yet another would be to establish a simplified procedure for submitting an affidavit of indigency.

Emergency Protection

Many—perhaps most—victims of abuse are threatened or attacked during evenings and weekends when courts are ordinarily closed. For this reason, 23 states provide for emergency civil protection orders after court hours (although any court on its own authority may make after-hours emergency relief available).[9] Despite this authority, most jurisdictions have not established a system for victims to secure emergency relief.[10] Two jurisdictions that have are Philadelphia and Colorado Springs.

Philadelphia. Pennsylvania provides for emergency relief, but only from the close of business on Friday until Monday morning, by authorizing municipal court judges to accept petitions. A Philadelphia ordinance extends availability by providing for emergency relief from 5:00 p.m. to 9:00 a.m. on weekdays and empowers municipal court bail commissioners who hear after-hour arraignments to act on petitions for emergency relief in the name of the administrative judge of the city's Family Court Division. After-hours bail commissioners are located at police headquarters in downtown Philadelphia. The emergency order expires when court reopens, at which time the victim may seek a temporary protection order from the Court of Common Pleas.

Although several women per week obtain emergency orders this way, it is difficult for many victims—especially those with children—to find affordable transportation downtown at night and on weekends. In addition, victims must appear in court at the beginning of the next business day to continue the protection. The burdens of this process may prohibit some victims from obtaining protection when they need it most.

Colorado Springs. According to Colorado statute, "The chief judge in each judicial district shall be responsible for making available in each judicial district a judge to issue by telephone emergency protection orders at all times when the county and district courts are otherwise closed for judicial business."[11] This mandate has been implemented in Colorado Springs. Once a police officer who is on the scene has determined that an emergency protection order is called for, the officer telephones the on-call judge and explains the situation. If the judge issues the order, the officer fills out a blank copy of an order and serves it on the defendant. The officer tells the batterer to leave the premises and warns that if he returns he will be arrested and held overnight without bond. The officer then allows the man to collect some personal belongings and waits until he has left.

Emergency orders remain in effect until the close of judicial business on the next day the court is open. Allowing a battered woman a full court day to seek extended relief alleviates the gap in coverage caused by emergency orders that expire at the opening of the next judicial day. Another advantage of the Colorado system is that petitioners do not have to leave home to get emergency protection. However, it is important that emergency protection orders not be issued as an alternative to arrest in situations where arrest is the appropriate response.

Several Colorado Springs officers noted they are very selective in deciding which cases are serious enough to warrant the immediate attention of an on-call judge. For example, although the law makes the threat of abuse grounds for issuing an emergency order, some officers report they will not call a judge unless they believe there has been actual violence. Some officers are also concerned about their liability in physically issuing a court order even though authorization has come from a judge. Others seem unsure about their authority to "bother" a judge late at night. However, officers who have used the system report that judges rarely turn down their requests for emergency orders except in situations concerning divorced or legally separated partners (although there seems to be no statutory basis for such a rejection).

Legal Representation for the Victim

No matter how simple the petitioning procedure or how much lay assistance victims receive, women who have the help of an attorney are not only more likely to get a court order but also to get one that contains all desirable provisions related to eviction, child support, and limitations on visitation rights. A few statutes recognize the desirability for legal counsel. Nebraska's statute requires the Department of Public Welfare to provide "emergency legal counseling and referral." Wyoming's law provides that "The court may appoint an attorney to assist and advise the petitioner."

Legal representation for the victim is particularly crucial if issues related to child custody, visitation rights, division of property, and spouse or child support are raised. Decisions in these areas may not only affect the victim's present well-being, they may also set precedents for subsequent protection order hearings or other domestic relations proceedings. For example, without an attorney a victim might request less support than she is entitled to and the resulting award might influence a subsequent support award in a divorce proceeding. Even with its comprehensive victim advocacy system, Duluth provides attorneys to only about 10 percent of petitioners because of complex legal issues that arise in these cases. Similarly, shelter staff advocates in Portland, Maine call the local legal aid society to help petitioners when the case involves a gay couple, when the abuser is out of state (and the judge may question the reasons for the woman's fear of abuse), or when the parties are not currently living together but once had an intimate relationship.

An attorney for the petitioner is especially important when the respondent has counsel. Without her own counsel, the victim must counter the defense attorney's rebuttals by herself. In one case, a respondent's lawyer sought to have a protection order vacated on the grounds that the victim did not remember the correct date when her husband allegedly battered her. The victim's attorney was able to have the order continued by arguing that the victim had met the statutory burden of proof by demonstrating by a preponderance of the evidence that the battery had occurred—regardless of the exact date.

Most judges prefer to have attorneys present because the evidence is generally presented more appropriately and efficiently than when petitioners proceed pro se. Many judges say they prefer not to have to question petitioners personally to obtain enough information to decide whether to issue an order or decide what provisions to include. Judges are sometimes concerned that such questioning might appear to violate fair procedure or be interpreted as implying bias.

Some judges arrange for victims to be represented. While not required by law, almost every petitioner for a protection order in Philadelphia is represented by an attorney because the judge who handles hearings has made it court policy for victims to have legal counsel. Most victims use one of the city's 1,000 attorneys who serve on a pro bono basis or one of the small number of attorneys who work for local legal aid and women's groups. In Ithaca, New York the Assigned Counsel Office in Family Court finds an attorney for every indigent petitioner. These private attorneys are paid a reduced fee by the county. In Chicago and Springfield, Illinois most women who petition for an order are represented by a prosecutor. The cities provide free and expedited service in issuing an order if the victim files a criminal complaint when she petitions for a protection order. When a victim files criminal charges, a prosecutor petitions for the protection order while representing the state in the criminal case. In several states, law school deans send state supreme courts the names of students who wish to work for legal services organizations as part of a clinical program. Many of these students represent battered women in court.

Even with strenuous judicial and community efforts to provide attorneys for petitioners, many victims still have to rely on lay assistance. Few jurisdictions have allocated funds to provide legal counsel for all indigent petitioners and many communities cannot recruit enough attorneys willing to provide assistance without charge. Furthermore, many battered women who cannot afford a private attorney do not qualify for free legal services—especially when a financially dominant husbands' income is included in the determination of their indigency status. While in Nashville and some other jurisdictions the court can order a husband to pay a victim's legal fees, lawyers are understandably reluctant to take on such cases because they may have to sue husbands to get their fees.

Pro Se Petitioning

Some victim advocates believe that one of the advantages of civil protection orders should be that women can secure them on their own. Being able to proceed pro se is seen as a way of opening the courts to the poor. Many civil protection order statutes authorize and facilitate pro se petitions. For example, Massachusetts requires administrative justices to promulgate a form of complaint in a form and language that permits a plaintiff to prepare and file a complaint herself.

The majority of women in many jurisdictions do petition on their own. For example, during a three-month period in 1987, 49 of 61 petitioners in Nashville—80 percent—appeared at the hearing for a permanent order without an attorney. However, most victims who proceed pro se can get adequate protection only if there is competent and experienced lay assistance available to help them. Lay help usually comes from two sources: victim advocates and court clerks.

Victim advocates. Many jurisdictions make extensive use of victim advocates to assist women in filing for a protection order. Hawaii's statute expressly requires that "[T]he family court shall designate an employee or appropriate non-judicial agency to assist the person in completing the petition." In several jurisdictions, lay advocates provide assistance to victims that extends beyond helping them complete petition forms. In Duluth, for example, an advocate determines the victim's eligibility for an order under state statute and explains the protection order process; assists in filling out the forms; explains the legal help available to the victim, the relief she can ask for, and the limitations of an order; joins the petitioner in the initial hearing for a temporary order; helps prepare the victim for the hearing for the full order; and attends the hearing with the victim. Seattle's Domestic Violence Coordinator stationed in the clerk's office provides victims with a packet containing petitioning information, forms, and a list of resources as well as access to a videotape on the petitioning process developed by the state bar association. Even in Springfield and Chicago, Illinois, where prosecutors represent most petitioners, victim advocates "officed" in courtrooms perform an indispensable function in helping women prepare petitions because the state's attorneys do not have time to provide this service.

In many respects, this combination of legal representation and lay advocacy provides women with the maximum protection because victim advocates can often assist petitioners in ways that most attorneys cannot. Advocates may have a better understanding of battering issues and battered women, greater ability to communicate with victims, a greater tendency to take the violence seriously, and more knowledge of the law than attorneys who handle only one or two cases a year. For example, an advocate in Portland, Maine spent time explaining to a victim the importance of restricting visitation rights to reduce the potential for renewed violence.

At the same time, victim advocates have limitations too. Because they are not attorneys, they must be careful not to engage in the practice of the law. In many jurisdictions, judges will permit advocates to sit in on the hearings but not allow them to participate. Even where advocates can participate fully in the courtroom, their effectiveness, as noted, is often limited when the respondent has an attorney.

However, some judges report that advocates expedite court proceedings by screening petitioners for eligibility and making sure that they complete petition forms before hearings. Permitting or inviting advocates to accompany distraught or intimidated victims in the courtroom also results in fewer interruptions in the proceedings. By arranging to have witnesses appear with a victim, advocates allow a judge to hear corroborating evidence to support a petitioner's claims of abuse. When they successfully encourage reluctant petitioners to show up for permanent hearings, advocates reduce judges' frustration at seeing victims drop their cases.

Because of these advantages, judges in Duluth encourage advocates to speak for petitioners in court and generally do not find their lay status a significant handicap. Judges there also meet quarterly with the local victim advocacy group to address mutual problems and preview changes in court procedures. The judges have provided training for advocates too.

Court clerks. When victim advocates or attorneys are not available, assistance from court clerks is a last resort. In recognition of this, several states require clerks to assist petitioners. In some jurisdictions, clerks play an extremely valuable role. They provide explicit instructions about the level of detail petitioners must use in describing the abuse in their petitions and make sure victims request all the protections to which they may be entitled. However, clerks in many other places are very cautious about providing help. In part, this hesitation reflects a lack of time to undertake this new responsibility. But clerks are also concerned that they will be accused of an unauthorized practice of the law. While some clerks overreact to this and provide much less help than they are legally allowed to furnish, there are often good reasons for concern. Nevada's statute expressly warns that "the clerk shall not render any advice or service that requires the professional judgment of an attorney." A sign in the clerk's office in Springfield informs petitioners that "By Law, Employees Are Not Permitted to Give Legal Advice." Clerks in Nashville provide virtually no help because they have been warned that they could be sued. The defense bar has registered complaints about clerk assistance in Chicago and Portland, Oregon.

It is difficult to generalize about what clerks may and may not do because the law varies from one jurisdiction to another. In addition, regardless of the law, clerks sometimes exercise substantial unsupervised influence in screening petitioners for eligibility and encouraging or discouraging them from seeking orders. In one jurisdiction, clerks mistakenly told each would-be petitioner that she was not eligible for an order if she had not lived with the batterer within the past year—when the state's statute had been amended to permit orders when the parties had lived together any time during the previous two years. Some clerks may act out prejudices against victims of abuse too. For example, some clerks discourage women who return several times for an order. And others may act as unauthorized victim advocates; one clerk, for example, tries to persuade women who want to have their orders vacated to have them modified instead.

Courts can significantly improve the assistance that clerks give petitioners by ensuring that clerks have written instructions for assessing petitioner eligibility for an order under state statute and firm instructions that they are not to assess a petitioner's credibility, advise her what course of action to follow, or give legal advice. The goal is to limit the role of clerks to screening for eligibility and providing assistance in filling out petitions in a helpful, thorough, welcoming manner, as permitted under law. To ensure proper case handling by clerks, Milwaukee and San Francisco hold training seminars for them. In Seattle, the Supervisor of the Family Court brings two or three clerks together periodically to discuss how to handle unusual cases.

Repeat Petitioners

Occasionally, victims return several times to petition for an order, either after failing to appear at a hearing or after withdrawing previous petitions. Some judges express concern that these repeat petitioners may be abusing the system to evict their abusers temporarily without any real intention of ending the abuse. As a result, if the need for an ex parte order does not appear compelling, judges may schedule the parties for a hearing on a full order without issuing a temporary order.

While some judges are unsympathetic to repeat petitioners, there are often good reasons for a victim's return. Sometimes a woman withdraws an earlier petition because she is convinced her partner will reform or because he promises to enter counseling. Recognizing this, a judge in Philadelphia granted a woman's request to vacate her permanent order because her alcoholic husband was improving with treatment, but the judge reminded the victim that "[Y]ou can always come back if you need to—the door is open to you. Do you understand that?" In addition, another judge observed that just as most cigarette smokers try to quit many times before they finally succeed, many abused women may make several false starts to try to stop the battering before they are emotionally and economically able to succeed.

Advocates report that some victims are physically unable to attend hearings for a permanent order, are confused about having to attend a second hearing, or have been intimidated by threats of more violence from batterers if they persist in court action.

Perhaps the wisest course of action is to grant an emergency order if it appears warranted on its face and to address the issue of repeat petitioning at the hearing on the permanent order by attempting to determine the exact nature of the problem and how to best protect the victim. The Colorado statute reflects this approach by requiring that "[I]f three emergency protection orders are issued within a one-year period involving the same parties..., the court shall summon the parties to appear before the court at a hearing to review the circumstances giving rise to such emergency protection orders."

ADVANTAGES AND LIMITATIONS OF PROTECTION ORDERS

Properly issued and enforced, protection orders can be useful. Improperly issued and poorly enforced, they can expose battered women to greater risk by giving them the illusion of being protected. The principal benefits and limitations of civil protection orders are reviewed below.

Advantages

Victims, victim advocates, and judges report that proceeding civilly may have a number of advantages for victims. First, civil protection orders generally enjoin borderline criminal behavior such as harassment and intimidation which state criminal codes may not define as "arrestable" offenses. These orders also provide the only remedy in misdemeanor abuse incidents where insufficient evidence exists for charging or conviction (e.g., threats, shoving).

In addition, most women are interested in stopping the battering, not punishing their partners. And because of a fear of retaliation, many women do not want their partners arrested. If the men are given a criminal record or jailed, they might lose their jobs and their children might turn against their mothers for "throwing dad in jail." This may explain why so many women in some jurisdictions seem to prefer to seek civil protection orders to prevent being battered than to file criminal complaints. Tucson issues about 1,000 orders a year, Milwaukee 3,000, and Portland, Oregon, over 4,000. Chicago issued 9,000 orders and extensions of orders in 1987.

By enjoining any contact and evicting batterers from the home, civil protection orders can address some unique circumstances. The specific dynamics of abuse create havoc with the criminal justice system because, unlike most other types of violent crime, the offender is motivated to retaliate against a specific victim. And as a cohabitant of the victim, he has a unique opportunity to continue to abuse her and to play on her sympathy ("It won't ever happen again! What would the kids do without me?"). Evicting batterers can have tremendous shock value by forcing them to realize that their partners will no longer tolerate being abused. Evicting batterers and providing for child support and structured visitation also give victims a breathing spell in which to gather some resources and decide what to do next. Finally, some police officers report they are more likely to arrest men who violate an order than other batterers.

The remedies provided by protection order legislation are separate from and not replicated by existing divorce and separation procedures. Returning to court to petition for an order may be the only recourse for many victims whose abusers violate their conditions of divorce. The immediate enforcement available with a protection order is crucial because, absent effective protection, the danger of abuse may increase rather than decrease directly after separation. Thus, a strong civil protection order system is necessary as an alternative and supplement to both criminal prosecution and divorce proceedings.

Limitations

All observers agree that—at least until they are violated—civil protection orders are useless with the "hard core" batterer for whom nothing short of incapacitation with a jail sentence would be effective. Any abuser who is determined to batter—or kill—his partner will not be deterred by a piece of paper.

Some observers also think that bringing the less determined batterer into criminal court with its stern, coercive atmosphere has a more chilling effect on his behavior than an appearance in civil court. Civil protection orders are sometimes seen as a "soft" response to criminal behavior and as sending a message that abuse is less serious than nonstranger violence. However, these critics also point out that the sanctions for violating an order can be as severe as the punishment imposed for assault and battery—and in most cases they are applied more quickly with a protection order violation. This observation leads directly to the most serious deficiency of protection orders: widespread lack of effective enforcement by both the police and the courts.

Law enforcement. Police officers and deputy sheriffs can stymie the effectiveness of a protection order at three different points. First, many victims who are unfamiliar with legal remedies will never even learn that protection orders are available unless police officers responding to an abuse complaint tell them. In recognition of this dependence on the police for information, 15 states require law enforcement officers to tell victims about available legal remedies. This obligation may be incorporated into a police department's general orders. For example, a Philadelphia Police Department directive requires officers to explain to victims the civil protection order option and the procedure for obtaining an emergency order after normal court hours. Police departments in some jurisdictions give officers information sheets or cards about protection orders to distribute to victims.

Many victims do learn about protection orders from police officers. Ninety percent of the women who petition the Philadelphia Family Court for protection orders say they have been referred by the police. However, reports from victims and victim advocates suggest that most officers do not provide this information.

In most jurisdictions, law enforcement officers are also responsible for serving protection orders. Because an order is not enforceable until it has been served—and the intervening time can create serious danger of renewed or even increased violence—quick service is critical. As a result, a number of statutes have expedited service requirements. However, while some sheriff's deputies report that service is given top priority, many battered women's advocates and victims complain of having to make repeat requests for service over many days, each time with detailed information on the whereabouts of batterers, in order to prod the serving of protection orders.

The most serious enforcement deficiency is the widespread failure to arrest batterers once a protection order has been issued, even when there are clear signs of physical abuse or other violations of the order. There appear to be several explanations for this. Two common ones given by police are the belief that arrest is too drastic a recourse for what officers may perceive as a "trivial" offense and the belief that arrest is a waste of time because victims will later ask that the charges be dropped. Some officers in some situations do not believe a victim's story or think she is to blame if she appears to have invited or permitted the batterer to take up residence with her again after having been evicted. In other cases, the victim herself does not want the batterer arrested. If the batterer has fled, few officers—even with a felony-level battery—will take the time to find him. In some states, police do not have the legal authority to arrest for a protection order violation not committed in their presence.

However, statutes and case law in most states support a strong arrest policy. Twenty-four states provide for warrantless arrest for a violation of a civil protection order—including intimidating behavior like standing in the hallway outside a victim's apartment or approaching her at her workplace—that would not otherwise be an arrestable offense. Thirteen states require arrest for violating an order. In some of these jurisdictions, batterers have learned to claim that the woman was assaulting them, so that the police think the law requires them to arrest both parties. This discourages victims from calling the police because they fear they will be arrested along with the batterer. This problem has been solved in Duluth through special training for police to explain that arrest without a warrant must be based on probable cause and that in almost every instance there is no probable cause to conclude that the woman was assaulting the man.

A number of court decisions confirm the legal authorization of police to arrest batterers who violate protection orders. In a widely publicized case, a Connecticut appeals court ruled that the nonperformance or malperformance of official duties by a municipality and its police officers denied a victim of abuse equal protection of the law.[12] The court ruled that police may not treat abuse less seriously than other types of battery simply because of the relationship between the persons involved. A municipality and its law enforcement officers may no more refrain from interfering in abuse than in any other kind of violence. The court upheld a $2 million damage award to the victim. Several courts have also ruled that law enforcement officers have a duty specifically to enforce civil protection orders.[13]

There are a number of ways to improve the enforcement of civil protection orders. Judges can help ensure prompt service by making sure sheriffs know they consider this responsibility a top priority. When service is delayed, some judges make clear to petitioners that a protection order is not enforceable until it has been served to avoid giving the victim a false sense of protection.

When delays in service occur in some jurisdictions, police officers can handle situations that constitute violations of outstanding protection orders that have not yet been served. State statutes or local practice may establish proper police procedures in such cases. In Springfield, Illinois, officers at the scene have been instructed to detain the offender until a sheriff's deputy can arrive to serve the order.

In cases where officers cannot accomplish personal service, alternatives include public posting, sending the order by certified mail, or permitting personal service by other parties. For example, the Minnesota Domestic Abuse Act permits service by publication of the full notice in a qualified newspaper when other attempts at service have failed. The District of Columbia permits service by leaving copies of the order at the offender's home or usual place of abode "...with a person of suitable age and discretion then residing therein who is not a party."

One key to effective police enforcement of civil protection orders is a formal and closely monitored court policy regarding expected police handling of abuse calls. However, police training is equally essential to inform officers of their responsibilities. Lisa Lerman recommends specific training topics and specific numbers of training hours for recruits and veteran officers. She emphasizes that training should focus on law enforcement rather than on communication skills or crisis intervention, thus reversing " ...the notion that the primary task in responding to an abuse call is to mediate rather than to protect the victim from abuse."[14]

Most police training explains that abuse is not a problem of neighborhood annoyance, mutual combat, or verbal abuse, but a problem of persistent intimidation that typically involves or escalates into severe, even fatal, physical injury as well as emotional damage. Training also tries to help officers understand the control, intimidation, and economic and societal issues that lock women into abusive relationships. How this sort of information is received depends on the attitudes individual officers already have about abuse and male-female relationships. As a result, police trainers who consider exposure to the kinds of important issues just mentioned often focus primarily on changing police *behavior* and hope that attitudes will change over time.

One goal of police training is to impart knowledge about civil protection orders so officers can explain the legal options available to victims. A more difficult goal of training, however, is to make sure police officers enforce protection orders. Training can help accomplish this objective by explaining statutory requirements regarding enforcement and police liability for failure to enforce.

Police training can also emphasize that civil protection orders can help officers handle abuse cases. For example, officers have reported that being able to offer a victim information about civil protection orders reduced their frustration over not being able to do anything to help in situations where a victim was unwilling to file criminal charges against her batterer. Some officers express concern when they are required to arrest a batterer who has not further abused his partner but who has violated the order by appearing in the home. Trainers can make clear to these officers that this type of violation merits arrest because it represents clear contempt for the criminal justice system. Furthermore, even though there has been no physical violence, the mere presence of the man in the home may be terrifying to the victim and, indeed, may be intended to intimidate her. In addition, the man's presence creates a tremendous opportunity for him to resume his abuse at any time. One purpose of evicting him is precisely to remove this opportunity.

Other officers prefer a mandatory arrest requirement because it clarifies the appropriate police response when probable cause is met and reduces the "gray area" they say they often encounter in responding to many abuse calls. Statutory language on police behavior in specific situations can be enhanced by police department general orders which further clarify possible areas of confusion arising under statute. For example, the Duluth Police Department general order on abuse specifically defines probable cause and, on a related issue of concern to officers, emphasizes that "...state law requires an arrest regardless of whether or not the offender was invited back into the home...."

Finally, many police report that one of their reasons for not arresting violators is that prosecutors and judges do not seem to take these cases seriously and follow up arrests with swift and meaningful sanctions. Clearly, if law enforcement is to do its part, the courts must be equally conscientious in performing their responsibilities.

Courts. Unfortunately, many courts are not making a serious effort to use protection orders effectively. There are a number of steps judges can take to reverse this situation. One concerns admonishing defendants. Lectures from the bench can be eye-opening to some batterers. The Attorney General's Task Force on Family Violence urges judges "not to underestimate their ability to influence the defendant's behavior" and notes "a stern admonition from the bench can help deter the defendant from future violence."[15] A study of nonstranger violence sponsored by the National Institute of Justice found that "...judicial warnings and/or lectures to defendants concerning the inappropriateness and seriousness of their violent behavior apparently improved the future conduct of some defendants."[16] Thus, a judge in Portland, Maine makes a practice of informing respondents that while the order is for the protection of the victim, it is an order of the court and is taken very seriously by the court.

Admonishments can also benefit victims when they instruct victims that they do not have to tolerate assaultive behavior. Some judges direct victims to report any violations to the police and other appropriate agencies. Some judges also warn victims that they may find the police uncooperative if they experience more violence after inviting abusers back without first having their orders modified. Making such a warning meaningful requires a simplified modification procedure like Duluth's. Many women there seek modifications because the court has set up a procedure that is free, quick, and encouraged by judges and advocates alike.

In addition, judges can monitor compliance to improve the effectiveness of protection orders. In most jurisdictions, this is now left to victims. However, if judges did it they would send a message that violating an order is a criminal offense. For this reason, judges in Duluth have an arrangement with the Domestic Abuse Intervention Project to monitor respondents in three ways. Project staff review police records each day and inform the court if an incident involving a protection order violation has occurred. Project staff also contact victims once a month to inquire about renewed violence and check offender attendance at counseling sessions. Project staff request a court hearing if they find a violation. If the offender is found in contempt of court, he is usually sentenced to jail; however, for a first violation, he is given the option of completing the program while serving a probated sentence. Judges also inform victims that they should contact the Intervention Project if defendants violate their orders.

Judges can advocate the arrest of violators too. As noted, police often fail to make an arrest even when there are clear signs of physical abuse or other violations of a protection order. Therefore, it is critical for judges to inform law enforcement agencies that they must arrest batterers who violate protection orders and that statutes and case law in most states support this response. To show that they mean business, judges must impose meaningful penalties for violations.

Some judges order jail time for even first-time protection order violators if the severity of the abuse warrants incarceration, such as forced entry or any type of physical abuse or threats. These judges view a jail sentence as a necessary step to protect victims from further abuse. They also know that while this may be the first time the offender has violated the protection order, it is at least the second time he has committed assault and battery against the victim. These judges believe it is important to impose a jail sentence because an order of the court has been ignored.

Most state statutes limit the length of a jail sentence to six months or one year (See Figure 8.1). California mandates a minimum sentence of 48 hours if a violation involves an injury. Ohio authorizes a severe sanction for multiple offenders by making a conviction on a third violation a felony of the fourth degree.

Especially in jurisdictions where jail crowding is a problem, judges must make sentencing determinations with several concerns in mind. Some judges think it is more important to jail violent offenders like batterers than nonviolent offenders like prostitutes and public drunks. Some judges have also experimented with alternative sanctions. In Philadelphia, the judge has used intensive probation supervision and gives offenders a choice between regular attendance at counseling or a jail sentence. In Portland, Maine and Springfield, Illinois some cases are plea bargained down to probation and a 6- or 12-month suspended jail sentence; if no further violation occurs during this time, the offender is dismissed with no criminal record.

Several judges try to protect victims between the time a violation occurs and the offender's hearing in court. For example, batterers arrested for order violations in Portland, Oregon are not released on their own recognizance and bail is usually set at $5,000. In Denver, abuse has been taken off the bond schedule and suspects must stay in jail from a few hours to three days until the next court business day. In Duluth, violators are usually held overnight; this lets shelter advocates contact and help victims. Minnesota allows jailers to hold an assailant arrested under the probable cause arrest statute for 36 hours if a jailer believes an assailant is likely to be a danger to a victim.

As with police, training may be an indispensable component of any effort to improve the judicial use and enforcement of protection orders. While some judges are comfortable implementing civil protection order statutes, many have questions about their statutory authority or how they should handle certain cases. Some judges, while familiar with the powers granted them by statute, are uneasy exercising their full authority.

As a result, most judges would benefit from training on the use and enforcement of civil protection orders. Judges themselves suggest that training should include a thorough analysis of the law determining conditions of eligibility, relief that can be granted in a protection order, and standards of evidence to be applied in issuing orders and holding violation hearings. Training should also concern the proper handling of civil protection order petitions. Hearings should not be considered an extension of divorce court, in which a negotiated settlement of a private problem is called for, or a "normal" family court problem in which keeping families together is the judge's principal objective. Because it involves criminal behavior, abuse should be treated as a public problem requiring unilateral intervention by the state on behalf of the battered woman. Mediation is a disservice to victims that leaves them vulnerable to more criminal violence.

In addition, judicial training should explain how civil protection orders, by evicting batterers and giving police increased authorization to arrest them, contribute to maintaining law and order. This would involve an explanation of the dynamics of battering and the psychosocial and institutional factors that sustain it. Other important topics are why it is often difficult for women to leave their abusers; why victims sometimes return to abusive relationships; why victims may return to court repeatedly for new protection orders; victims' risks of being assaulted again; batterers' easy access to their victims; and how judges can use their authority in the courtroom to intervene effectively.

Judicial training opportunities vary across jurisdictions. In Portland, Oregon the chief administrative judge has arranged for both a Legal Services attorney and a private attorney experienced in dealing with battered women to provide 3 to 4 hours of training for judges. The chief administrative judge in Baltimore requires all new judges to attend a half-day orientation on abuse at a local shelter. Other judges receive training at state judicial conferences.

CONCLUSION

Enforcement is the Achilles' heel of the civil protection order process because an order without enforcement at best offers scant protection and at worst decreases the victim's safety. Batterers may routinely violate orders if they believe there is no real risk of being arrested. Enforcement can break down if the courts do not monitor compliance, if victims do not report violations, and, most of all, if police, prosecutors, and judges do not respond sternly to violations that are reported. There is considerable anecdotal evidence that batterers routinely flout civil protection orders—and scorn the authority of the court—with impunity. It will take a concerted and coordinated effort in every community to develop and implement a consistent enforcement policy in which each component of the justice system supports the others.

Of course, judges and police officers cannot fully improve the use and enforcement of protection orders by themselves. The judiciary and law enforcement need cooperation from each other—and from the social service system and advocacy group representatives. Civil protection orders, as part of the solution to domestic abuse, cannot be used and enforced fully by any one of these groups without cooperation from the others. For example, law enforcement officers are reluctant to file reports or make arrests if they do not believe the prosecutor will follow through or the judge will impose appropriate sanctions. Judges, in turn, are unlikely to mandate batterer counseling for the respondent unless the community provides quality services in this area.

Duluth is a case in point. Its Domestic Abuse Intervention Project, a local non-profit community-based organization, strives to make the community responsible for imposing sanctions on batterers by working with both the justice system and the social service system to send a consistent message that abuse is a crime that will not be tolerated. The project also provides counseling groups for batterers, support groups for victims, and training for judges and police. Since its inception, it has worked with the court system to establish, implement, and monitor court standards and procedures for handling abuse cases.

The Community Response Program in Portland, Maine has used Duluth as a model. It is following a three-year plan. The first year, which has been completed, focused on improving law enforcement responses by developing effective procedures and providing officer training. The goal of the second year was the establishment of counseling programs for batterers and improved coordination of social service agencies (including religious and charitable organizations). The focus of the third year is to develop a better system of communication and coordination between social service and community organizations, on the one hand, and judges and prosecutors on the other. The future of civil protection orders as an effective response to abuse rests largely on the ability of individual communities to implement this kind of collaborative arrangement.

NOTES

1 Stark, E., A. Flitcraft, D. Zuckerman, A. Grey, J. Robuson & W. Frazier (1984). *Wife Abuse in the Medical Setting*. Washington, DC: Office of Domestic Violence, U.S. Department of Health and Human Services, cited in L. Lerman, "A Model

State Act: Remedies for Domestic Abuse." *Harvard Journal on Legislation*, 2(1):74, n. 52.

State ex rel. Williams v. Marsh, 626 S.W.2d 223 (Mo. 1982).

Fitzgerald v. Fitzgerald, 406 N.W.2d 52 (Minn. Ct. App. 1987).

Mathews v. Eldridge, 424 U.S. 319 (1976).

Fuentes v. Shevin, 407 U.S. 67 (1972).

Mitchell v. W.T. Grant Co., 416 U.S. 600 (1974); *Boyle v. Boyle*, 12 Pa. D. & D.3d 676 (1979).

Boyle v. Boyle, 12 Pa. D. & C.3d 676 (1979).

State ex rel. Williams v. Marsh, 626 S.W.2d 223 (Mo. 1982).

In Ohio and possibly other states, criminal protection orders are available on evenings and weekends—but only if a charge has been filed and is pending.

When arrest is possible, a policy that keeps the batterer locked up overnight has been suggested as an alternative to calling judges in the middle of the night. Having secured immediate protection, the victim can petition for a protection order the next day for long-term relief.

Since July 1, 1988, police in California have been authorized under the revised Code of Civil Procedure [546(b)] to telephone a judge evenings and weekends for an emergency protection order. The officer has the victim fill out an application and reads it to the judge. The order may include evicting the batterer from the residence.

Thurman v. City of Torrington, 595 F. Supp. 1521 (D. Conn. 1984).

Baker v. City of New York, 25 A.D.2d 770, 269 N.Y.S.2d 515 (1966); *Nearing v. Weaver*, 295 Or. 702, 670 P.2d 137 (1983); *Kubitscheck v. Winnett et al.*, No. 8587, slip op. at ___ (Or. Feb. 10, 1980); *Soto v. County of Sacramento*, No. 332313, slip op. at ___ (Cal. Sup. Ct., 1986).

Lerman, L. (1984). "Remedies for Domestic Abuse." *Harvard Journal on Legislation*, 2(1):87.

Attorney General's Task Force on Family Violence, Final Report. Washington, DC: U.S. Department of Justice, 1984, p. 36.

Smith, B.E. (1983). *Non-Stranger Violence: The Criminal Court's Response*. Washington, DC: National Institute of Justice, p. 96.

9

Responding to Domestic Violence

Anthony Bouza
formerly of the Minneapolis Police Department

INTRODUCTION

A man comes home in a drunken, jealous rage and batters his wife with a cast iron frying pan. In the next room their eight-year-old son tries to escape in the blaring nonsense of the television set. Three women are stalked, run down, and slaughtered in suburban Suffolk County, New York. Outrage swells over officialdom's sluggishness in dealing with the warnings along the way. The women had repeatedly sought help but reluctant police officials had declined to interfere in "domestic squabbles." In Torrington, Connecticut another woman, fleeing from a murderously assaultive husband, pleads for police protection and does not get it. She is finally tracked down and violently assaulted.

This is the reality behind the sterile abstraction known as woman battering. It begins with angry words, then maybe a shove or a slap. If it is not treated at this crucial juncture, it escalates, frequently culminating in murder. Alcohol or drugs usually accompany the tragedy. Both the batterers and the battered are often themselves victims of child abuse or witnesses of family violence. It is a cyclical family problem. Sometimes it is connected to a mental disorder and sometimes it flows from the paranoic disorders associated with drug abuse.

While some men have argued to the contrary, the reality of battering in America is men beating up women. The occasional exception is remarkable enough to constitute the exception that proves the rule. Too much energy has been spent on the smoke screen that this is not a gender-specific crime. It is.

The family has always been a sort of sacred enclave. We have historically been reluctant to invade it. It is the essential core of societal organization; yet it can encompass child abuse, incest, violence against parents, murder, and the epidemic of child-thefts we seem determined to believe are occasioned by strangers. As we kick over the rock we are beginning to discover that the family can be a place of pure terror as well as the center of caring and nurturing.

How often have teachers, doctors, family, friends, welfare and social workers, or cops ignored the telltale signs of abuse? How often have emergency rooms patched up and ignored injuries that should have raised an alarm that a crime may have been committed? The tales of victims are frequently dotted with references to such official interventions as police responses to the home, medical treatment in hospital emergency rooms, complaints to a teacher, or the observations of a social worker. Yet most cases of abuse seem to elude these people.

BATTERING

Battering encompasses a wide range of behaviors. Almost 2 million women are battered each year and some form of violence occurs in one-fourth of all marriages. About 1 out of every 5 women seeking emergency medical aid are victims of abuse. More than 2 million children were reported abused in 1986 and more than 100 children a month die through abuse or neglect. Parents who were abused as children are 6 times more likely to abuse than those who have not been abused, and at least 4 out of 10 of all abuse cases involve alcohol or drugs.

The police, as the first responders to many abuse situations, are centrally important. Yet they, like others, have been very slow until recently to take action to protect women and children. Under pressure from the feminist movement and abetted by such whopping lawsuits as the one that almost broke Torrington, the police finally bestirred themselves to reluctant action.

Why this reluctance? One reason is that police chiefs have a lot of claims on their energies. They often scurry from squeaking wheel to squeaking wheel. That abuse and family violence claim their attention now suggests that other urgent concerns are being neglected too.

Another explanation for police inaction is that they do not understand the internal dynamics in abusive relationships that frequently involve escalating levels of violence. Their ignorance about abuse is reinforced by the psychological ploys employed by batterers that hold victims responsible for their own abuse: "She asked for it." The victim may even come to accept the blame. Her resistance is overborne, her self-esteem is shattered, and she gradually becomes a captive, physically and psychologically. She may even come to believe that she deserved her abuse or that abuse is normal.

One of the most celebrated cases in recent history, Joel Steinberg's abuse of Hedda Nussbaum and his murder of their "adopted" daughter Lisa, illustrates the complexity of the physical and psychological dynamics at work. This case is a textbook example of what is often concealed under the rubric of "family." Steinberg's Svengali-like control was so powerful that Nussbaum was unable to break it and reach out for help even when she was taken to a hospital after a beating and had to have her spleen removed or when she lay paralyzed, watching her "daughter" die. Steinberg's paranoic obsession over being stared at and his vicious abuse of his wife and children for doing it also demonstrate the strong effects of cocaine.

Once brought to her senses through the awful tragedy of the child's death, Nussbaum managed to see the depths to which she had been taken, through drugs and conditioning, into the sickest relationship imaginable. Her descent was inexorable as well as gradual, involving instinctively applied psychological rewards and punishments that ultimately gave her lover guru-like power over her. Isolation was a key element in her domination.

Yet evidence of this developing situation was available to others. Teachers should have noted Lisa's telltale marks and behavior. Nussbaum was treated by doctors for beating injuries. Family members were exposed to signs of abuse, neighbors must have heard things, and cops might have been called to prior incidents.

This case helps to show that battering and child abuse occur at all levels of society including highly educated, upper-middle-class whites. Every study of battering discloses its incidence in higher as well as lower social strata. Thus practitioners in the field were not shocked by disclosures that a high-ranking official at the Securities and Exchange Commission was a wife beater.

The central lesson here is the critical need to interrupt the cycles of battering and child abuse. This may be the one area of police work where homicide prevention could become a reality.

ADOPTING AN APPROACH

The adoption of a workable approach to treating battering requires the following:

(1) Usually a peace officer can only make an arrest for a misdemeanor without a warrant if it is committed in his presence. Since most domestic abuse (punches, slaps, non-permanent in-

juries, etc.) involves misdemeanors, the cops' hands have been tied. States are now passing laws enabling the police to make an arrest for a misdemeanor assault that did not occur in their presence. Usually it must have occurred during the preceding four hours. This definition has been expanded to include threats with dangerous weapons or placing the person "in fear of immediate bodily harm... ."

(2) Having legislation in place enables the adoption of policies that mandate arrest if there is evidence that the crime of abuse took place and if there is probable cause to believe in the guilt of the accused. Arrests are expected when there are visible signs of injury; if a dangerous weapon is involved; if officers believe the violence will continue; if officers have prior knowledge of an offender's predilection for violence; if there has been a violation of a protection order; or to protect anyone from further acts of violence. Even threats or a victim's warranted fear should result in an offender's arrest.

(3) The definition of a victim must include not only spouses but anyone with whom the batterer resides or has resided. Victims can share the offender's gender as well as be present or former lovers or roommates. Defining relationships narrowly may exclude a significant population of sufferers.

Policies must state clearly and in writing that battering is a crime and must be treated as such. They also must refer to other services that victims may need including shelters, counseling agencies, and advocates. The policies must be supported by comprehensive training programs for police too.

The police role, as part of a coordinated, systemic response, has to be described so that officers understand what is needed and how their actions relate to what others do. There must also be audits of dispatches to abuse calls to verify compliance with policies.

The problem of abuse is most frequently encountered first by responding cops. They must be especially sensitive to the importance of quick, effective action. If they fail, tragedy results. The adoption of a written policy helps ensure a uniform response consistent with a department's philosophy. There was a time when bureaucracies eschewed putting too much down in writing because of a fear of lawsuits and external criticism. Things are different now and failure to have written policies almost automatically renders an agency vulnerable to the charge that it is indifferent to pressing problems.

Police chiefs are discovering, as one did in Torrington, Connecticut, the difference between an insurer's and a steward's responsibilities. They have always known that it is unreasonable to expect any police executive to anticipate or prevent a particular crime and that they cannot be held liable for it; now they are learning that they are expected to act like good stewards in cases where they should have known and could have acted because of repeated prior incidents that pointed to continuing breaches.

Thus, the victim of a robbery would probably lose if he sued a chief for failure to prevent it. The frequent victim of batterings who reported them to the police and who demanded action without getting it will have a case when the next assault takes place. An insurer assumes responsibility for every single event and is required to restore the situation. A steward manages the enterprise and is guided by what he should have known, when he should have known it, what he should have done about it.

WHY ARREST?

Arresting an offender is a societal statement that his behavior is a crime, that it must stop, that punishment will follow, and that it is sensible to secure treatment to avoid repeating the behavior.

Many acts that produce long-term benefits produce short-term anguish. The assaulted woman can readily see many immediate problems. The long-term possibility of a safe, tranquil, "normal" life is often dimly perceived if at all. She can see that calling the police means that her abuser may lose his job, go to jail, get angrier and more dangerous, or cease to care for her or love her. Her mind is a confused mix of emotions and fears. As a result, she often finds it difficult to insist on an arrest. The process is not without risk. Many women risk or encounter poverty when they leave their abusers.

The cop, still reluctant to interfere, is not much help. The early introduction of a strong advocate holds the best hope for getting a victim to follow through with the prosecution that brings the full weight of government behind the effort to stop the battering. Someone who has been in her situation before can offer credible advice. The existence of a refuge—a women's shelter—is essential. The victim has to have somewhere to go immediately and frequently has children who must be safeguarded and sheltered. The shelters are a stopgap haven, serving for the days or few weeks it takes the woman to find more suitable and permanent quarters. Yet this brief respite is crucial, both for the protection it offers and for the advice and emotional support extended by those working or staying there.

The threat of jail coerces some batterers into treatment, frequently of the sort offered by Alcoholics Anonymous (AA). Recent court decisions have, however, called this approach into question because of the strong religious component of AA.

It is amazing how many batterers testify that they never thought of themselves as abusers. Over and over one hears the refrain "I never considered myself a wife beater. Sure we fought, but everybody has their little tiffs." No one ever stopped them. The system never seemed to say, unequivocally, "this is wrong and it must stop." That is the prime function of an arrest policy.

The police culture, still largely male and white, has traditionally been uncomfortable with the notion of intruding into the family. "A man's home is his castle." "Don't come between a man and his woman." "She probably had it coming." "They'll kiss and make up by morning, and then I'll be the villain." "She's not going to sign the complaint in court." These are the attitudes that have helped shape policy. In order to reshape behavior the attitudes of both the police and the victim must be changed.

In order to establish a workable policy regarding battering, the Minneapolis Police Department participated in an experiment in 1981 and 1982. Responding cops either mediated disputes, excluded the male from the home for at least 8 hours, or arrested him. The cops were given no choices. Their actions were dictated by an instruction booklet that assigned responses randomly. As most readers of this already know, the follow-up study revealed that arrest held the best hope for reducing violence for the six-month period after the interventions.

Was this playing with people's lives? Was it sensible police procedure to eliminate officer discretion? Was it even legal? The press can have a good time with such questions. Few chiefs are willing to take this kind of heat. This goes a long way toward explaining why most police departments are loath to undertake something as universally admired as scientific experimentation. Even though it holds the promise of revealing new and better ways of doing things, the risks involved look pretty daunting.

Doing things by the seat of the pants or doing nothing at all are responses too. Police departments have been following time-honored, but not tested or verified, approaches. Neglect is a form of treatment too. Its consequences are being paid for in a series of lawsuits alleging police inaction.

The police cannot, of course, break the law so the question of the legality of the experiment had to be resolved. Like everyone else in the justice system, the police are allowed enormous latitude. To resolve the question of legality, I arrogated this latitude to my own use and mostly deprived my charges of the right to employ it. This is not a popular act among the rank and file. In the main, however, the cops followed instructions faithfully.

GETTING THE COPS TO ARREST ABUSERS

Cops may fail to record a battering incident, listing it in their logs as a "dispute, gone on arrival" or "unfounded" or anything else that gets them out of recording a crime on an official form. It is just more paperwork about something they do not take very seriously.

Merely exhorting cops to follow written policies will not be enough; nor will perfunctory training sessions work. Police administrators need to put teeth into both compliance and educational programs. Officers have to be disciplined for failures to respond; training programs must be serious and deviations from the practices taught have to be punished.

What is needed and works is a system of verification that plainly advises cops that they risk being discovered if they fail to comply. Randomly checking dispatches to abuse locations offers the best hope for correcting a compliance problem. A woman or neighbor calling 911 and alleging a domestic incident should have the call dispatched in just that manner. Then calls can be checked and investigators can be assigned. "Was there an incident here the other night? What happened? Did the police respond? What did they do?" Responses can be matched with the reports the cops submitted or failed to submit and follow-up action can be taken. Cops respond energetically to such proddings and tasks can be assigned to existing personnel.

There is often a struggle between the cops on the street and their chief for power. The cops want maximum latitude to handle calls their own way. Each case is different and cops guard their discretionary power jealously.

Discretion does not need to be eliminated but it must be limited and channeled. This is a push-pull struggle between the chief and the troops that is ultimately resolved through the imposition of disciplinary measures. In the world of the police, where the greatest power is centered on the lowest rank level, the only practicable method of control is to convince cops that they will be disciplined for failing to conform to policies. If cops do not fear a chief then they will handle calls according to their prejudices, convenience, or personal perspective. Curiously, not many actions against cops have to be taken. A few cops being brought up on charges is usually more than enough to capture everyone's attention.

Abuse calls pose dangers for responding police because of the violence and drugs usually involved in these highly unpredictable situations. Responding cops are thrust into scenes of escalating violence, frequently involving heavy drinking and mindless, reflexive actions sometimes with weapons. Interrupting these events, early in the violence cycle before they escalate, holds the best hope for everyone's safety. Although cops know all of this, their affection for their discretionary power is so great that many would rather risk the dangers than be restricted.

One way to protect cops responding to abuse calls is to keep chronic trouble spots in a "dangerous location" file. Cops can be informed of the dangers and nature of the previous problems at each site before they respond to new incidents at them.

Following the adoption of what we all felt was a workable and enlightened policy of requiring arrests in abuse cases, prosecutions soared. Other departments quickly adopted our methods and approach. However, reality intruded months later when an audit revealed that many of the cases the cops were responding to had not even been recorded. Disciplinary action followed swiftly and was itself followed by more general compliance with requirements. This illustrates the importance of verification and the folly of accepting anything on face value in a police bureaucracy.

Training is needed too. There is hardly a study that does not stress the necessity of further training. Yet, in abuse cases, training is not only needed to teach cops how to deal with cases but, perhaps even more important, to change their attitudes. Training is usually geared towards improving operational techniques. Training is normally content to leave attitudes alone and usually that is a wise decision. Attitudes usually take too long to change. It is a lot easier to change behavior. But abuse is an area where attitudes drive actions and, unless the former are changed, performance will be pro forma and fail.

In order to bring verisimilitude to the process, advocates, victims, and former batterers must participate. Their's is the credible testimony that holds the greatest promise for convincing skeptical cops that the problem is real, serious, and needs to be treated. It would not be an exaggeration to say that abuse is one area of police operations where a significant change in approach will never be possible until underlying prejudices are overcome. Remembering that cops are part of the general population too, a training program ought to consider the probability that some police may be batterers themselves.

The best training reinforcement is success. If an arrest takes place, the woman follows through, the prosecutor and judge take it seriously, the batterer goes into treatment, and the violence stops, then the program will work. It is a lot easier to sell the idea then than it would be if the horizon were littered with obvious failures. Jailing a batterer for the time after his arrest helps to ensure a program's success. It sends a dramatic and clear message that society considers abuse both important and wrong. Jailing also offers victims some measure of protection from batterers, serves as a cooling-off period, and strengthens a judge's hand in getting batterers into treatment.

OTHER CRIMINAL JUSTICE PLAYERS

The cooperation of the other elements of the criminal justice system must be secured or a program will fail. District attorneys worried about conviction rates will not be eager to prosecute such difficult cases as those involving abuse. Judges working to clear their calendars will resist having them clogged with abuse cases. And jailers will not be pleased to see their crowded domains jammed further with assaultive males.

An arrest policy is not an automatic winner. It must be supported by other justice officials to be successful. For example, prosecutors should consider establishing special units to prosecute abuse cases. Continuances and repeated exposures to testifying must be minimized as well as the use of videotaped statements to spare victims from the ordeal of repeated cross-examinations.

Moreover, judges are in the best positions to control an offender's behavior through the coercive power of incarceration. They need to use this power to protect victims and secure a cessation of the abuse. Compelling treatment for substance abuse, issuing orders, and ensuring an orderly court process will help to communicate the seriousness of the process to the offender. Above all, judges must understand the issues and take them seriously. They and prosecutors should also pursue cases in which victims are reluctant to participate through the use of photos, taped calls to 911, witness testimony, or other evidence. Prosecutions can proceed absent the direct involvement of the victim, but they are rarely successful. Direct testimony is the most powerful and allows the jury to evaluate the principals.

Defense attorneys have obligations too that go beyond their obsession with winning. They must also be committed to discovering the truth and to stopping the violence. They must represent the interests of their clients; but these interests must be broadly (the preservation of the family's peace and stability) rather than narrowly (getting his client off the hook) construed. A good deal of the problem of eroding public confidence in the legal profession today can be blamed on the lawyer's concern for victory as opposed to the search for a just solution to a problem.

Follow-up monitoring is especially critical when dealing with chronic and escalating violence. A system of verification is needed to protect victims. Probation officers are the eyes and ears of the court and can accomplish this through impromptu visits, verification of employment, checking medical records for injuries that might indicate abuse, watching for compliance with treatment programs, encouraging charges into furthering their education, and generally overseeing the activities of those they are assigned to supervise. Excessive caseloads that subvert this process must be avoided.

TREATMENT PROGRAMS

Treatment programs are crucial too. The point of the arrest process is to stop the violence by either jailing the batterer or forcing him into treatment. This makes the existence of useful, relevant programs essential. The range of programs has to be broad because the problems driving abusive behavior can range in variety and complexity from alcoholism to drug addiction and from mental disturbance to any of the scores of ills that attend the human condition.

It is in these follow-up areas that the system fails so often because many elected officials find it difficult to get excited about programs that do not play well on television or on the front pages of newspapers. They are much more comfortable pointing to the Willie Hortons than to the thousands of successes behind occasional failures. Maybe the essential problem of the criminal justice system is that we send very poor-quality people into public life and they are the ones who make policy. It is an old saw that in a democracy the people get the government they deserve. If we insist on sending feckless caretakers and survivalists to city halls, we will continue to receive the sort of deplorable "service" or outright betrayal of trust that our newspapers report to us daily.

THE VICTIM'S RESPONSIBILITY

Advocates of tough policies regarding abuse have persistently searched for a way to extricate the victim from the dilemma of coming forward. The most recent wrinkle is the move to secure evidence, independent of her testimony, to prosecute the batterer. Such evidence might be photographic, recorded telephone calls to 911, the testimony of witnesses, visible injuries, statements of the offender, etc. In fact, there are no legal impediments to using these strategies except that, in the real world, they encounter a lot of resistance.

Ours is an adversarial system of justice. The accused faces his accuser and a search for the truth follows. The absence of an accuser in all cases (except the clearly understood case of murder) where the state stands in for the victim is usually fatal to the prosecution. Judges and prosecutors are very reluctant to proceed absent the determined presence of the complainant. Juries expect the accuser to confront her abuser.

Victim advocates are not likely to find an alternative solution. They have to face the economic, emotional, and physical risks of coming forward and pointing the finger at their tormentors if they want justice to prevail. The system, nevertheless, must still do its best even when she fails to cooperate and this may mean proceeding with an unpromising case for the prosecution. This is where feminist consciousness-raising groups could be coordinated to work with the police.

The system's need for and insistence on confrontation may well be the great divide between the problem of abuse and the system's effective response to it. A police chief trying to do something about abuse will fail if he does not secure the cooperation of other justice officials. Judges, prosecutors, jailers, etc. will not cooperate unless they see some prospects for success. Current discussions often center on arrest because an arrest must be made for the entire process to work.

As police resistance to arrest is overcome, and it is happening rapidly, failures will come downstream in the district attorneys' offices or judges' chambers. A failure anywhere will still produce the same tragic results. The batterer must be arrested and learn through his experience with the process that he must either change his behavior or face painful consequences.

The victim must escape the psychic thrall of abuse before she can hope to deal with its reality. She must learn that it is not only abnormal but unacceptable. She must find the courage to confront it and insist on stopping it. As progress mounts, the central importance of the woman will inevitably become clearer. Feminists who hope to spare the victim the additional pain of having to come forward and point the finger at her batterer are wasting energy on a well-intentioned search for a legal remedy they will not find. They would be better off ensuring that the system is sensitive to the victim's needs, that it does not subject her to ordeals that might be avoided through the use of videotaped testimony and that it offers her the necessary support and protection.

CONCLUSION

A lot of progress has been made in recent years. Research, experimentation, litigation, interest group pressures, and the simple desire to promote the public's safety have all contributed to the forward movement now under way. But a lot remains to be done.

Domestic abuse is complex human behavior. Its cure will require complex solutions. The determination to attack the problem is a key step that has to be accompanied by concerted action.

Hanging over the issue is the specter of ruinous litigation. A police chief cannot be held responsible for every failure but each failure should be examined to determine how much the police knew and what they did about it. If the record is marked with indifference, the city and the chief are going to be in trouble. It is too bad that negatives drive so much of our public policy but it is far better to be driven to do some good by a negative force than to do nothing at all.

The traditional police approaches of ignoring abuse, trying to mediate or massage disputes into non-events, excluding the male, or doing nothing have plainly not worked. Arrest seems to offer the best hope for reducing domestic violence. The instinctive sense is that direct action offers the best hope for success. Ignored problems tend to fester and rarely dissolve. The chief's responsibility is to take whatever legal measures he believes wisest, based on something better than seat-of-the-pants feelings, to promote the safety of his community.

REFERENCES

A Silence Too Loud: Family Violence (1984). Minneapolis: University of Minnesota.

Bard, M. (1970). *Training Police as Specialists in Family Crisis Intervention.* Washington, DC: U.S. Department of Justice.

Blumstein, A., et al. (1986). *Criminal Careers and Career Criminals. Volumes 1 and 2.* Washington, DC: National Academy Press.

Goolkasian, G. (1986). *Confronting Domestic Violence: A Guide for Criminal Justice Agencies.* Washington, DC: U.S. Department of Justice, May.

Lempert, R.O. (1987). "Spouse Abuse: Ann Arbor Rushed Into Arrest Ordinance Without Studying Side Effects." *Ann Arbor News.* June 21.

Peters, R.D. & R.K. McMahon (eds.) (1986). *Social Learning and Systems Approaches to Marriage and the Family.* New York: Brunner/Mazel.

Petersilia, J. (1985) *Guideline-Based Justice.* Santa Monica: The RAND Corporation.

Police Executive Research Forum (1989). *Innovative Programs, Policies, Procedures and Experiments from PERF Members' Agencies.* Washington, DC: Police Executive Research Forum.

Sherman, L.W. & A.V. Bouza (1984). "The Need to Police Domestic Violence." *Wall Street Journal.* May 22.

Sherman, L.W. & E.G. Cohn (1989). "The Impact of Research on Legal Policy: The Minneapolis Domestic Violence Experiment." *Law and Society Review*, pp. 118-144.

U.S. Attorney General's Office (1984). *Attorney General's Task Force on Family Violence.* Washington, DC: U.S. Department of Justice, September.

U.S. Department of Justice (1987). *Principles of Good Policing: Avoiding Violence Between Police and Citizens.* Washington, DC: Community Relations Service.

Victim Services Agency (1989). *The Law Enforcement Response to Family Violence: The Training Challenge.* New York.

10

Coordinated Community Responses

Jeffrey L. Edleson
University of Minnesota and the Domestic Abuse Project

INTRODUCTION

Previous chapters in this book have examined recent developments involving the efforts of police, prosecutors, judges, probation officers and social service workers to end woman abuse. Unfortunately, the interventions of many different agencies often create inconsistent responding. For example, Ford (1983:463) found that prosecution of woman abusers was "governed as much by chance as by rational procedures." His study of 325 battered women who sought prosecution revealed that only 30 of their cases eventually reached court for a hearing. Similarly, Dutton (1987:189) estimated that perpetrators of woman abuse had only "a 0.38% chance of being punished by the courts."

The difficulties many communities have experienced in changing their responses to abuse have generated a new type of organization, the Community Intervention Project (CIP) staffed primarily by battered women's advocates. In recent years, CIPs have been established across the United States to coordinate multisystem efforts aimed at achieving more consistent responses among different interveners.

This chapter begins with a description of model efforts to develop coordinated community interventions. It continues with a discussion of policy and practice issues regarding coordinated efforts and current evidence concerning the effectiveness of CIPs.

Community Intervention Projects

CIPs have been established in Colorado (Domestic Violence Manual Task Force, 1988), California (Soler & Martin, 1983), and elsewhere (see Goolkasian, 1986). They exist in a variety of forms ranging from independent non-profit organizations to victim services programs within city or county attorneys' offices. Most are staffed by trained legal advocates who help battered women interact with criminal justice and social service agencies and work at a systems level to change policies and procedures towards all battered women.

Over 20 CIPs currently operate in Minnesota alone and several of the country's oldest are located there. Two of them, the Domestic Abuse Intervention Project (DAIP) in Duluth (Pence, 1983; Pence & Shepard, 1988) and the several CIPs administered by the Domestic Abuse Project (DAP) in the Minneapolis metropolitan area (Brygger & Edleson, 1987; Gamache, Edleson & Schock, 1988), have been emulated by other communities across the country. Both operate as independent, non-profit organizations and it will be this type of CIP that will be the focus of this chapter.

Context In Which CIPs Developed

The context in which intervention projects have developed has been an important influence on the forms they now take. Zvi Eisikovits and I have reviewed the published literature on intervention with men who batter (Eisikovits & Edleson, 1989). Our review indicated that over the past two decades a great deal of attention has been placed on changing police department responses to a variety of community events including domestic violence. Homant (1985) grouped changing police responses to woman battering into two categories; counseling-oriented and arrest-oriented. Through the 1970s and into the early 1980s, police responses to domestic disputes were guided primarily by a counseling orientation and the concept of "family crisis intervention." Bard (1970, 1977; Bard & Berkowitz, 1967) was one of the earliest and strongest proponents of this approach. He argued that police use of crisis intervention techniques would enhance the management of domestic disputes. Walsh and Witte (1975) discuss this view of the police role in terms of improving the overall mental health of a community. This approach was, at the time, consistent with the public's quest for more "progressive" and responsive police departments. As a result of it, law enforcement's boundaries began to overlap with those of other helping professions. For example, officers began to receive training in family mediation and specialized crisis intervention units were created that included social workers paired with responding officers.

In the early 1980s new pressures began to build on police departments. Pressures from women's organizations and victim rights groups grew and their agendas converged to bring about a major shift in police and judicial responses to battering. Their influence was reinforced by successful suits against police inaction brought by several battered women around the country (e.g., *Thurman v. City of Torrington*, 1984). Victim rights advocates pushed for more severe punishment of offenders by courts while women's groups advocated for a consistent police and judicial response to crime regardless of where it occurs. The literature detailing the decision-making processes and inaction of police also grew rapidly (e.g., Berk & Loseke, 1980-81; Brown, 1984; Pastoor, 1984; Waaland & Keeley, 1985). Police who arrested perpetrators of violence on the street but did not arrest them for violence in the home were seen by women's groups as perpetuating domestic violence and the unequal treatment of women.

The foci of research shifted as these new pressures began to intensify. The relevance of deterrence theory to intervention with men who batter was reexamined (e.g., Sherman & Berk, 1984). Carmody and Williams (1987), among others, argued that deterrence does not simply rely on the effect of a delivered punishment but also relies on the degree to which offenders perceive sanctions as both certain and severe. Their research showed that of several possible forms of deterrence, police arrest was perceived as most severe but very unlikely.

Increased public pressures, landmark cases, and the application of deterrence theory to battering led to an increased use of arrest by police. As a result, increasing numbers of offenders entered court systems for arraignment, trial, and sentencing. For the first time, many prosecutors and judges were forced to deal directly with large numbers of battering cases.

The interests of victim rights advocates and women's groups converged again in the courts. The push for victim rights reinforced pressure from women's groups to make battered women's wishes more influential on court decisions. As with police actions, public attention again led to a growing literature on the victim's role in court (e.g., Ford, 1983; Ford & Burke, 1987; Galaway, 1985; McLeod, 1983; Sebba, 1982). Many courts, hoowever, have avoided using punishments like jail sentences and have favored a rehabilitation approach that diverts or mandates batterers into treatment.

Interestingly, the use of deterrence by police and stayed sentencing with mandated rehabilitation by the courts is advocated by many CIPs (see Brygger & Edleson, 1987; Pence, 1983). While seemingly inconsistent, this approach appears to offer perpetrators clear and immediate sanctions through arrest (deterrence) as well as motivation to enter treatment to avoid serving a jail sentence (rehabilitation).

In short, changing public attitudes, the outcomes of several landmark cases, pressure from battered women's advocates, and new research on police responses to domestic calls and on the victim's role in court have led to a greater readiness among criminal justice agencies to work with CIPs.

Design Assumptions

Within this historical context, several explicit assumptions have formed the basic design elements in most Minnesota CIPs. A study I co-authored (Gamache et al., 1988) summarized these assumptions including those about the causes of woman battering and types of desirable intervention goals. The assumptions are based on a feminist analysis of woman battering (see Schechter, 1982; Yllo & Bograd, 1988) and three in particular have shaped the design of many CIPs.

First, it is assumed that neither men nor women have a right to use violence except to remove themselves, in self-defense, from a physical assault. The use of physical violence to maintain power over others, to punish another person, or to obtain one's desires is viewed as illegitimate. Even if such violence takes place in the privacy of one's home, societal intervention to end it is considered desirable.

A second assumption is that "domestic" violence is rooted in a societal norm that has permitted males, as a class, to use violence to maintain their power and control over the family. Thus, any attempt to address the issue of woman battering effectively must necessarily challenge this norm. The historical reluctance of our response systems to do so and their currently inconsistent interventions are believed to contribute directly to the perpetuation of battering. This second assumption also raises the issue of women's "empowerment." The term "empowerment" is used widely and with differing meanings. However, it is clear that increasing a woman's power to control her own life is a guiding value for many CIP interventions.

This leads to a final assumption. If woman battering is rooted in societal norms then social systems must bear the responsibility for confronting men who batter and maximizing the protection of victims. To address the issue of woman battering effectively, efforts must be aimed at changing the responses of our social systems.

These assumptions lead to a set of design guidelines that influence decisions about policy development, project procedures and individual case management. Briefly, these guidelines generally seek to end battering by exposing abusers to the same sanctions that offenders in other assault cases experience and to remove the responsibility for confronting assailants as much as possible from victims who often bear this burden alone. The success of these efforts are judged not only by their ability to maximize the immediate protection available to victims but also by their ability to empower battered women and to minimize further danger or victimization.

These guidelines were developed for CIPs trying to coordinate criminal justice and social service interventions. They also facilitate evaluations of the consistency and effectiveness of different but related efforts to resolve problems related to battering.

Operational Procedures

Finn's chapter discusses in more detail the importance of creating legal environments for effective intervention projects. Statewide legal changes, a political climate supportive of women's and victims' rights, and the assumptions mentioned above have played a critical role in Minnesota's development of CIPs. The statewide Minnesota Coalition for Battered Women (MCBW) has, since 1978, led a series of successful lobbying efforts to change state laws regarding probable cause arrest, the levels at which woman battering crimes are charged, the terms under which protection orders are issued, child support and custody considerations, and other matters. It has also successfully lobbied the state legislature to fund a variety of CIPs and other domestic violence programs with tax dollars distributed by the Minnesota Department of Corrections. Thus, much of the underlying legal framework and core funding for Minnesota CIPs came from state government.

While Minnesota's experience depended heavily upon state-level changes, other communities have created similar coordinated efforts without them. For example, in Lincoln, Nebraska, the local police chief initiated an arrest policy after negotiating an agreement with the county attorney's office to prosecute offenders (Steinman, 1989).

With legal remedies and initial funding in hand, Minnesota CIPs have set out to establish a network of new policies and procedures for criminal justice and social service agencies. These efforts most often start with the local police department. In each CIP community, advocates work to obtain agreements with the local police administration to adopt policies requiring officers to make an arrest when probable cause exists that a domestic assault has occurred or when a protection order has been violated.

Once an arrest has been made, the police department agrees to notify the local CIP office immediately. In order to offer victims increased protection, local jails often agree to hold men for several hours or until an arraignment is made the next morning. During this time, trained paid or volunteer advocates are dispatched for separate visits to both the victim and, where permitted, the assailant. Male volunteers, some of whom are former batterers, visit the jail to encourage the man to acknowledge the severe negative results of his violent behavior, provide information about the range of treatment options available in the community, and offer support in seeking help through the court process. At the same time, a pair of women's volunteer advocates visit the victim at home while the man is in jail. During such visits or over the telephone, advocates offer support and information about subsequent court proceedings, shelters, and other available services. Time permitting, advocates also attempt to contact and provide services to women in homes where police intervened but did not make an arrest.

CIP advocates work with prosecuting attorneys in each community too in an effort to establish procedures for handling battering cases and to work out agreements that prosecutors will aggressively pursue these cases when an arrest occurs or a complaint is filed. With the victim's permission, CIP advocates assist prosecutors by supplying victim information during the court process. The goal at this point is to obtain judicial outcomes that help end the violence and increase both the victim's safety and her satisfaction with the criminal justice system's response.

Upon entry of a guilty plea by the man or his conviction by the court, judges participate in coordinated efforts by agreeing to order presentence investigations. During these investigations, probation officers participate by agreeing to incorporate information on the history of the man's violence and the battered woman's wishes into their presentence recommendations to the court. Where intervention projects exist, judges and referees are asked to pronounce a sentence that includes imprisonment and then to stay part or all of the sentence pending successful completion of a batterers' treatment program as a condition of probation.

Throughout these legal proceedings, advocates work closely with and on behalf of the battered woman. They work with prosecutors and probation officers and help victims secure or renew protection orders, temporary child custody, and child support. They also help the women link up with shelter or community-based support and education groups for them and their children, post-shelter housing, job training programs and the like.

Typically, criminal justice systems where CIPs exist mandate men to batterers' treatment programs. These programs participate in CIPs by giving priority to men referred by court order and by submitting regular reports on a man's progress in counseling. Where men's treatment programs are inadequate or unavailable, CIP advocates work with local mental health agencies and professionals to develop a violence-focused program. Advocates continue to monitor each man's compliance with probation conditions and regularly report to the court on his progress in treatment.

The network of relationships among criminal justice and social service agencies is complex. Figure 10.1 illustrates, albeit in simplified and idealistic terms, the processes described above.

Figure 10.1
Advocates' Roles in System Coordination

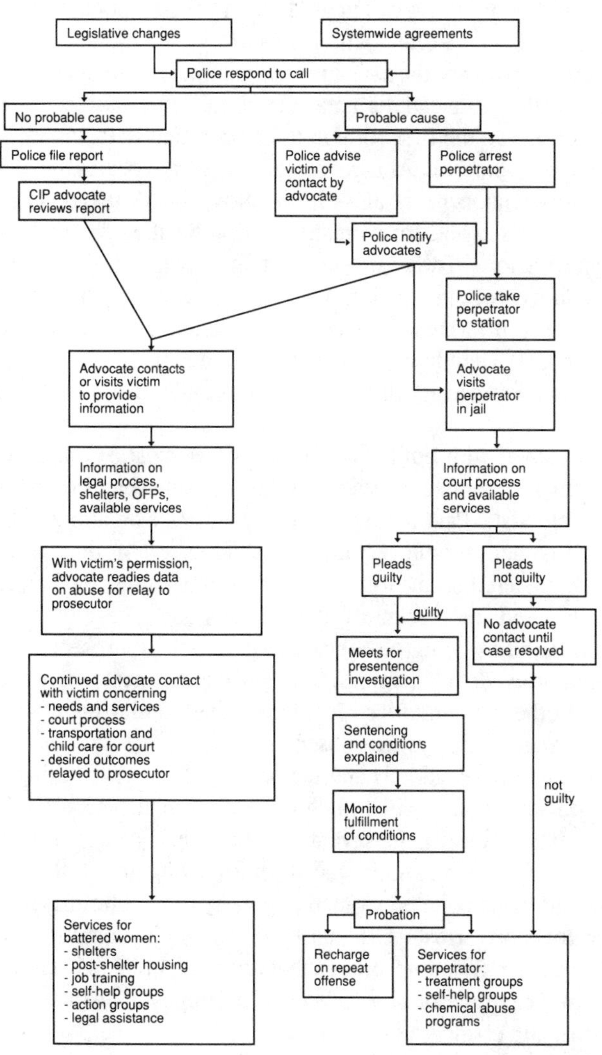

Problems in Establishing Coordination

Gaining the cooperation of police officers, prosecutors, judges, probation officers, and social service professionals is a time-consuming and resource-intensive process. Changing attitudes requires CIPs to engage in continual advocacy and monitoring during which consistent and clear community sanctions for violent behavior are repeatedly negotiated. In large metropolitan areas, such activities include regular monitoring of hundreds of criminal justice professionals involved at many levels in handling battering cases.

Added to this complexity are the ever-growing numbers of men arrested for battering offenses. In the Minneapolis area, the rise in the number of arrest cases has been staggering. In the first 16 months of operating CIPs in three suburban communities, the Domestic Abuse Project's three advocates received a total of 98 arrest cases (Gamache et al., 1988). Now, in Minneapolis alone, there are over 3,000 arrests a year for woman battering handled by 6 advocates and 1 volunteer coordinator. These staggering numbers are being replicated across the country and overwhelm small CIP staffs. As a result, CIP advocates have been forced to set priorities among the individual cases and systems changes on their agendas. They have, however, resisted calls for greater use of diversion prior to conviction because it lets a perpetrator avoid conviction and a criminal record.

To assist more women with limited resources, the Domestic Abuse Project is experimenting with a monitoring project in several suburban communities where CIPs do not yet exist. Paid and volunteer advocates ride along with police on domestic calls and monitor court proceedings on a regular basis. Monthly statistics are gathered on the total number of arrest cases, the percent of offenders found guilty, and the percent of cases dismissed. These data are reported to all the communities being observed and give police, prosecutors, and judges in each community detailed information on their system's response in comparison to that of other communities. It is hoped that monitoring alone may create a substantial change in the systems observed.

The shortage of space in local jails and the backlog of cases awaiting prosecution also create difficult issues with which CIPs must deal. Recently, in an effort to lessen crowding in local jails, several local criminal justice officials in Minnesota proposed reforms (e.g., shorter jail stays following arrest) that victim advocates feared would place battered women at greater risk. After having successfully advocated for more arrests, CIP staff had to organize against counter-pressures to revert to earlier system responses that did not require substantial jail space. This is just one example of how advocates are repeatedly forced to expend resources to maintain changes already in place.

Conflicts with prosecutors over what constitutes consistent and empowering social responses also have arisen in several localities around the country. As stated earlier, empowerment of women in society, and particularly of battered women, is a strong value for many CIPs that seek to protect victims from immediate danger and to minimize the chances of further victimization. At the same time, prosecutors seek winnable cases (Rauma, 1984). To win cases, a number of prosecutors have suggested (Lerman, 1986) that battered women unwilling to testify against their perpetrators be served a subpoena forcing them to do so. Such recommendations are sometimes intended to relieve women of the responsibility (and blame) for deciding to testify. Forcing battered women to testify, however, creates the potential for a great deal of tension between prosecutors and battered women's advocates. On the one hand, battered women's advocates value active efforts by prosecutors to bring sanctions to bear on perpetrators. On the other hand, forcing a battered woman to testify is seen by many advocates as disempowering and revictimizing women who are already in low power positions. A study by Ford (1984) supports this view. Ford found that battered women viewed control over the court process as a power resource in negotiating a resolution with their partners. Removing women's control over the process through subpoenas and forcing them to testify may, in fact, lessen the usefulness of the court process to them.

Recently, some Minnesota localities have begun to subpoena battered women after their second failure to appear voluntarily in court to testify. Some localities have also adopted a policy of dismissing a case if a woman fails to show after being subpoenaed regardless of the circumstances. To win cases, some defense attorneys have advised abusers to keep their partners away from the court in order to invoke the dismissal rule. In another extreme case, a judge ordered the police to seek out and arrest several women who did not appear after being subpoenaed and some spent the weekend in jail after being arrested late on a Friday afternoon. These events are sad examples of how a policy intended to relieve battered women of the decision to testify is easily turned against them.

Biased practices that discriminate against persons because of their race, sex, ethnic origin, sexual preference, or age are also problems repeatedly confronted by advocates. As part of their monitoring and system change efforts, they attempt to lessen the effects of discrimination wherever they find it. This is particularly important when procedures are implemented differentially based on a woman's status. For example, given the number of calls to police, a greater number of arrests might occur in minority neighborhoods than in white ones or prosecutions may be lower among white perpetrators than black ones. Persistent monitoring of police, prosecutor, court and probation activities and regular meetings with individuals and supervisors are major parts of an advocate's work.

Finally, there is a danger that CIPs will be coopted by the criminal justice system. Increasingly, CIP budgets are being supplemented by tax dollars while other programs are being incorporated into city or county attorneys' offices. As this occurs, there is a distinct danger that CIPs will lose their independence and their ability to monitor systems and apply pressure for change. Already, some criticize the common practice of collecting witness data for prosecutors as doing work they should perform. It is not hard to envision how programs could become extensions of existing bureaucracies by being restricted to focus solely on individual case advocacy. The importance of placing continued emphasis on system change rather than acting as a permanent supplement to existing offices is clear.

Evaluations of Coordinated Interventions

To date, very few evaluations of coordinated community interventions have been completed. What does exist can be grouped into three categories including evaluations of: (1) system-level activity change; (2) court-mandated batterers' treatment programs; and (3) coordination efforts.

System-Level Changes

The number of arrested and prosecuted perpetrators appears to be rising dramatically around the country. Only one study, however, has linked coordination efforts to these system-level changes in activity. My colleagues and I (Gamache et al., 1988) retrospectively studied the first three communities in which the Domestic Abuse Project established CIPs. These communities were small (15,000 to 36,000 people), suburban cities in the Minneapolis metropolitan area, relatively homogeneous (97% white) and prosperous (70% to 80% held white-collar positions).

The Domestic Abuse Project had established each CIP approximately three months apart. This created the opportunity for a naturally occurring, multiple-baseline study comparing the same three communities before intervention to activity levels during intervention. Archival police and court records were examined and charts constructed depicting changes in arrests, convictions, and perpetrators mandated to treatment by the courts.

Our analyses showed that CIPs had a significant impact on arrests, convictions, and court mandates to treatment. They also showed that the larger the system, the more difficult the coordination. What this study did not indicate was whether all this significantly increased activity was associated with changed rates of violence against women.

Court-Mandated Treatment

A number of studies have examined the effects of court-mandated batterers' treatment on recidivism of rates. In general, these studies have found that court-mandated men are as responsive to treatment as those referred through other means and that court-mandated participants who complete treatment are less likely to re-offend during follow-up periods than those who do not participate or who drop-out of treatment.

Dutton (1986) compared police reports on 50 men who had completed a 16-week court-mandated treatment program to police reports on a matched group of batterers convicted on battering charges but not mandated to receive treatment. He examined police reports for a post-treatment period averaging 2 years and found that only 4 percent of the treated batterers recidivated compared to 40 percent of the matched, untreated batterers. Dutton also examined wives follow-up reports for treated batterers who were married throughout treatment and follow-up. Eighty-four percent of the wives reported that their partners were not violent since the end of treatment. Thus, one can conclude from Dutton's study that batterers who are both arrested and receive subsequent treatment are less likely to re-offend than those who are just arrested.

Shepard (1987) conducted a cross-sectional study of 92 men who were at the beginning, middle or end of CIP associated treatment programs in Minnesota or had completed treatment three months earlier. Most of the men in this study were court-involved. Using self-reports and reports from their partners, she found that men in later phases of treatment were less violent than those in earlier phases. The most dramatic decreases in violent and psychologically abusive behavior occurred in the first 3 months of treatment. Shepard contacted 39 of the men's partners a year after the men completed treatment and found that 70 percent of the women reported they were no longer being battered.

Shepard points out, however, that approximately 25 percent of the men who attended intake sessions dropped out of treatment. The successful outcomes found by Dutton and Shepard, while promising, are somewhat tempered by this percentage and by other studies that have found little relationship between court-orders to treatment and men's compliance with the orders. Such findings are especially important considering that several other studies (Edleson & Grusznski, 1988; Hamberger & Hastings, 1988) have found less recidivism among program completers than noncompleters.

If perpetrators are mandated to treatment but do not follow it through to completion there is a risk that increased court activity may create false hopes and expectations. To date, studies completed both at the Domestic Abuse Project (Grusznski, 1985; Lund et al., 1982) and elsewhere (Kelso & Personnette, 1985; Parker & Saunders, 1989) have found court-mandated batterers no more or less likely to complete treatment than those referred through other means.

To address the issue of program completion, Saunders and Parker (1989) recently conducted two studies examining the association of legal sanctions and the completion of treatment programs. They found a relationship between mandated referral and treatment completion only within particular subgroups of abusers. They found that mandated referral was related to completion among young, non-college-educated men and that, among men over 25 with at least some college, voluntary referral was related more strongly with completion. Moreover, among men who did not report severe violence, voluntary referral was more highly related to completion than involuntary referral.

Another recent study (Tolman & Bhosley, 1989) compared recidivism rates among 3 groups of men who participated in treatment: men who participated voluntarily, men who were recommended to treatment by either the police or courts, and men who were court-mandated to treatment. They found that men who were recommended to treatment by the criminal justice system were less likely to be violent than the others as reported by victims after following treatment. Men whose treatments were court-ordered or voluntary were not differentially associated with changes in recidivism rates. Tolman and Bhosley argue that recommended men may be motivated by a perception that more serious negative consequences may occur in the future if they do not succeed in treatment.

Finally, in a recent study that randomly assigned 283 men to 1 of 6 treatment programs, Maryann Syers and I found that the men who reported court-mandates to treatment were no more or less likely to succeed in treatment than those who were not court-mandated. In general, we found that men who participated in and completed structured treatment groups, regardless of referral source, had a 2 out of 3 chance of being reported not violent at follow-up (Edleson & Syers, 1989).

Taken together, these studies indicate that court mandates and recommendation for treatment may be effective methods of getting men into treatment and, if the men complete a program, there is a likelihood that they, as often as others, will end their violence during follow-up periods. It may be that court involvement is an effective source of referrals to treatment but that its "power" to lower recidivism is generally no greater than other means of referral such as pressure from informal social networks.

Coordinated Efforts

Measuring the overall effect of Duluth's coordinated intervention effort, Pence, Novack and Galaway (1982) reported that 6 months after men completed a treatment program, 51 percent of their victims reported no subsequent violence compared to 41 percent of a comparison group of victims from the same community. Unfortunately, the contributions of the specific criminal justice and social service components were not tested.

While this book's editor reports his research later, a brief summary of 2 of his studies adds important data to those thus far reviewed. His study of 183 victims and their partners in Lincoln, Nebraska found that post-arrest sanctions applied in a CIP-like effort had little influence on recidivism beyond what was achieved through arrest (Steinman, 1988). Recidivism was measured with archival data from the county attorney; victims were not contacted. He also found that some post-arrest sanctions, e.g., fines, were marginally associated with lower rates of recidivism.

To investigate these possible associations, Steinman (1990) examined recidivism among 2 groups of batterers who were arrested or received a citation. One group was involved in cases that occurred before the implementation of a coordinated community effort (n=48) and the second was involved in cases that occurred after the establishment of the coordinated effort (n=156). Controlling for a number of variables including time between arrest and follow-up interviews of victims, Steinman found that police actions not coordinated with other sanctions produced more violence. Police action, especially arrest, in coordination with other criminal justice efforts became a significant deterrent. He also found, however, that coordinated efforts are not consistently effective. For example, victims who called the police themselves and who were not living with their perpetrators tended to be at greater risk. Thus, bringing advocates, police, and others into a situation may put some women at a heightened level of risk. At the same time, however, these women may already be in a high-risk situation and the violence they suffer may grow regardless of criminal justice efforts. Steinman's studies suggest that coordinated criminal justice responses that include arrest policies and post-arrest sanctions can be effective but that some women may face increased risk by actively seeking the aid of criminal justice professionals.

The arrest of perpetrators and the completion of treatment groups, as indicated in the above studies, do seem to contribute to lower recidivism rates. The relative contributions of other components of coordinated post-arrest responses such as advocacy, prosecution, conviction, diversion, and court-mandates are, at this moment, unknown.

DISCUSSION

New, coordinated community responses to battering are being established across the country. They exist as programs of the criminal justice system and as independent, non-profit organizations. The experience of Minnesota's intervention efforts indicates the importance of building networks not only within specific criminal justice systems but also across the state and with legislative bodies. Minnesota's experience also highlights some of the difficulties CIPs face because of the success of their efforts, e.g., rapidly growing arrest rates that place new demands on the criminal justice system.

Most troubling is the little we currently know about the effects of all this activity. We have some indications that it can change system responses and lead to less violence against women. We are very far, however, from understanding exactly what works, with whom, and under what conditions.

At the Domestic Abuse Project, we are currently analyzing data from a large set of 6- and 12-month follow-up interviews of battered women who had some contact with police. Out of approximately 1,000 women who had some contact with police, we have interviewed about 500. Hopefully, their responses and other data will allow a quasi-experimental comparison of the additive effects of coordination components both on the violence that the women continued to experience and on their satisfaction with various aspects of coordinated interventions.

REFERENCES

Bard, M. (1970). *Training Police as Specialists in Family Crisis Intervention.* Washington, DC: U.S. Department of Justice.

_____ (1977). "Family Crisis Intervention: From Concept to Implementation." In M. Roy (ed.) *Battered Women.* NY: Van Nostrand Reinhold.

Bard, M. & B. Berkowitz (1967). "Training Police as Specialists in Family Crisis Intervention: A Community Psychology Action Program." *Community Mental Health Journal,* 3:315-317.

Berk, S.F. & D.R. Loseke (1980-81). "'Handling' Family Violence: Situational Determinants of Police Arrest in Domestic Disturbances." *Law & Society Review,* 15:317-346.

Brown, S.E. (1984). "Police Responses to Wife Beating: Neglect of a Crime of Violence." *Journal of Criminal Justice,* 12:277-288.

Brygger, M.P. & J.L. Edleson (1987). "The Domestic Abuse Project: A Multisystems Intervention in Woman Battering." *Journal of Interpersonal Violence,* 2:324-336.

Carmody, D.C. & K.R. Williams (1987). "Wife Assault and Perceptions of Sanctions." *Violence and Victims,* 2:25-38.

Domestic Violence Task Force (1988). *The Denver Domestic Violence Manual.* Denver, CO: City of Denver.

Dutton, D.G. (1986). "The Outcome of Court-Mandated Treatment for Wife Assault: A Quasi-Experimental Evaluation." *Violence and Victims*, 1:163-175.

_____ (1987). "The Criminal Justice Response to Wife Assault." *Law and Human Behavior*, 11:189-206.

Edleson, J.L. & R.J. Grusznski (1988). "Treating Men Who Batter: Four Years of Outcome Data from the Domestic Abuse Project." *Journal of Social Service Research*, 12:3-22.

Edleson, J.L. & M. Syers (1989). "The Relative Effectiveness of Group Treatments for Men Who Batter." Manuscript submitted for publication.

Eisikovits, Z.C. & J.L. Edleson (1989). "Intervening with Men Who Batter: A Critical Review of the Literature." *Social Service Review*.

Ford, D.A. (1983). "Wife Battery and Criminal Justice: A Study of Victim Decision-Making." *Family Relations*, 32:463-475.

_____ (1984). "Prosecution as a Victim Power Resource for Managing Conjugal Violence." Paper presented at the annual meeting of the Society for the Study of Social Problems, San Antonio, Texas, August.

Ford, D.A. & M.J. Burke (1987). "Victim-Initiated Criminal Complaints for Wife Battery: An Assessment of Motives." Paper presented at the Third National Family Violence Research Conference, Durham, New Hampshire.

Gallaway, B. (1985). "Victim Participation in the Penal-Corrective Process." *Victimology*, 10:617-630.

Gamache, D.J., J.L. Edleson & M.D. Schock (1988). "Coordinated Police, Judicial and Social Service Response to Woman Battering: A Multi-Baseline Evaluation Across Three Communities." In G.T. Hotaling, D. Finkelhor, J.T. Kirkpatrick & M. Straus (eds.) *Coping with Family Violence: Research and Policy Perspectives*, pp. 193-209. Newbury Park, CA: Sage Publications.

Grusznski, R.J. (1985). "Court-Ordered Treatment of Men Who Batter." Unpublished dissertation, University of Minnesota, Minneapolis.

Goolkasian, G.A. (1986). *Confronting Domestic Violence: A Guide for Criminal Justice Agencies*. Washington, DC: National Institute of Justice.

Hamberger, L.K. & J.E. Hastings (1988). "Skill Training for Treatment of Spouse Abusers: An Outcome Study." *Journal of Family Violence*, 3:121-130.

Homant, R.J. (1985). "The Police and Spouse Abuse: A Review of Recent Findings." *Police Studies*, 8:163-172.

Kelso, D. & L. Personnette (1985). *Domestic Violence and Treatment Services for Victims and Abusers: An Analysis of Violent Behavior of Abusers and Victims in Relation to AWAIC Treatment Services (Research report).* Anchorage, AK: Abused Women's Aid in Crisis.

Lund, S.H., N.E. Larsen & S.K. Schultz (1982). *Exploratory Evaluation of the Domestic Abuse Project (Research report).* Minneapolis, MN: Domestic Abuse Project.

Lerman, L.G. (1986). "Prosecution of Wife Beaters: Institutional Obstacles and Innovations." In M. Lystad (ed.) *Violence in the Home.* NY: Brunner/Mazel.

McLeod, M. (1983). "Victim Non-Cooperation in the Prosecution of Domestic Assault." *Criminology*, 21:395-416.

Parker, J.C. & D.G. Saunders (1989). "Sociodemographic Factors and Treatment Follow-Through in Groups for Men Who Batter." Manuscript submitted for publication.

Pastoor, M.K. (1984). "Police Training and the Effectiveness of Minnesota 'Domestic Abuse' Laws." *Law & Inequality*, 2:557-507.

Pence, E. (1983). "The Duluth Domestic Abuse Intervention Project." *Hamline Law Review*, 6:247-275.

Pence, E., S. Novack & B. Galaway (1982). "Domestic Abuse Intervention Project: Six Month Research Report." Unpublished manuscript from the Duluth (Minnesota) Domestic Abuse Intervention Project.

Pence, E. & M. Shepard (1988). "Integrating Feminist Theory and Practice: The Challenge of the Battered Women's Movement." In K. Yllo & M. Bograd (eds.) *Feminist Approaches on Wife Abuse*, pp. 282-298. Newbury Park, CA: Sage Publications.

Rauma, D. (1984). "Going for the Gold: Prosecutorial Decision-Making in Cases of Wife Assault." *Social Science Research*, 13:321-351.

Saunders, D.G. & J. Parker (1989). "Legal Sanctions and Treatment Follow-Through Among Men Who Batter: A Multivariate Analysis." Manuscript submitted for publication.

Schechter, S. (1982). *Women and Male Violence.* Boston, MA: South End Press.

Sebba, L. (1982). "The Victim's Role in the Penal Process: A Theoretical Orientation." *American Journal of Comparative Law*, 3:217-240.

Shepard, M. (1987). "Intervention with Men Who Batter: An Evaluation of a Domestic Abuse Program." Paper presented at the Third Family Violence Conference for Researchers, Durham, New Hampshire, July.

Sherman, L.W. & R.A. Berk (1984). "The Specific Deterrent Effects of Arrest for Domestic Assault." *American Sociological Review*, 49:261-272.

Soler, E. & S. Martin (1983). *Domestic Violence is a Crime*. San Francisco: Family Violence Project.

Steinman, M. (1988). "Evaluating a System-Wide Response to Domestic Violence: Some Initial Findings." *Journal of Contemporary Criminal Justice*, 4:172-186.

_____ (1989). *Final Report to the Lincoln/Lancaster County Domestic Violence Coalition*. Lincoln, Nebraska.

_____ (1990). "Lowering Recidivism Among Men Who Batter Women." *Journal of Police Science and Administration*, 17(2):124-132.

Thurman v. City of Torrington, 595 F. Supp. 1521 (D. Conn. 1984).

Tolman, R.M. & Bhosley, G. (1989). "The Impact of Criminal Justice System Involvement on the Outcome of Intervention with Men Who Batter." Manuscript submitted for publication.

Waaland, P. & S. Keeley (1985). "Police Decision-Making in Wife Abuse: The Impact of Legal and Extralegal Factors." *Law and Human Behavior*, 9:355-366.

Walsh, J.A. & P.G. Witte (1975). "Police Training in Domestic Crises: A Suburban Approach." *Community Mental Health Journal*, 11:301-306.

Yllo, K. & M. Bograd (eds.) (1988). *Feminist Approaches on Wife Abuse*. Newbury Park, CA: Sage Publications.

11

Coordinated Criminal Justice Interventions and Recidivism Among Batterers

Michael Steinman
University of Nebraska—Lincoln

INTRODUCTION

A major theme of this book is that treating woman battering effectively requires agencies with different roles and kinds of expertise to coordinate their efforts. Using a before and after research design, this chapter examines whether arrest policies coordinated with other criminal justice interventions are related to recidivism among batterers.*

POLICY RESPONSES TO BATTERING

The Minneapolis domestic violence experiment raised expectations that a single intervention, arrest, and temporary incarceration, could lower battering rates (Sherman & Berk, 1984). However, findings from the Omaha replication of this experiment (Dunford, Huizinga & Elliott, 1989) and conversations with researchers involved in other replications indicate that police action alone is not a panacea.

This news will disappoint those who were influenced by publicity about the Minneapolis experiment to think that the police could lower battering rates sig-

* This study was funded by state and local government agencies, businesses, and foundations in Lincoln, Nebraska and by the National Institute of Justice.

nificantly by themselves. It will not disappoint conservatives committed to patriarchal authority and to traditional roles for women. They are likely to use the replications' findings to criticize arrest policies and to demand that police chiefs do away with them.

The results of the replications will not surprise students of the policy process familiar with the difficulties of treating complex problems. Nor will it surprise personnel in shelters and men's anger control programs who are sensitive to the many causes, symptoms, and effects associated with battering. They know how little any one intervention can accomplish by itself.

Complex strategies are needed to treat complex problems. Earlier chapters have reported the benefits of coordinated, multiagency efforts. This chapter's purpose is to see if coordination between the police and other criminal justice agencies is associated with recidivism rates.

Three kinds of police intervention are examined: arrest, citation, and responding to a call for service but taking no formal action. Information on these interventions comes from two periods. One is an experimental period marked by the enforcement of arrest policies coordinated with aggressive prosecution; the other is a baseline period before arrest policies and aggressive prosecution went into effect. The three police interventions represent a continuum of potentially deterrent costs. Arrest imposes the most costs and no formal action imposes the fewest. The costs imposed by arrest include a brief time in jail or the chance of it and the possibility of being prosecuted and suffering court-mandated penalties like a fine or a jail term. Arrest may also trigger indirect costs for offenders such as humiliation, divorce or separation from their partners, and loss of job (Williams & Hawkins, 1989).

Aggressive prosecution means more than prosecutors deciding to charge offenders. It also includes commitments to work with victims to gain their trust and cooperation, to prosecute offenders when they cannot get victims' cooperation, and to seek appropriate treatment for each offender (e.g., pretrial diversion services or court-ordered penalties). Thus, aggressive prosecution imposes its own costs which may include interventions by other criminal justice agencies.

Effective coordination between police and prosecutors requires certain actions. For example, police chiefs must define battering as a crime, be willing to promote this view in their departments and communities, adopt arrest policies, and monitor rank and file compliance with the policies. Chiefs must also require officers to undergo training about the dynamics of abusive relationships and why arrest policies are needed and how to implement them. Moreover, chiefs must work with prosecutors to make sure the enforcement of arrest policies is supported by prosecutions and that a track record of support is documented and publicized to officers and the community. In addition, prosecutors must take similar steps. They must define battering as a crime, charge batterers with criminal offenses, educate their staffs and the community about battering, and make sure staff are aware of police efforts.

Studies reported in earlier chapters indicate that police officers who do not see prosecutions flowing from arrest are less apt to consider battering a crime and more likely to think that arrest wastes time and contributes to more violence. Likewise, prosecutors are unlikely to give battering much time if they think they are acting alone. Taking the actions noted in the preceding paragraph forces line personnel to decide for themselves whether battering is a crime and how to respond to it. Confronted with these choices, line personnel tend to arrest and prosecute more offenders when they know others are treating battering like a crime too.

This chapter examines whether police action coordinated with other criminal justice interventions is related to recidivism rates. It is expected that coordinated interventions will be related to less recidivism when policies, training, and experience indicate to line police and prosecutors that their superiors want them to treat battering as a crime and that their efforts will be supported. This chapter also examines the relationship between coordinated criminal justice interventions and recidivism controlling for evidence that offenders have violent histories and for the nature of victim/offender relationships.

RESEARCH SETTING

The research setting is Lincoln/Lancaster County, Nebraska which has a mostly white (96%), middle-class population of over 200,000 people. Its white-collar economy is based on state government, the main campus of the state university, insurance companies, banks, and a variety of service industries. It also has a highly regarded public school system.

Coordinated efforts to stop battering began in 1985 when representatives of the local commission on the status of women, a victim support program, and a shelter approached Lincoln's police chief to persuade him that battering is a problem and that officers could reduce its incidence and protect victims by arresting offenders. These advocates for change had information from victims indicating that officers responded slowly to calls for help and that their typical response was to separate offenders and victims so the former could "cool off." These advocates argued that the police were not protecting victims from more harm.

The chief responded by identifying problems that prevented him from adopting arrest policies. Foremost among them were a disinclination among officers to get involved in what they considered domestic "disputes" and a concern that arresting or citing offenders would be wasted effort because most would avoid prosecution. At this time, most battering cases in which police did arrest or cite offenders were sent to the city attorney's office which typically gave them a very low priority. The chief's concerns led advocates for change to talk to the county attorney who said he would not give battering a priority because most victims did not cooperate with his office by filing charges when told they had to pay a $50 filing fee.

While these reactions were disappointing, the police chief and county attorney did agree that battering is a public problem and called for a multiagency approach to treat it. They pointed to the work of their own agencies to argue that policy changes in one or a few agencies would be ineffective without the cooperation of all agencies with relevant missions. With their encouragement, the Justice Council, a local criminal justice coordinative body, created a special task force to develop and promote the adoption and implementation of appropriate policy options. Many agency heads were asked to serve on it in addition to those involved in earlier discussions: the county sheriff, the chair of the Judges Council, the city attorney, the public defender, the head of corrections, the head of the probation office, and the top counselor of a private men's anger control program. Since its creation, what has come to be known as the Domestic Violence Coalition (DVC) has grown to include pretrial diversion programs, the Lincoln Council on Alcoholism and Drugs, other men's anger control programs, and the police department's Victim Witness Unit. The DVC is an example of what Edleson calls a Community Intervention Project.

A major DVC-supported innovation was the adoption of arrest policies. The police department's policy states: "When violence has occurred or been threatened, irrespective of the victim's wishes, the primary responsibility of the responding officers is to investigate a crime, and if probable cause exists, to arrest the person responsible." It notes that many victims have "strong and complex reasons" not to report and testify against offenders and that the proximity of those involved makes more abuse possible. It also notes that not taking action can produce liability problems. The county sheriff's policy is similar.

The policies require officers to file reports on all incidents, including those in which they take no formal action, and to note explicitly when cases involve battering. This is meant to encourage effective enforcement and to stop officers from using radio reports when they take no formal action, a much-used practice before the policies were adopted that leaves no paper trail. Officers are also directed to give victims cards noting the telephone numbers and addresses of agencies that provide victim services. Both the police chief and sheriff require in-service training for their officers that stresses the criminal nature of battering. They did not do this before DVC efforts began. Neither department reports serious compliance problems.

The police chief and sheriff were moved to adopt arrest policies by a combination of influences including local demands for change, the well-publicized findings of the Minneapolis experiment (Sherman & Berk, 1984), and the possibility of judicial penalties for not protecting victims. In addition, they were influenced by the county attorney's decisions to handle misdemeanor cases and to prosecute offenders without requiring victims to file charges and pay a fee. The latter decision was an important step to take the onus of prosecuting off victims, to protect them from reprisal, and to inform offenders that the community does not tolerate battering. The latter decision was a major change since most cases are misdemeanors and had been handled by the city attorney's office.

The county attorney assigned all battering cases to one deputy and directed her to prosecute whenever possible, even when victim cooperation is doubtful or absent. Part of her standard operating procedure is to subpoena victims to encourage their cooperation and inform offenders that the decision to prosecute is not the victims'. She does not penalize victims who ignore the subpoenas.

The county attorney's new policies were key because they removed a significant police objection to arresting batterers by promising to support officers whenever possible. These policies and arrest policies went into effect on June 1, 1986. The DVC is committed to implementing as many coordinated interventions as possible. Its goals include putting larger numbers of carefully selected offenders in pretrial diversion programs and ensuring that other offenders appear in court to be judged guilty and punished. As will be shown later, this expectation has been realized to a large degree. In addition, DVC goals originally included commitments by one public and one private agency to contact victims within two days of every incident to make sure they get whatever help they need. Available evidence indicates that few victims, especially those in misdemeanor cases, have been contacted. As a result, this chapter focuses exclusively on criminal justice interventions. The DVC is currently considering ways to contact and service victims more effectively.

METHODOLOGY

This study compares associations between criminal justice interventions and recidivism before and after policies governing arrest and prosecution went into effect. Police incident reports and county attorney files were used to collect archival data on the first case in which every male offender was involved after June 1, 1986. Archival information was also collected from police reports when officers took no formal action. From July, 1987 to May 31, 1989, archival data on initial incidents were collected one year after each occurred. The data describe factual details about cases, the parties involved, how cases were handled by law enforcement officers, the county attorney, and other agencies, and whether the county attorney charged men with battering in subsequent cases.

After collecting archival data, efforts were made to locate and interview victims on the telephone. In addition to collecting information about initial incidents, interviews identified which victims were attacked again by offenders using a modified version of Straus's Conflict Tactics Scales (1979). Interviews were conducted by the Bureau of Sociological Research at the University of Nebraska-Lincoln. Interviewers were middle-aged women with considerable experience with telephone interviews. Their scripts introduced them to victims by stressing their university employment and invited respondents to verify their identity and purpose by calling a university extension.

Archival and interview data were also collected on cases from a 12-month baseline period running from June 1, 1985 to May 31, 1986. These cases were identified by a Lincoln police officer working in her spare time. She reviewed all police reports from this period and collected archival data on cases she believed involved battering. Given the time it took to do this, efforts to interview baseline victims did not begin until the spring, 1988.

Bureau staff located 322 victims from the experimental period, 47 of whom refused to be interviewed. The 275 victims who were interviewed represent 28.2 percent of the 974 victims in cases from this period. Interviews were conducted from 12 to 33 months after the incidents took place. The average number of months between initial incident and interview is 14.7. In addition, Bureau staff located 91 baseline victims, 28 of whom refused to be interviewed. The 63 who were interviewed represent 24 percent of the victims in 262 baseline incidents. Interviews of baseline victims were conducted from 24 to 48 months after initial incidents. The average number of months between initial baseline incident and interview is 33.1.

As with other samples of reported cases of battering in other studies, disproportionately high percentages of cases involved minority group members and low-income people. While 4 percent of the local population is minority, minorities were involved in 27 percent of the experimental and 32 percent of the baseline cases on which archival data were collected. That most experimental (76%) and baseline (78%) incidents occurred in low-income census tracts suggests that they involved low-income people too. The often transient residential and employment histories of low-income/minority group people, their relative inability to pay for telephone service, and waiting a year to do the interviews made it difficult to find many victims. To interview as many of them as possible, Bureau staff contacted their neighbors, searched marriage license applications, used telephone and city directory records, called individuals with victims' last names hoping they were relatives and knew victims' whereabouts, and contacted victims' employers if they were noted in archival records and hospitals if victims used them after the incidents.

Very few important differences distinguish victims who were interviewed from those who were not. Not surprisingly, these few differences concern minority group status and income. Compared to figures in the above paragraph, smaller percentages of minority group members are in the experimental (18%)

and baseline (16%) samples of interviewed victims; there are smaller percentages of cases from low-income census tracts (64% and 67% respectively) too. Nevertheless, minority and low-income people are still represented disproportionately compared to the community's minority and low-income populations.

The DVC's mission statement calls for the reduction of "domestic violence and its recidivism rate in Lincoln and Lancaster County." The statement defines domestic violence as abuse "of any kind [i.e., verbal abuse and intimidating behavior as well as physical assault]...between two adults living under the same roof." This definition is expanded for this study to include adults who are or were in any intimate relationship, that is adults who are dating as well as those who had dated, lived together, or been married.

Recidivism is defined in this study using victim reports of physical battering. The reason for this is related to a core policy goal: protecting victims from physical violence and injury. Examining associations between interventions and post-incident physical assaults may help achieve this goal by contributing to the design and implementation of more effective policy responses.

Table 11.1 **Victim Reports of Post-Incident Battering Using a Modified Version of Straus' Conflict Tactics Scales***

	Baseline Period (n = 63) %	Experimental Period (n = 275) %
Has (the offender) :		
Pushed, grabbed, or shoved you?	65	50
Hit or tried to hit you with something?	54	29
Slapped or spanked you?	40	27
Punched or kicked you?	41	24
Thrown you bodily?	43	27
Thrown something at you?	35	26
Bitten or scratched you?	22	11
Choked or strangled you?	25	17
Forced sex on you or forced you to do something sexual you didn't want to do?	18	14
Used a knife, gun, or other weapon on you?	6	6
Beat you until you were unconscious?	5	4
Burned you?	5	2
Hurt you with some other physical battering?	11	6

*The author is grateful to Jeffrey Edleson for advice in modifying and administering these items.

Table 11.1 identifies the kinds of physical battering victims were asked about and the percentages of victims from both samples that reported experiencing them. That the percentages are larger in the baseline data for most types of battering is a welcome finding. According to victims, 71 percent (n=45) of the offenders from baseline cases repeated by engaging in at least 1 kind of post-incident physical abuse compared to 53 percent (n=146) of the offenders from experimental cases.

Archival data were used to measure recidivism too. Six baseline and 11 experimental offenders whose victims did not report post-incident violence to interviewers were charged with more battering by prosecutors. Among the 11 from experimental cases, the county attorney charged 3 with attacking different victims. Information is unavailable on how many of the 6 baseline offenders attacked different victims because the city attorney's records are incomplete.

A dummy dependent variable was created and coded "1" for offenders who recidivated according to victim reports or prosecutors' files and "0" for offenders who did not. Among offenders from experimental cases, 57 percent (n=157) were coded "1" compared to 83 percent (n=51) of the baseline offenders. All offenders are men and all victims are women.

The major independent variables are dummy variables indicating 3 police responses: taking no formal action, issuing citations to offenders, and arresting and transporting offenders to police headquarters where they were booked and often jailed for a time. In addition, the police took no action in a few cases but sent reports on them to the county attorney's office for prosecutors to decide whether to file charges. The men in these cases were grouped in the analysis with men who were cited. While they were not charged by police, their experience resembled those who were cited because they did not experience immediate costs but faced potential costs later. Finally, it was not possible to distinguish arrestees who were released after being booked from those who were jailed. However, police executives who monitor daily operations report that most arrestees spend at least a brief time in jail.

Table 11.2 reports police responses in the baseline and experimental periods to calls for service related to battering. While DVC innovations seem to have had little impact on whether officers took formal action in the experimental period, their effects were major but impossible to document. Officers in the baseline period did not have to tag cases as battering-related or write reports when they took no formal action. Because they typically used their radios to report taking no formal action, the paper trail describing baseline police responses is incomplete. The actual number of battering cases is unknown as is the number of cases in which police took no formal action. This means that the percentage of baseline cases in which police took no formal action is understated in

Table 11.2 and the percentages of baseline cases in which citations were issued and arrests were made are much smaller than reported.

Table 11.2 Police Actions

	Baseline Period (n = 63) %	Experimental Period (n = 275) %
No formal police action	19	22
Citation issued	52	46
Suspect arrested	29	32
Total:	100	100

Analysis compared associations between police responses and recidivism controlling for whether coordinated interventions were in place, whether offenders had criminal records or had been accused of battering before incidents, and type of victim/offender relationship. A one-tailed test of significance was applied in multiple regression analyses because it was expected that arrest policies coordinated with other interventions would be related to less recidivism.

FINDINGS

The DVC's goal is to expose offenders to certain and consistent sanctions to motivate them to avoid more sanctions by not repeating their violence. Table 11.3 describes the handling of offenders during the baseline and experimental periods. It shows that more offenders were exposed to more criminal justice sanctions in the experimental period. For example, fewer men had the charges against them dismissed by prosecutors in the experimental period and more men in this period were put in pretrial diversion programs or court-ordered counseling services and were fined than in the baseline period. Additionally, 19 percent of baseline offenders were only contacted by police and not arrested or cited according to police reports. As was noted earlier, this percentage would be much larger than its experimental counterpart if the number of baseline cases in which police took no formal action was known. Likewise, the percentages of men who were only cited or arrested in the baseline period would be smaller.

Table 11.3 Degrees of Offender Exposure to the Criminal Justice System*

	Baseline Period (n = 63) %	Experimental Period (n = 275) %
Only contacted by police	19	22
Cited only	27	14
Arrested only	6	4
Put in pretrial diversion	0	20
Charged by prosecutors but charges were dropped later for various reasons	33	19
Found not guilty in court	0	< .5
Put in probation or men's anger program	0	2
Fined under $100	5	5
Fined over $100	6	13
Jailed: For up to 90 days	2	3
For over 90 days	2	0

* Rounding off and the fact that some offenders received more than one punishment (e.g., some were fined and jailed) explains why the percentages in the experimental period total more than 100 percent.

The data in Table 11.4 suggest that coordinated efforts are useful. They show significantly less recidivism (Pearson's $r=-.19$, $p \leq .000$) among offenders from the experimental period. Eighty-three percent of the men in baseline cases re-offended compared to 57 percent of the men in experimental cases.

Determining if police responses are related to this finding required analysis regressing recidivism on them controlling for general experimental effects. A dummy variable was created measuring whether cases occurred before (=0) or after (=1) DVC efforts began. Table 11.5 reports the results of regressing recidivism on police responses and that dummy variable. Compared to no formal action, arrest and citation lack significant associations with recidivism although arrest's is deterrent and strong. While this analysis explained very little variance, it produced a significant coefficient indicating that offenders in experimental cases were 24 percent less likely to re-offend controlling for police responses. To understand this finding, recidivism was regressed on police responses separately for baseline and experimental cases. Table 11.6 reports the results.

Table 11.4 **DVC Interventions and Recidivism**

	Baseline Period (6/1/85 to 5/31/86)	Experimental Period (After 6/1/86)
No Recidivism	12 (19%)	118 (42.9%)
Recidivism	51 (83.3%)	157 (57.1%)
Totals:	63 (100%)	275 (100%)

Pearson's r = -.19, p ≤ .000

Table 11.5 **Regression of Recidivism on Police Actions Controlling for Experimental Effects (n = 338)**

Police Actions:	b	t
No formal action	-- omitted--	
Citation	- .01	- .10
Arrest	- .11	- 1.44
Cases occurred in the experimental period	- .24	- 3.52*
Constant	.84	10.62*

* ≥ 1.64 significant at .05, one-tailed test

Findings in Table 11.6 show that arrest is associated with about 18 percent less re-offending in the experimental period compared to no formal action; the direction of citation's relationship with recidivism is the same but insignificant. In baseline cases, both arrest and citation are significantly related to more recidivism compared to no formal action. These results indicate that arrest coordinated with other interventions is related to significantly less recidivism and that uncoordinated police action, both arrest and citation, is related to significantly more recidivism. These are interesting findings but low rates of explained variance indicate that other influences are at work.

Table 11.6 **Regression of Recidivism on Police Actions in Baseline and Experimental Periods**

	Baseline Period (n = 63)		Experimental Period (n = 275)	
	b	t	b	t
Police Actions:				
No formal action (constant term)	.58	5.24*	.66	10.30*
Citation	.30	2.27*	-.07	-.91
Arrest	.25	1.74*	-.18	-2.15*
	$R^2 = .08$		R^2 -.02	

* ≥ 1.64 significant at .05, one-tailed test

One such set of influences may be other criminal justice interventions. A dummy variable was created to identify men who were prosecuted (=1) and men who were not (=0). Bivariate analysis indicated that the decision to prosecute was not related to recidivism in experimental cases. However, a relationship emerged between the prosecution of cases and more violence in the baseline period (Pearson's r=.26). Since the city attorney handled most of these cases and gave battering a low priority, his office may have tended to prosecute men who committed more serious or violent offenses and who were less treatable. That no relationship emerged between prosecution and recidivism in experimental cases suggests that prosecution has an indirect utility because it reinforces the effects of police action.

Another bivariate analysis examined whether judicial findings of guilt and court-ordered penalties (fines, jail, or probation) were related to recidivism. A dummy variable was created to measure whether men were found guilty and sentenced (=1) or not (=0). Too few men received each kind of penalty to examine its independent association with recidivism. For example, only 7 men from experimental cases were jailed, 5 for 30 days, 1 for 60 days, and 1 for 90 days. Although all 22 percent (n=61) of the offenders coded "1" from experimental cases had time to repeat, no relationship emerged between the dummy variable and recidivism. As with decisions to prosecute, the association between judicial actions and recidivism may be indirect. The courts may influence recidivism by taking battering cases seriously, thereby encouraging prosecutors to file charges and police to take formal action. Too few offenders were coded "1" (n=9) to report findings from the baseline period.

Thus far, analysis has focused on DVC interventions in the expectation that their costs will deter men from re-offending. However, some offenders may be more or less treatable. Others have reported that men with more violent histories tend to be more difficult to treat (e.g., Dutton & McGregor in this book; Sonkin et al., 1985). Two measures of whether offenders have violent histories are whether they had a criminal record at the time incidents occurred or had been accused of battering in the past. This information was available from archival sources. It is possible that men without criminal records or men who had not been accused of battering before incidents are more likely to be deterred by criminal justice interventions.

A dummy variable was created measuring whether men had a criminal record or had been accused of battering before incidents. Men with such records were coded "1" and men without them were coded "0". Fifty-four percent (n=34) of the men from baseline cases were coded "1" as were 48 percent (n=133) of the men from experimental cases. Bivariate analysis indicated that men coded "1" did not re-offend significantly more than men coded "0" in the baseline sample. Eighty-two percent (n=28) of the baseline offenders coded "1" repeated as did 79 percent (n=23) of the men coded "0". However, a small relationship (Pearson's r=.12) emerged in the experimental data: 63 percent (n=84) of the men coded "1" repeated compared to 51 percent (n=73) of the men coded "0".

Finally, analysis examined whether the nature of victim/offender relationships affects associations between interventions and recidivism. Marriage and cohabitation generally involve longer, more intimate relationships than dating and give offenders more opportunity to develop violent habits of interacting with their partners. As a result, men who were or had been in these relationships may be less treatable than daters. This possibility was tested in a bivariate analysis including only offenders who were or had been married to or living with victims when incidents occurred. Another analysis examined only offenders who were dating or had dated victims when incidents occurred. Table 11.7 reports that DVC interventions are still related to significantly less recidivism when only offenders with marital or cohabiting histories with victims are included. The same association emerges in Table 11.8 regarding daters. That just eight pairs of daters are in the baseline period limits the drawing of hard and fast conclusions, however.

Table 11.7 DVC Interventions and Recidivism Among Offenders Who Were or Had Been Married to or Cohabiting with Victims When Incidents Occurred

	Baseline Period (6/1/85 to 5/31/86)	Experimental Period (After 6/1/86)
No Recidivism	11 (20%)	101 (43.7%)
Recidivism	44 (80%)	130 (56.3%)
Totals:	55 (100%)	231 (100%)

Pearson's r = -.19, p ≤ .000

Table 11.8 DVC Interventions and Recidivism Among Offenders Who Were or Had Been Dating Victims When Incidents Occurred

	Baseline Period (6/1/85 to 5/31/86)	Experimental Period (After 6/1/86)
No Recidivism	1 (12.5%)	17 (38.6%)
Recidivism	7 (87.5%)	27 (61.4%)
Totals:	8 (100%)	44 (100%)

CONCLUSION

This chapter examined the association between police responses and recidivism among batterers when the enforcement of arrest policies is coordinated with other criminal justice interventions. It compared this association with one from a baseline period before arrest policies and other new criminal justice responses were adopted and coordinated. As reported in Table 11.4, bivariate analysis indicated that the enforcement of arrest policies in coordination with other interventions is related to significantly less re-offending.

Regressing recidivism on particular police responses revealed that coordination was indeed related significantly to recidivism. As reported in Table 11.6, this analysis showed that, compared to taking no formal action, arresting and citing offenders were related to significantly more re-offending in baseline cases. It also showed that arrest was related to significantly less re-offending when the enforcement of arrest policies was coordinated with other criminal justice responses. That no police training on battering occurred in the baseline period may be important too. Bard argues that intervention by poorly trained officers can produce more violence (1971:3).

That uncoordinated police intervention is tied to significantly more recidivism shows that a traditional police argument for not taking action has some merit. Police intervention can be linked with more violence. As Chief Bouza noted in an earlier chapter, arrest policies are not an "automatic winner." However, this chapter's findings indicate that police action need not have this effect. Coordinating hierarchically supported arrest policies with prosecution and other interventions can turn police action into a deterrent. In fact, bivariate analyses suggested that the major value of other interventions is that they encourage the enforcement of arrest policies and strengthen their deterrent effects. These analyses found that prosecutors' decisions to charge offenders and judicial sanctions were not related to recidivism directly.

Other bivariate analyses indicated that coordinated effort is related to less recidivism among men who do not have a criminal record or a history of battering. This is consistent with findings reported elsewhere that interventions tend to be more effective among men who do not have violent histories. Other bivariate analyses also found that coordinated interventions were related to significantly less recidivism controlling for the kind of relationships offenders had with victims when incidents occurred. There was significantly less recidivism in the experimental period than in the baseline period among offenders who were or had been married to or living with victims when incidents occurred. The same association emerged among men who were or had been dating victims.

Finding that coordinated criminal justice interventions are related to less battering is good news. However, two caveats must be noted. The first is that the findings reported here may not be generalizable to more socioeconomically and racially heterogeneous communities than Lincoln. The other is that low reported levels of explained variance indicate that stronger correlates remain to be found. Nevertheless, these findings are welcome because replications of the Minneapolis experiment revealing the inutility of isolated police action may produce a conservative reaction demanding a repudiation of arrest policies and the need for government intervention.

Finally, researchers looking for stronger policy correlates of recidivism should remember that identifying useful policies does not ensure their adoption or use. Service providers with responsibilities related to battering will continue to do their jobs according to their own styles and priorities. Given public expectations that the many parts of our fragmented policy system represent diverse views, most Americans would not have it any other way.

REFERENCES

Bard, M. (1971). "Iatrogenic Violence." *The Police Chief*, January:16-17.

Dunford, F.W., D. Huizinga & D.S. Elliott (1989). *The Omaha Domestic Violence Police Experiment: Final Report.* Washington, DC: National Institute of Justice.

Sherman, L.W. & R.A. Berk (1984). "Deterrent Effects of Arrest for Domestic Assault." *American Sociological Review*, 49:261-272.

Sonkin, D.J., D. Martin & L. Walker (1985). *The Male Batterer: A Treatment Approach.* New York: Springer Publishing.

Straus, M.A. (1979). "Measuring Intrafamily Conflict and Violence: The Conflict Tactics (CT) Scales." *Journal of Marriage and the Family*, 41:75-88.

Williams, K.R. & R. Hawkins (1989). "The Meaning of Arrest for Wife Assault." *Criminology*, 27:163-181.

12

Research on the Effects of Witnessing Parental Battering: Clinical and Legal Policy Implications

Mary Kenning
University of Nebraska—Lincoln
Anita Merchant
University of Nebraska—Lincoln
Alan Tomkins
University of Nebraska—Lincoln

INTRODUCTION

Approximately 3.3 million children witness their parents' interpersonal violence each year (Carlson, 1984). Despite clinical reports of mothers attempting to hide their battering from their children, one study found that children are present during almost half of all battering incidents (Steinman, 1989). Goodman and Rosenberg (1987) believe that when children are present, they actually witness or are at least aware of nearly all such violent episodes.

Despite their numbers, children of violent families have often been called the "forgotten victims." The effects on children of witnessing battering are understudied and research indicates that there has been little action to treat them or to intervene on their behalf. This is unfortunate considering that the research indicates that adult batterers are likely to have grown up in families in which battering occurred (Kalmuss, 1984; Rosenbaum & O'Leary, 1981; Stahly, 1977-78; Star, 1978). In fact, based on estimates from a national sample, sons who had witnessed their fathers' violence had a 1000 percent greater battering rate than those who had not (Straus, Gelles & Steinmetz, 1980). The purpose of this chapter is to review the available research in this area and to explore the clinical and legal implications suggested by this research.

PSYCHOLOGICAL AND BEHAVIORAL EFFECTS: THE EMPIRICAL EVIDENCE

A review of the relatively sparse literature on this topic suggests that witnessing battering has a measurable effect on children. Jaffe, Wolfe, Wilson and Zak (1986b) found that boys who witnessed battering have a pattern of clinically significant adjustment problems which are similar to those of physically abused boys, but which are significantly different from those of children of nonviolent parents. This finding indicates that witnessing battering, by itself, is harmful to children and that effects similar to those experienced by abused children may emerge among child witnesses. In their study of 198 children aged 4 to 16 from violent and nonviolent families, Wolfe, Jaffe, Wilson and Zak (1985) found that battered mothers rated their children as lower in social competence and higher in symptoms of maladjustment and emotional distress (e.g., anxiety, depression, aggressive behavior, school problems, overactivity, and difficulty in getting along with others). Another study by these researchers showed that children exposed to battering were reported by their mothers to have fewer interests, fewer social activities, and lower school performance (Wolfe, Zak, Wilson & Jaffe, 1986). The authors conclude that these children were highly distressed as a result of witnessing parental violence and that their distress was evidenced in concrete ways such as decreased school performance and lowered social competence.

Other studies have also noted behavioral problems that may be symptomatic of distress related to witnessing family violence. Hershorn and Rosenbaum (1985) found significantly more personality problems (shyness, depression, and anxiety) and conduct problems (disruptiveness, impulsivity, and irritability) among child witnesses than were present among children who had not witnessed parental discord or violence. Hilberman and Munson (1977-78) observed school-related problems among children in shelters such as erratic attendance, poor performance, distractibility, and school phobias. These authors also cited a variety of physical problems in these children. Specifically, they noted such health complaints as headaches, stomachaches, diarrhea, ulcers, intestinal difficulties, asthma, enuresis, and sleep difficulties such as insomnia, sleepwalking, and nightmares.

In a related line of inquiry, Kosky (1983) examined the families of adolescents who had attempted suicide and compared them to families of non-suicidal children under age 14 with mental health problems such as anxiety disorders, depressive illnesses, obsessive-compulsive disorders, and anorexia nervosa. The variables Kosky investigated included child IQ scores, history of illness, schooling, experiences of loss, family illness, intra-familial aggression, and perinatal difficulties. The results showed that intra-familial aggression was rare in the families of the non-suicidal children whereas 65 percent of the families of children who had attempted suicide reported that children had witnessed physical violence between their parents. Although this does not imply a causal relationship between witnessing battering and increased rates of child suicide, it is an interesting finding nonetheless.

Not surprisingly, several studies have found that children who witness parental verbal fighting and battering are less competent in social situations than non-witnessing children (Hershorn & Rosenbaum, 1985; Jaffe, Wolfe, Wilson & Zak, 1986a; Wolfe, Jaffe, Wilson & Zak, 1985). In their study of 25 child witnesses (ages not given), Pfouts, Schopler and Henley (1982) noted that 53 percent acted out violently with parents, 60 percent acted out violently with siblings, 30 percent with peers, and 33 percent with teachers. This finding is interesting because the children appear to be copying the violent behaviors they witnessed between their parents. In addition, 16 percent had appeared in juvenile court, 20 percent were characterized as truants, and 58 percent were rated as below average or failing in school. However, Koski's (1987) review of the research on the association between parent-parent violence and nonfamily delinquent crime indicated there was no clear pattern regarding the relationship between witnessing battering and later involvement in violent or delinquent crime.

Post, Willett, Franks, House and Back (1983) and Steinmetz (1977) have hypothesized that children who witness intra-familial battering have not been exposed to more constructive ways of resolving conflicts. Consequently, researchers have focused specifically on child witnesses' ability to resolve interpersonal conflict. Rosenberg (1987a) found that children from violent families tended to choose either passive or aggressive (angry or demanding) strategies when trying to resolve interpersonal conflict, rather than choosing more assertive strategies. A follow-up study by Groisser (1986) found that child witnesses did not resolve interpersonal conflict well, particularly when they encountered obstacles to their initial solution. A study by Burnett and Daniels (1985) compared young adult men from violent families with young adult men from nonviolent families, examining their abilities to resolve conflict in constructive ways. The results showed that the young men from nonviolent families were able to resolve significantly more conflict situations in a constructive way than were the men from violent families. The researchers explain this finding in terms of differential learning. That is, the men from nonviolent families used the more appropriate and constructive skills exhibited by their parents.

In their study of 16 preschool children from homes where battering had occurred, Hinchey and Gavelek (1982) found that their subjects showed a deficit in abilities commonly associated with the concept of empathy, or "the ability of an individual to identify the feelings or emotional state of another, assume his or her role or perspective, and then act accordingly" (p. 400). They suggest that this deficit may have caused these children to have difficulties in developing intimate relationships. Rosenberg (1987a) also found that child witnesses performed less well on a measure of interpersonal sensitivity which would appear to corroborate Hinchey and Gavelek's findings. These findings will be discussed later in relation to the generational transfer hypothesis.

FACTORS INFLUENCING THE EFFECTS OF WITNESSING BATTERING

Most studies to date have examined the question of whether or not children who witness battering suffer any negative effects. Generally, specific antecedents or mediating factors have not been explored except as they have been noted incidentally. Stressful life events of many types, (e.g., divorce, severe parental alcohol abuse, and serious medical procedures) affect children in highly variable ways. This variability may be a partial function of the child's temperament, social support, and acquired skills. The impact of these factors has not been well researched on children who witness battering.

One finding noted by Jaffe, Wolfe, Wilson and Zak (1986a) is that girls tend to show more internalizing symptoms, such as depression and anxiety, than do boys who tend to display higher degrees of externalizing symptoms. Hershorn and Rosenbaum (1985) found that abused mothers describe their sons as aggressive in their acting out and their daughters as exhibiting more passive-aggressive refusal behavior. This gender difference may follow a pattern similar to the effects on children of other disruptive and traumatic events, such as divorce, serious medical procedures and sexual abuse (Emery, 1982; Rogers & Terry, 1984). These authors also note that there is evidence that adjustment problems in girls tend to have a later onset than for boys. This raises the importance of follow-up studies to determine whether the impact of witnessing battering appears at a later age for females, such as in adolescence or adulthood (Wolfe, Jaffe, Wilson & Zak, 1988).

Jaffe, Wolfe, Wilson and Zak (1986a) also found that the overall adjustment of boys was significantly related to the degree of battering they had witnessed. Hershorn and Rosenbaum (1985), in their study of sons of battered women, found there was a significant relationship between the degree of exposure to marital violence and conduct and personality problems. Jaffe and his colleagues (1986) suggest that their findings support others by Wallerstein and

Kelly (1980) and Straus (1979) that boys may be more vulnerable to family discord than girls. However, other studies have not found these sex differences (Davis & Carlson, 1987; Friedrich, Urquiza & Beilke, 1986).

Children's ages are a factor too. In a study of shelter children by Hughes and Barad (1983), researchers found that on self-esteem measures, older school-aged children (grades 4-7) scored in the average range; younger school-age children (grades 1-3) scored at the lower end of the average range; and preschool children scored well below average. A later study by Hughes (1988) found that preschool child witnesses were reported by their mothers to have the most behavioral problems, more than those reported by mothers of non-witnessing children. Hughes' findings are consistent with studies that documented greater behavioral problems among younger rather than older children (Cass & Thomas, 1979; Lapouse & Monk, 1964; Schechtman, 1970; Weiner, 1982).

Experiencing physical abuse may also influence the way in which a child is affected by witnessing battering. The extent of the overlap between battering and child abuse has been estimated to be as high as 40 to 60 percent (Straus et al., 1980). In their study of over 60 child witnesses, Davis and Carlson (1987) found that the children who had both witnessed abuse and were themselves victims of abuse had significantly lower scores on a measure of social competence than the children who witnessed parental violence. They concluded that the combination of witnessing and receiving abuse has more serious consequences for children than witnessing alone.

A study by Hughes (1988) also documented this pattern. She studied 97 children between the ages of 3 and 12 who were witnesses of battering and victims of abuse, witnesses but not victims of abuse, and non-witnessing, non-abused children. The problems assessed included behavioral problems, anxiety levels, self-esteem, and depressive symptoms. Her methodology was noteworthy because it used children's self-reports in addition to those of parents. Results of this study showed that non-abused witnesses exhibited fewer problems than the abused witnesses but more than children who were neither witnesses nor abused. In addition, she noted that nonabused witnesses did not differ significantly from the comparison group on a measure of problem behavior, but did differ on measures of anxiety. The abused witness sample was significantly different from the comparison group, however, on the measure of problem behavior. Thus, it is important for researchers to know whether the children they are studying have witnessed battering and/or whether they have been the victims of physical abuse.

In homes where children are witnesses to battering as well as victims of physical violence, mothers are responsible for child abuse as well as fathers. Straus, Gelles and Steinmetz (1980) report that battered women are 150 percent more likely to use severe violence with their children than are non-battered women. However, despite the high rate of violent discipline among battered women, researchers find that it is still the male batterer who is more likely to abuse children physically. In a study by Stark and Flitcraft (1988) of a sample of 116 battered women and their abused children, approximately 50 percent of the children were abused by the male batterer and 35 percent were abused by the battered mother. The remaining 15 percent were abused by others or by both the male batterer and the battered mother. Wolfe (1987) reported that the perpetrator of physical abuse is 1.5 times more likely to be male than female.

Another factor that may influence how child witnesses are affected by battering concerns their battered mothers. Some researchers believe that having a psychologically healthy relationship with a caregiver may buffer children against some of the possible effects of witnessing battering (Emery, 1982). Wolfe, Jaffe, Wilson and Zak (1985) suggest that maternal stressors, such as physical and emotional problems or financial or housing crises, may be mediating factors, given that stress accounted for 19 percent of the variance in explaining child behavior problems. They suggest that the final impact of witnessing battering on a child may be influenced by the mother's degree of impairment following violent episodes. They also note that increased measures of maternal stress appear to be related to the occurrence of other forms of physical violence occurring in the family.

This relationship may not exist solely with respect to the mothers. Kratcoski (1984) found that family violence was more likely to occur in families generally characterized by low levels of family functioning. "Family functioning" was defined as the degree to which all family members were mutually supportive of each others' social-emotional goals and needs. Thus, maternal stress may coexist with stress for other family members when they are not functioning as parts of a cooperative family unit.

A related study by Jouriles, Barling and O'Leary (1987) suggested that battering may affect children negatively because it profoundly affects parents' ability to comprehend and respond to their children's needs. These researchers studied 45 children of women who had been victims of battering and examined the relationships between battering, child physical abuse, and the behavior problems of the children. Using standardized measures of family violence and children's behavior problems, they noted that battering is associated with physical child abuse and child behavior problems, but that witnessing battering was not significantly related to child behavior problems. Therefore, marital problems predict child behavior problems by virtue of their association with parenting. Although the results of this study must be replicated, it does suggest that researchers can err in identifying the causes of child behavior problems in homes where battering occurs.

In a summary of the literature in this area, Elbow (1982) suggests several reasons for parental denial or ignorance of the impact of parental violence on children. Recognition of the problem can cause a mother to feel guilty or, because she may be worried about her own survival or depressed, she may be unable to attend to the needs of her children. The mother's psychological problems may prevent her from understanding her children's behavior. Thus, it is possible that the way in which an abused parent is affected by violence can influence how child witnesses of abuse are affected by it. The extent to which an abused parent becomes psychologically or emotionally unavailable to her child needs to be explored as a possible additional stressor for children or as the removal of a buffer that protects children from some of the effects of witnessing parental violence.

It is important to remember that although maternal stress is one mediating factor, it would be inappropriate to "blame the victim" and ignore other mediating factors. There is little clinical or practical benefit from blaming battered women for increases in their levels of stress or decreases in psychological functioning as results of being battered.

TREATMENT RESEARCH

There has been very little published regarding the treatment of children who witness battering. Stullman, Schoenenberger and Hanks (1987) have conceptualized the assessment of violent families and varying types of treatment for them by categorizing them into three types. In a Type I family where violence has occurred no more than once and with less severity, short-term crisis-oriented therapy may help the child witness most. Any evidence of post-traumatic stress disorder can be assessed by exploring the child's subjective experiences of the event and other symptoms such as nightmares, anger, and fears. A Type II family in which violence is episodic, explosive, and cyclic requires both an initial crisis-oriented intervention as well as a complete evaluation to determine appropriateness for individual therapy for the child and/or parents and for family and/or marital therapy. A Type III family, where multiple problems exist and violence pervades members' interactions, may require placing a child in a foster home or treatment facility. Long-term treatment plans may also be needed for the entire family.

Research findings on mediating factors in the development of negative effects on child witnesses (i.e., the mother-child relationship, conflict resolution skills, post-traumatic stress) can be used to design treatment programs. Indeed, some treatment programs for children are based on empirical findings and mental health professionals have begun designing and implementing others. One program described by Gentry and Eaddy (1980) is based on a family systems approach in which all members of the family are treated, including the abuser. Appropriate precautions may be required but the authors contend that including the abuser in treatment helps children learn that problems can be resolved within the family. They suggest that removing the perpetrator may simply cause the child to experience further loss, confusion, and guilt. Further, if the abuser is not involved in treatment, he may seek revenge against the family, become violent toward others, or move on to a new family and re-offend. Treatment can teach family members appropriate ways to resolve conflict and child therapy can help children feel more positively about themselves. Cooperative play, art therapy, and bonding exercises are used in this program to help children develop trusting relationships with others.

Another program to treat child witnesses is described by Grusznski, Brink and Edleson (1988). Using a group-therapy format, children met for 1 hour for 10 weeks. Family sessions also met directly following children's groups. In the children's groups, the expression of feelings and self-disclosure were encouraged so that children could begin to deal with issues that revolve around responsibility for the violence, shame and isolation, protection planning, conflict resolution, gender role, and self-esteem. Group leaders used clinical rating scales to assess whether children met each of four program goals. The results showed that the majority of the children acknowledged that violence in the family was not their fault, enjoyed increased self-esteem, learned new resources and ways to protect themselves, and learned nonviolent ways of resolving conflict. This study did not include a control group and the group leaders rated outcomes.

The results of a pilot intervention project have been reported by Jaffe, Wilson and Wolfe (1986) in which 18 boy and girl battering witnesses between the ages of 8 and 13 were followed over 10 weeks of group counseling sessions. One-hour structured interviews were conducted with the children and their mothers before the group began and after it ended. The main focus of the groups was to bring about attitude change and enhance skills. Results from interviews with the mothers showed that 93 percent thought their children enjoyed participating in the group and 62 percent believed their children had learned something from the group. However, only 34 percent thought their children showed significant behavior changes. Results from interviews with the children indicated that more children could identify appropriate strategies to handle an emergency situation, that they could identify more positive things about themselves, and that there was a decrease in the extent of violence the child condoned in the family following group counseling.

Cassady, Allen, Lyon and McGeehan (1987) designed what they called a Child-Focused Intervention Program based on a recognition that children are often confused and stressed when they enter shelters and may need to learn new coping skills. Children therefore attended a psychoeducational support group focused on raising self-esteem, helping them to understand responsibility for violence, helping them to express emotions, and developing feelings of trust. Preliminary results of this pilot program indicated that, in a sample of 33 children between the ages of 2 months and 12 years, the children exhibited better social skills, screamed less, and reported fewer physical complaints.

Silvern and Kaersvang (1989) suggest that treatments should focus on encouraging the child to disclose what he has witnessed to others. They argue that questions about children's reactions may prevent them from communicating information and that a better approach may be to concentrate on details mentioned by the children and to let them elaborate. Mowbray (1987) suggests that long-term treatment goals include helping the child face the truth about battering, dealing with the "damaged goods syndrome," identifying guilt and blame, dealing with the expression of emotions, and helping the child access supportive resources for the future. The process of working with children who have been traumatized requires patience and researchers mention the need for training for those who work with these children to avoid traumatizing them again. It is important to remember that there is hope for child witnesses. A comparison of children from non-violent families, recent witnesses of violence, and previous witnesses indicates that the effects of parental conflict and separation can be ameliorated if the violence is eliminated and opportunities for recovery are provided (Emery, 1982; Walker, 1979; Wolfe, Zak, Wilson & Jaffe, 1986).

LIMITATIONS OF THE RESEARCH

Although available research suggests that witnessing battering does have a negative impact on children, a review of the literature reveals several methodological limitations. Often, mothers' reports are the primary or sole source of information regarding the effects of witnessing battering on children's behavior. Wolfe, Jaffe, Wilson and Zak (1985) suggest that mothers' reports could be negatively biased if they associate their sons with their violent fathers. In addition, Hughes (1988) suggests that mothers also may be biased depending upon their own defensiveness or desire for help and that their own level of psychological distress may contribute. Hughes and Barad (1983) found that mothers, in general, tend to rate their children more negatively than other observers. Although this may reflect mothers' greater familiarity with and sensitivity to their children's behavior, as these researchers suggest, it is important to balance the mothers' reports with reports from other sources such as teachers, other caretakers, other family members, or shelter staff.

Another limitation is that most studies have been done with shelter residents. Since children whose mothers do contact and find shelter may have witnessed more, less, or different types of battering than children whose mothers never contact or take up residence in a shelter, these children may not be a representative sample of all child witnesses. A related problem is that children of violent families may suffer from a variety of other stressors which come with being the child of a violent family (e.g., frequent moves, frequent temporary stays away from home, erratic school attendance, inability to maintain long-term friends, parental separation or loss, child abuse, and economic disadvantage) which may affect them in complex ways (Jaffe, Wolfe, Wilson & Zak, 1986a). Because of the possible existence of multiple stressors, it may be difficult to identify exactly what effect witnessing battering has over and above the effects of these other stressors. Children in shelters often are studied over a brief length of time, owing partly to the norm of short-term stays in shelters. Thus, many children are often not available for study for more than a few days and follow-up studies become virtually impossible if frequent moves occur following the shelter stay. As a result, there have been very few longitudinal studies and very little is known about possible long-term effects. There is a great need to study children from violent families through their developmental years into adulthood. In addition, data will be of greater utility if they are used to test theoretical hypotheses. It is to the topic of explanatory theories that we now turn.

EXPLANATORY THEORIES FOR THE EFFECTS OF WITNESSING PARENTAL VIOLENCE

Much of the research in the field of domestic violence has conceptualized the development of physical violence in families in terms of social learning or modeling theory (Bandura, 1977) which is more formally known as the generational transfer hypothesis. It states that children learn to be violent by participating in a violent family where the emotional and moral meaning of violence is taught implicitly and explicitly by parents (Straus et al., 1980). Violence between family members provides a model for learning violent behavior as an acceptable means of expressing anger, reacting to stress, or controlling others (Kalmuss, 1984). As aggressive behavior by children in violent families is often unpunished, there is ample opportunity to adopt and practice violent interpersonal skills, (Patterson, 1982). Many studies show that batterers are more likely to come from families where they witnessed parental violence (Hilberman & Munson, 1977-78; Kalmuss, 1984; Rosenbaum & O'Leary, 1981; Schechter, 1982; Stahly, 1977-78; Star, 1978). Fagan, Stewart and Hansen (1983) found that exposure to violence in childhood is a strong predictor of both the prevalence and severity of later family violence. Sons who witnessed their fathers' violence had a 1000 percent greater rate of wife abuse than sons who had not (Straus et al., 1980). For females the picture is less clear, although some studies have found that girls who have witnessed parental violence are more likely to become victims of violence by their partners (Hotaling & Sugarman, 1986; Walker & Browne, 1985). These correlational studies do not give us solid information regarding the long-term effects of witnessing battering on children;

however, they do suggest that short-term effects may eventually play a role in the development of family violence in the next generation.

How is family violence transmitted from one generation to the next? One possible path involves the lower rates of social competence and the decreased empathic and constructive conflict resolution skills which have been noted in child witnesses of family violence. Assuming that nonviolent and more appropriate patterns of interpersonal interaction require partners to recognize and respond in assertive ways to the emotional states of others, decreases in ability to do this as children may set the stage for the development of later interpersonal difficulties (Rosenberg, 1987a). In addition, the modeling of violent behaviors, which can be seen in the higher rates of behavior problems in boys who witness battering, may extend into adulthood and become the only learned option for dealing with interpersonal conflict. The preliminary work on the mechanisms by which generational transfer may occur needs to be extended to examine whether there are particular characteristics or situations which make it more likely that children will develop battering behaviors in adulthood.

Some researchers, such as Stark and Flitcraft (1989), argue that the generational transfer hypothesis does not account for the large number of men who batter their partners and who neither witnessed nor experienced physical violence in childhood. They argue that the hypothesis "pathologizes abuse by attributing it to a subset of deviants from bad (or violent) homes" (p.15) and ignores the fact that although both boys and girls are exposed to battering, it is most often men who use battering to control their partners. Other researchers point out that the social learning model does not explain findings regarding diverse affective symptoms such as low self-esteem and depression (Silvern & Kaersvang, 1989). These may best be accounted for by the theory of post-traumatic stress syndrome. Witnessing battering may evoke trauma in children and feelings of anxious excitement, terror, or helplessness may account for children's reactions.

Adult reactions to traumatic events include sleep disturbances, traumatic nightmares, daytime preoccupation with the event, startle reactions, and flashbacks. Some symptoms of post-traumatic stress disorder in children are physical problems, an increase in fears or worries, feelings of guilt, behavioral disturbances including acting out or withdrawal, regression to the behaviors of an earlier stage of development, and denial (Mowbray, 1987). In studies by Hershorn and Rosenbaum (1985), Hilberman and Munson (1977-78), and Jaffe, Wolfe, Wilson and Zak (1986a), these latter symptoms are among those reported by mothers of child witnesses of battering. Thus, the act of witnessing battering may qualify as an event profound enough to cause a child to experience a form of post-traumatic stress disorder.

SUMMARY

Three general patterns of findings emerge from this review of the literature. First, witnessing battering can have a negative impact on children, comparable in type although not in severity to the effects of physical abuse. The impact of exposure to violence may be indirect rather than direct and may be mediated by mothers' health and availability to their children, stressful life events, and family crises (Wolfe, Jaffe, Wilson & Zak, 1985) as well as by temperamental differences, acquired skills or social influences on the child (Garmezy, 1983; Rosenberg, 1987a). Two studies indicate that the level of marital conflict and disharmony witnessed by children is critical in predicting children's later adjustment, too (Emery, 1982; Wolfe et al., 1985). However, no research finding directly relates the level or amount of battering witnessed by children to behavioral or psychological sequelae.

The second pattern is that children in violent homes are at high risk of being physically abused. Although all male batterers do not abuse their children, woman battering and child abuse overlap by as much as 40 to 60 percent (Straus et al., 1980). Men are more likely than women to abuse their children physically, a surprising finding given that fathers typically spend much less time with children than mothers and are less responsible for direct child care. However, battered women are much more likely to use harsh physical punishment or to be abusive physically than non-battered mothers (Straus et al., 1980). Although it is likely that such abuse is related to maternal stressors and problem-solving skills as well as financial disadvantage and family crises, there are no data to confirm this directly.

Finally, although much of the data on the adjustment of child witnesses to battering come from mothers, the types of problems reported (poor conflict resolution and interpersonal problem-solving skills, lowered empathy, and decreased social competence) are all closely related to the types of problems seen in adult batterers and to some extent victims. Research has not yet established direct links between these problems and adult behavior; but studies completed thus far suggest that the kinds of social skills and anger control deficits seen in adult batterers may be present early on rather than simply appearing in adult relationships.

A neglected related area of interest involves the incidence of child sexual abuse which takes place in violent families. It is not known whether child sexual abuse is related to parental violence. However, the attitudes of a parent who batters his partner may be similar to those of a parent who sexually abuses his child. He may relate to both family members by remaining very distant emotionally or by attempting to control their behavior. It is also possible that battering, with its frequent concomitant stressors such as moving, separation, etc., may decrease the parent's and especially the mother's availability to the child.

Research by Finkelhor (1986) suggests that such unavailability places a child at greater risk for sexual abuse. Research needs to explore the possible relationship between battering in the home and the risk of sexual abuse for children.

What implications do these findings have for intervention and prevention? One prevention strategy is to encourage mental health professionals—whether they are treating children, families, battered women, or batterers—to investigate the presence or extent of violence between parents as well as the possibility that a child may be physically abused. This is particularly important when a child is identified as having poor social skills or other behavior problems. Parents could then be told the consequences for children exposed to battering and encouraged to examine the impact of their behavior on their children (Jaffe, Wolfe, Wilson & Zak, 1986a). This strategy may be more effective in situations where there have been few episodes of violence of low to moderate severity, i.e., Type I families (Stullman et al., 1987).

Shelter treatment and follow-up treatment programs for children that try to address the common problems of children exposed to battering are an additional intervention strategy. Alessi and Hearn (1984) and Jaffe, Wilson and Wolfe (1986) have suggested that strategies which include both immediate assistance and training in longer-term problem-solving skills have the greatest potential to prevent serious adjustment difficulties for child witnesses. Immediate assistance can include crisis management to help the child adapt to the rapid and intrusive changes that may occur after the battering. This can involve helping the child stay in the same school or with the same group of friends, encouraging one or both parents to maintain a relationship with the child and explaining the nature and responsibility of the violence in an age-appropriate manner. Longer term interventions include helping the child maintain previous social support systems with peers or adults and education on appropriate interpersonal problem-solving strategies. Although it is paramount to ensure the child's ongoing safety, simply isolating him or her from the perpetrator may inadvertently contribute to more long-term adjustment problems (Jaffe, Wilson & Wolfe, 1986).

Early intervention programs in schools to teach children about ways to respond in a crisis and coping skills might also be used. Such programs have been used in the Los Angeles area (Timnick, 1989). They allow services to reach children who may be witnesses to battering but whose mothers are unlikely to use shelter facilities, the main current resource for child witnesses.

LEGAL AND POLICY IMPLICATIONS

Traditional legal constructs have too often been inadequate to stop or prevent violence. Because of their limitations, social scientists and legal commentators have called for legal changes to address the reality of violence in the home. In light of emerging empirical evidence on the effects of witnessing battering reviewed in this chapter, what legal and policy innovations might be appropriate?

Two analogies to the child witnessing context are (1) viewing violence on television and in the movies and, (2) psychological maltreatment. Both television/movie violence and psychological maltreatment have been recognized as controversial targets for legal reform. A cursory review of these two contexts is a useful part of any discussion of law and policy regarding interventions for child witnesses.

People have worried for years that a child's viewing of broadcast violence will be harmful. Although there is concern that viewing some forms of violence (e.g., sexual violence) is associated with tendencies for viewers to become insensitive to violence and more likely to subscribe to antisocial attitudes (e.g., Malamuth & Briere, 1986), there are strong, constitutional reasons to prefer a limited role for government in regulating broadcasts because of an even greater concern about censorship and other restrictions to free speech (e.g., Campbell, in press; Linz, Penrod & Donnerstein, 1986). Thus, there is a contradiction between the desire to reduce the potential for violent behavior and the desire to protect freedom of speech. Judicial reviews of government regulations of violent content in the media (whether broadcast or print), typically give freedom of speech a higher priority (e.g., *Winters v. New York*, 1948; *Writers' Guild of America, West v. FCC*, 1976; see generally, Krattenmaker & Powe, 1978).

Psychological maltreatment offers a similar policy problem. It is somewhat simpler to identify what is "violent" television than it is to identify what is "psychological" abuse. A parent who constantly belittles a child, yells at the child, tells the child that he is worthless, and otherwise acts to undermine the child's sense of self and sense of potency is clearly mistreating the child psychologically. But what about the unsupportive parent? What about parents who tell their teenagers that their school grades, friends, or activities are not quite good enough? Is this psychological maltreatment? As Garrison (1987:157) points out, it is critically important to know what we are looking for when we label behaviors as psychologically abusive: should we focus on "perpetrators' acts or on psychological harm to the child?" The difficulty of defining psychological maltreatment and the low probability that legal intervention can treat it has produced calls for caution in policy-making (e.g., Melton & Thompson, 1987; Melton & Davidson, 1987).

The difficulty in pinpointing the behaviors that harm children makes it unwise to adopt laws allowing government intervention based on "psychological maltreatment" theory. Moreover, the research on psychological maltreatment is scant. Even clinical "interventions have been based more on intuition than on empirical findings" (Rosenberg, 1987b:166). This is an area where more empirical evidence is needed before policies are adopted and enforced that articulate the kinds and ranges of permissible state-sponsored interventions.

In summary, there has been a reluctance to support extensive legal intervention regarding broadcast violence and psychological maltreatment. Should the same reluctance be exercised when a child has witnessed the battering of his/her mother? We think not. Unlike the viewing of television/movie violence, there is not the same explicit, fundamental, constitutional right at stake to mitigate against intervention. Broadcasters have explicit First Amendment protections; in order to overcome such protections, "compelling interest" must be shown. The literature on the effects of media violence is not definitive enough yet to justify using the law to punish or regulate broadcasters (Campbell, in press). This also mitigates against extensive regulation regarding psychological maltreatment.

The United States Supreme Court has accorded family and marital privacy significant protections under the Constitution in numerous cases over the past half-century (see Developments in the Law, 1980; Mnookin, 1978). For example, in *Meyer v. Nebraska* (1923), the Court held that a state may not unreasonably interfere with parental right to make educational choices for their offspring; *Pierce v. Society of Sisters* (1925) stated that parents, not the state, are responsible for a child's upbringing; in *Skinner v. Oklahoma* (1942) the Court indicated that there are constitutional protections to the integrity of family life that include the right to procreate; *Griswold v. Connecticut* (1965) ruled that the use of contraceptives is protected under marital privacy rights; and *Loving v. Virginia* (1967), provided constitutional freedom of choice to marry whomever one pleases.

Nevertheless, privacy rights have, during the same period, regularly been subordinated to other ends such as promoting community health or welfare interests through laws mandating smallpox vaccinations (*Jacobson v. Massachusetts*, 1905), limiting access to pornography (e.g., *Paris Adult Theatre v. Slaton*, 1973), or requiring the use of motorcycle helmets (e.g., *Everhardt v. City of New Orleans*, 1968). Indeed, the U.S. Supreme Court has even held that the right to procreate can be subordinated to a state's interest in protecting mentally infirm, institutionalized women with a limited capacity to make reproductive decisions (*Buck v. Bell*, 1927). In *Buck*, the Commonwealth of Virginia decided that sterilizing these women was in their best interests to protect their health and welfare and the Court, in a decision that is still controversial, affirmed the state's decision. The implication of these Supreme Court decisions is that the right to privacy that provides parents with general protections from state intrusion into child-rearing activities and the privacy of family life does not completely restrict the state from protecting the safety and welfare of children (e.g., *Prince v. Massachusetts*, 1944).

The recent abortion decision in *Webster v. Reproductive Health Services* (1989) again addressed the issue of whether privacy rights are fundamental rights that require any intrusion to be justified by compelling reasons (see especially the plurality opinion of Chief Justice Rehnquist, pp. 3054-3058, which discusses this issue directly). In the aftermath of the *Webster* decision, it seems certain that whenever a fundamental right is not at stake, the state is legally justified to intervene as long as there is a "reasonable relationship" between the actions mandated and the rationales underlying the state's actions. Moreover, even without a reversal of the right to privacy analysis underlying *Roe v. Wade* (1973), it is permissible to intrude into family "privacy" if such interventions promote a greater good, if there are compelling reasons for the intrusion, and if there are not other means available to accomplish the laudable purposes promoted by the intervention (e.g., *Roe v. Wade*, 1973:152-153).

The recent decision in *Baltimore City Department of Social Services v. Bouknight* (1990) underscores the fact that when a child's health and well-being are at stake, fundamental rights may be subordinated to the child's interests. In *Bouknight*, the Court held that a mother's Fifth Amendment privilege against self-incrimination (a fundamental constitutional right) did not shield her from disclosing the whereabouts of her son to the juvenile court judge when the judge was trying to protect the child's well-being. The mother's constitutional interest in avoiding self-incrimination was at stake because there was ample evidence to suggest that by revealing the location of her son, Bouknight would be giving evidence that she had beaten her son to death.

Although written as a Fifth Amendment analysis, the *Bouknight* case reinforces the view that child safety issues justify intervention into the sanctity of parents' constitutional rights. Regarding child witnesses, we think it is reasonable—and probably even compelling—to allow a diminution of family privacy in order to protect the welfare of children who might be at risk (see Feshbach & Feshbach, 1978). Although the literature may not yet offer conclusive findings, we think it shows a sufficient scientific basis to presume that children who view severe or very frequent battering of their mothers or other adult females are at risk of undesirable behavioral and psychological sequelae.

Moreover, unlike the situation regarding psychological maltreatment, the precipitating event is not without a specific, physical referent. Where a woman's battering has been documented (or is a reasonable certainty), we think that this "observable event" justifies state and clinical investigation of trauma to the witnessing child. Because the consequences of witnessing in many of their manifestations mirror those of actual abuse, we think that the same types of interventions allowed under abuse and neglect laws are applicable. Thus, therapeutic interventions are warranted, including removal in the most severe cases. As a matter of policy, however, we recommend adopting the "least intrusive alternative" (see Tomkins & Kepfield, in press, for a similar policy argument in a different child welfare context.)

To begin with, we suggest that mental health professionals be required to conduct an evaluation of the family when there is documentation of woman battering in the home. Just as there are requirements for any social service, mental health, medical, or other professional to make a report when there is a suspicion of direct child abuse in a home, a report should also be required when woman battering is involved. This involves limited intrusion. Rather than remove youngsters from their homes, it is preferable to work with them in their homes and in their schools using the types of clinical interventions previously described. Violence is a part of many children's lives. The presence of violence, however, does not obviate the need for policies that provide for the least restrictive intervention available that might best address the impact of this violence on the children who view it.

We also think more intrusive interventions are supportable when less onerous means are not practical. Clearly, if women's rights can be infringed to promote the health and welfare of their offspring (e.g., *International Union, UAW v. Johnson Controls*, 1989; In re Ruiz, 1986, see generally Tomkins & Kepfield, in press), then parental privacy can be invaded to protect the safety and psychological well-being of children who view violence in their homes.

Several state court opinions seem to support this conclusion. For example, using neglect jurisdiction, some courts have upheld extremely intrusive interventions (i.e., removal of a child from the home) in instances when the removed child had not been identified as a direct victim of parental neglect. In one case, an intermediary appellate court in Illinois upheld a child's removal from her home under a neglect theory. Her siblings appeared to be victims of physical abuse but she did not appear to be an abuse victim herself. The appellate court held that it was reasonable to remove a non-abused child from her home given the substantiated violence against her siblings. The court refused to wait until an actual episode of violence was substantiated against the youth herself before removing her from the home for her protection. The court noted that given the evidence of "abuse in the home," protective removal was legally justified under an Illinois statute providing that a youth is neglected if she is in an "environment injurious" to her welfare (*In Interest of Brooks*, 1978:879-881).

Other state court cases have referred more directly to child witnessing of woman battering (typically the mother, a stepmother, or a girlfriend) to justify custody decisions. *In re Marriage of Godwin* (1982), child custody was awarded to the father; among the factors considered by the court was the fact that the child was a witness to violence between the father's ex-wife and her new husband. In *Blackburn v. Blackburn* (1983), child custody was also changed from mother to father; among the factors considered was that the child witnessed physical pushing and fighting between his mother and the mother's live-in boyfriend. In *Feltman v. Feltman* (1984), a father petitioned for custody of his daughter because her mother's beatings by her live-in boyfriend were witnessed by her and she "worried about her mother and sometimes had trouble sleeping" (p. 620). Finally, in *Wolfson v. Minerbo* (1985), the court had to deal with children's refusal to visit their father after witnessing him fight physically with their mother. The court ordered family therapy.

CONCLUSION

What the law will support and what makes good public policy are not necessarily coterminous. A major problem with trying to use the law to prevent or remedy the harms that children may experience after witnessing battering is that the law can be a blunt instrument. Thus, as we have discussed, the courts will probably uphold laws that allow the removal of a child from the home in substantiated instances of woman battering when there have been efforts to use less intrusive means prior to removal. But what would be the impact of a policy that allows removal as a final response when a woman has been battered? Although precise evaluation requires empirical support, we speculate that an unintended consequence might be revictimization for battered women by a judicial system that tacitly holds them to blame for not having left the battering relationship and not having protected their children from witnessing or experiencing physical abuse. Thus, care needs to be taken in promoting policies that treat battered women, as well as their children, as passive objects of violent forces. Nonetheless, taking the evidence available to date along with the laws relevant to child witnesses, we think it is better to err on the side of implementing policies that allow early intervention for the benefit of children that may stigmatize and disadvantage battered women further rather than let children face more exposure to situations producing known adverse sequelae for them. As the Court indicated in *Prince v. Massachusetts* (1944:166-167), although "[i]t is cardinal... that the custody, care and nurture of the child reside first in the parents.... the state has a wide range of power for limiting parental freedom" when parental behaviors overstep permissible bounds. Substantiated instances of woman battering should be prima facie evidence that permissible bounds have been overstepped.

REFERENCES

Alessi, J.J. & K. Hearn (1984). "Group Treatment of Children in Shelters for Battered Women." In A.R. Roberts (ed.) *Battered Women and Their Families*, pp. 49-61. New York: Springer Publishing.

Baltimore City Department of Social Services v. Bouknight, 58 U.S.L.W. 4184 (U.S. February 20, 1990) (Nos. 88-1182 & 88-6651).

Bandura, A. (1977). *Social Learning Theory*. Englewood Cliffs, NJ: Prentice-Hall.

Blackburn v. Blackburn, 168 Ga. App. 66, 308 S.E.2d 193 (1983).

Buck v. Bell, 274 U.S. 200 (1927).

Burnett, E.C. & J. Daniels (1985). "The Impact of Origin and Stress on Interpersonal Conflict Resolution Skills in Young Adult Men." *American Mental Health Counselors Association Journal*, 7:162-171.

Campbell, E. (1990). "Television Violence: Social Science vs. the Law." *Loyola Entertainment Law Journal*, 7:413-466.

Carlson, B.E. (1984). "Children's Observations of Interpersonal Violence." In *Battered Women and Their Families: Intervention Strategies and Treatment Programs*. New York: Springer Publishing.

Cass, L.K. & C.B. Thomas (1979). *Childhood Pathology and Later Adjustment*. New York: John Wiley.

Cassady, L., B. Allen, E. Lyon & D. McGeehan (1987). "The Child-Focused Intervention Program: Treatment and Program Evaluation for Children in a Battered Women's Shelter." Paper presented at the Third National Family Violence Researcher Conference, Durham, New Hampshire, July.

Coleman, D.H. & M.A. Straus (1986). "Marital Power, Conflict, and Violence in a Nationally Representative Sample of American Couples." *Violence and Victims*, 1:141-157.

Davis, L.V. & B.E. Carlson (1987). "Observation of Spouse Abuse: What Happens to the Children?" *Journal of Interpersonal Violence*, 2:278-291.

"Developments in the Law: The Constitution and the Family" (1980). *Harvard Law Review*, 93:1156-1383.

Dobash, R.E. & R.P. Dobash (1984). "The Nature and Antecedents of Violent Events." *British Journal of Criminology*, 24(3):269-288.

Elbow, M. (1982). "Children of Violent Marriages: The Forgotten Victims." *Social Casework*, 63(8):465-471.

Emery, R. (1982). "Interpersonal Conflict and the Children of Discord and Violence." *Psychological Bulletin*, 92:310-330. University Press.

Everhardt v. City of New Orleans, 253 La. 285, 217 So. 2d 400 (1968), *appeal dismissed*, 395 U.S. 212 (1969).

Fagan, J.A., D.K. Stewart & K.V. Hansen (1983). "Violent Men or Violent Husbands?" In D. Finkelhor, R.J. Gelles, G.T. Hotaling & M.A. Straus (eds.) *The Dark Side of Families*. Beverly Hills, CA: Sage Publications.

Feltman v. Feltman, 99 A.D.2d 540, 471 N.Y.S.2d 619 (1984).

Feshbach, S. & N.D. Feshbach (1978). "Child Advocacy and Family Privacy." *Journal of Social Issues*, 34(2):168-178.

Finkelhor, D. (1986). *A Sourcebook on Child Sexual Abuse*. Beverly Hills, CA: Sage Publications.

Friedrich, W. N., A.J. Urquiza & R.L. Beilke (1986). "Behavior Problems in Young Sexually Abused Young Children." *Journal of Pediatric Psychology*, 2:47-57.

Garmezy, N. (1983). "Stressors of Childhood." In N. Garmezy & M. Rutter (eds.) *Stress, Coping and Development in Children*, pp. 43-84. New York: McGraw-Hill.

Garrison, E.G. (1987). "Psychological Maltreatment of Children: An Emerging Focus for Inquiry and Concern." *American Psychologist*, 42:157-159.

Gentry, C.E. & V.B. Eaddy (1980). "Treatment of Children in Spouse Abusive Families." *Victimology*, 5(2-4):240-250.

Goodman, G.S. & M.S. Rosenberg (1987). "The Child Witness to Family Violence: Clinical and Legal Considerations." In D. Sonkin (ed.) *Domestic Violence on Trial: Psychological and Legal Dimensions of Family Violence*, pp. 97-126. New York: Springer Publishing.

Griswold v. Connecticut, 381 U.S. 479 (1965).

Groisser, D. (1986). "Child Witness to Family Violence: Social Problem-Solving Skills and Behavioral Adjustment." Unpublished doctoral dissertation. Denver, CO: University of Denver.

Grusznski, R.J., J.C. Brink & J.C. Edleson (1988). "Support and Education Groups for Children of Battered Women." *Child Welfare*, CXVII:431-444.

Hershorn, M. & A. Rosenbaum (1985). "Children of Marital Violence: A Closer Look at the Unintended Victims." *American Journal of Orthopsychiatry*, 55:260-266.

Hilberman, E. & K. Munson (1977-1978). "Sixty Battered Women." *Victimology*, (2):460-470.

Hotaling, G.T. & D.B. Sugarman (1986). "An Analysis of Risk Markers in Husband to Wife Violence: The Current State of Knowledge." *Violence and Victims*, 1(2):101-124.

Hinchey, F.S. & J.R. Gavelek (1982). "Empathic Responding in Children of Battered Mothers." *Child Abuse and Neglect*, 6:395-401.

Hughes, H.M. (1988). "Psychology and Behavior Correlates of Family Violence in Child Witnesses and Victims." *American Journal of Orthopsychiatry*, 58:77-90.

Hughes, H.M. & S.J. Barad (1983). "Psychological Functioning of Children in a Battered Women's Shelter: A Preliminary Investigation." *American Journal of Orthopsychiatry*, 53:525-531.

In re Brooks, 63 Ill. App. 3d 328, 379 N.E.2d 872 (1978).

In re Marriage of Godwin, 104 Ill. App. 3d 790, 433 N.E.2d 310 (1982).

In re Ruiz, 27 Ohio Misc. 2d 31, 500 N.E.2d 935 (Ohio Comm. Pl. 1986).

International Union, UAW v. Johnson Controls, 886 F.2d 871 (7th Cir. 1989).

Jacobson v. Massachusetts, 197 U.S. 11 (1905).

Jaffe, P., S. Wilson & D.A. Wolfe (1986). "Promoting Changes in Attitudes and Understanding of Conflict Resolution Among Child Witnesses of Family Violence." *Canadian Journal of Behavioral Science*, 18:356-366.

Jaffe, P., D. Wolfe, S.K. Wilson & L. Zak (1986a). "Family Violence and Child Adjustment: A Comparative Analysis of Girls' and Boys' Behavioral Symptoms." *American Journal of Psychiatry*, 143:74-77.

_____ (1986b). "Similarities in Behavioral and Social Maladjustment Among Child Victims and Witnesses to Family Violence." *American Journal of Orthopsychiatry*, 56:142-146.

Jouriles, E.W., J. Barling & D.K. O'Leary (1987). "Predicting Child Behavior Problems in Maritally Violent Families." *Journal of Abnormal Child Psychology*, 15:165-173.

Kalmuss, D. (1984). "The Intergenerational Transmission of Marital Aggression." *Journal of Marriage and the Family*, 51:11-19.

Koski, P. (1987). "Family Violence and Nonfamily Deviance: Taking Stock of the Literature." *Marriage and Family Review*, 12:23-46.

Kosky, R. (1983). "Childhood Suicidal Behavior." *Journal of Child Psychology and Psychiatry and Allied Disciplines*, 24:457-468.

Kratcoski, P.C. (1984). "Perspectives on Intrafamily Violence." *Human Relations*, 37:443-453.

Krattenmaker, T.G. & L.A. Powe, Jr. (1978). "Televised Violence: First Amendment Principles and Social Science." *Virginia Law Review*, 64:1123-1297.

Lapouse, R. & M. Monk (1964). "Behavior Deviations in a Representative Sample of Children." *American Journal of Orthopsychiatry*, 34:436-446.

Linz, D., S. Penrod & E. Donnerstein (1986). "Issues Bearing on the Legal Regulation of Violent and Sexually Violent Media." *Journal of Social Issues*, 42:171-193.

Loving v. Virginia, 388 U.S. 1 (1967).

Malamuth, N.M. & J. Briere (1986). "Sexual Violence in the Media: Indirect Effects on Aggression Against Women." *Journal of Social Issues*, 42:75-92.

Melton, G.B. & H.A. Davidson (1987). "Child Protection and Society: When Should the State Intervene?" *American Psychologist*, 42:172-175.

Melton, G.B. & R.A. Thompson (1987). "Legislative Approaches to Psychological Maltreatment: A Social Policy Analysis." In M.R. Brassard, R. Germain & S.N. Hart (eds.) *Psychological Maltreatment of Children and Youth*, pp. 203-216. New York: Pergamon Press.

Meyer v. Nebraska, 262 U.S. 390 (1923).

Mnookin, R.H. (1978). *Child, Family and State: Problems and Materials on Children and the Law*. Boston: Little, Brown and Co.

Mowbray, C.T. (1987). "Post-Traumatic Therapy for Children Who Are Victims of Violence." In F.M. Ochberg (ed.) *Post-Traumatic Therapy for Children Who Are Victims of Violence*. New York: Brunner/Mazel, Inc.

Paris Adult Theatre v. Slaton, 413 U.S. 49 (1973).

Patterson, G.R. (1982). *Coercive Family Processes*. Eugene, OR: Castalia.

Pfouts, J.H., J.H. Schopler & C.H. Henley (1982). "Forgotten Victims of Family Violence." *Social Work*, 27:367-368.

Pierce v. Society of Sisters, 268 U.S. 510 (1925).

Post, R.D., A.B. Willett, R.D. Franks, R.M. House & S.M. Back (1981). "Childhood Exposure to Violence Among Victims and Perpetrators of Spouse Battering." *Victimology*, 6:156-166.

Prince v. Massachusetts, 321 U.S. 158 (1944).

Roe v. Wade, 410 U.S. 113 (1973).

Rogers, C. & T. Terry (1984). "Clinical Interventions with Boy Victims of Sexual Abuse." In I.R. Stuart & J.G. Geer (eds.) *Victims of Sexual Aggression: Treatment of Children, Women and Men*. New York: Van Nostrand Reinhold.

Rosenbaum, A. & K.D. O'Leary (1981). "Marital Violence: Characteristics of Abusive Couples." *Journal of Consulting and Clinical Psychology*, 49:63-71.

Rosenberg, M.S. (1987a). "Children of Battered Women: The Effects of Witnessing Violence on their Social Problem-Solving Abilities." *Behavior Therapist*, 10:85-89.

_____ (1987b). "New Directions for Research on the Psychological Maltreatment of Children." *American Psychologist*, 42:166-171.

Schecter, S. (1982). *Women and Male Violence*. Boston, MA: South Bend Press.

Schechtman, A. (1970). "Age Patterns in Children's Psychiatric Patterns." *Child Development*, 41:683-693.

Silvern, L. & L. Kaersvang (1989). "The Traumatized Children of Violent Marriages." *Child Welfare*, 68:421-436.

Skinner v. Oklahoma, 316 U.S. 535 (1942).

Stahly, G.B. (1977-1978). "A Review of Select Literature of Spousal Violence." *Victimology*, 2(3-4):591-607.

Star, B. (1978). "Comparing Battered and Non-Battered Women." *Victimology*, 3(1-2):32-44.

Stark, E. & A.H. Flitcraft (1988). "Women and Children at Risk: A Feminist Perspective on Child Abuse." *International Journal of Health Services*, 18:97-118.

Stark, E. & A.H. Flitcraft (1989). "Letter to the Editor." *Family Violence Bulletin*, 5:15.

Steinman, M. (1989). "The Effects of Police Responses on Spouse Abuse." *American Journal of Police*, 8:1-19.

Steinmetz, S.K. (1977). *The Cycle of Violence: Assertive, Aggressive and Abusive Family Interaction.* New York: Praeger.

Straus, M.A. (1979). "Measuring Intrafamily Conflict and Violence: The Conflict Tactics Scales." *Journal of Marriage and the Family*, (41):75-88.

Straus, M. A., R.J. Gelles & S.K. Steinmetz (1980). *Behind Closed Doors: Violence in the American Family*. New York: Doubleday.

Stullman, M.E., A. Schoenenberger & S.E. Hanks (1987). "Assessment and Treatment of the Child Victims of Marital Violence." Paper presented at the Third National Family Violence Research Conference, New Hampshire, July.

Timnick, L. (1989). "Children of Violence: What Happens to Kids Who Learn as Babies to Dodge Bullets and Step Over Corpses on the Way to School?" *Los Angeles Times Magazine*, 6 (available on NEXIS), Sept. 3.

Tomkins, A.J. & S.S. Kepfield (in press). "Policy Responses When Women Use Drugs During Pregnancy: Using Child Abuse Law to Combat Substance Abuse." In T. Sonderreger (ed.) *Perinatal Substance Abuse: Research Findings and Clinical Implications.* Baltimore: Johns Hopkins University Press.

Walker, L. & A. Browne (1985). "Gender and Victimization by Intimates." *Journal of Personality*, 53(2):179-195.

Wallerstein, J.S. & J.B. Kelly (1980). *Surviving the Breakup: How Children Cope with Divorce*. New York: Basic Books.

Webster v. Reproductive Health Services, 109 S. Ct. 3040 (1989).

Weiner, I. (1982). *Child and Adolescent Psychopathology*. New York: John Wiley.

Winters v. New York, 333 U.S. 507 (1948).

Wolfe, D.A. (1987). *Child Abuse: Implications for Child Development and Psychopathology*. Newbury Park, CA: Sage Publications.

Wolfe, D.A., P. Jaffe, S.K. Wilson & L. Zak (1985). "Children of Battered Women: The Relation of Child Behavior to Family Violence and Maternal Stress." *Journal of Consulting and Clinical Psychology*, 53:657-665.

_____ (1988). "A Multivariate Investigation of Children's Adjustment to Family Violence." In G.T. Hotaling, D. Finkelhor, J.T. Kirkpatrick & M.A. Straus (eds.) *Family Abuse and Its Consequences*. Newbury Park, CA: Sage Publications.

Wolfe, D.A., L. Zak, S.K. Wilson & P. Jaffe (1986). "Child Witnesses to Violence Between Parents: Critical Issues in Behavior and Social Adjustment." *Journal of Abnormal Child Psychology*, 14:95-104.

Wolfson v. Minerbo, 108 A.D.2d 682, 485 N.Y.S.2d 545 (1985).

Writers' Guild of America, West v. FCC, 423 F. Supp. 1064 (C.D. Cal. 1976).

About the Authors

Anthony Bouza is a former chief of the Minneapolis Police Department.

Naomi R. Cahn is the assistant director of the Sex Discrimination Clinic at the Georgetown University Law Center.

Christine DeRiso is an analyst with the Montgomery County, Maryland Police Department.

Dorothy Dionne is an assistant professor in the School of Psychology at Nova University and the clinical coordinator of its Family Violence Program. Her research centers on family violence, victims, and post-traumatic response following intimate violence.

Donald G. Dutton is a professor of psychology at the University of British Columbia. His research focuses on the etiology of wife assault and criminal justice policy.

Mary Ann Dutton-Douglas does research in family violence, victimization, and post-traumatic response following intimate violence. She is an associate professor and the director of the Family Violence Program and Clinical Training in the School of Psychology at Nova University.

Jeffrey L. Edleson is a professor in the School of Social Work at the University of Minnesota in Minneapolis as well as the director of Evaluation and Research at the Minneapolis Domestic Abuse Project.

Peter Finn is a senior research analyst at Abt Associates in Cambridge, Massachusetts.

J. David Hirschel is a professor of criminal justice at the University of North Carolina in Charlotte. Consistent with his research interests in spouse abuse, victimology, and legal issues, he is a principal investigator in one of the replications of the Minneapolis domestic violence experiment. He also has an interest in comparative criminal justice.

Ira Hutchison is an associate professor of sociology in the Department of Sociology, Anthropology, and Social Work at the University of North Carolina in Charlotte. He is a principal investigator in a replication of the Minneapolis domestic violence experiment and does research in family change and family problems.

Mary Kenning is the director of the Psychological Consultation Center at the University of Nebraska—Lincoln and does research in family violence and woman battering as well as in the sexual abuse of children.

Lisa G. Lerman is an assistant professor in the Columbus School of Law at The Catholic University of America.

Barbara M.S. McGregor is research director of the Family Violence Laboratory in the Department of Psychology at the University of British Columbia. Her research interest concerns child abuse.

Anita Merchant is a graduate student in clinical psychology at the University of Nebraska—Lincoln. Her research interests involve women's issues and battering.

Dennis Rogan is working on the Milwaukee replication of the Minneapolis domestic violence experiment and is Vice President of Research and Data Analysis in the Crime Control Institute.

Lawrence W. Sherman is a professor of criminology at the University of Maryland and is president of the Crime Control Institute. He was a principal investigator in the Minneapolis domestic violence experiment and is conducting the Milwaukee replication of that experiment.

Janell D. Schmidt is director of the Milwaukee office of the Crime Control Institute where she is working on a replication of the Minneapolis domestic violence experiment.

Michael Steinman is a professor of political science at the University of Nebraska—Lincoln and does research in police behavior and domestic violence.

Murray A. Straus is a professor of sociology and co-director of the University of New Hampshire's Family Research Laboratory.

Alan Tomkins is an assistant professor in the University of Nebraska—Lincoln's Psychology Department and an adjunct assistant professor in the College of Law. His research examines policy and legal issues related to family violence.

ADIRONDACK COMMUNITY COLLEGE
3 3341 00066399 6